PORTSMOUTH PUBLIC LIBRARY
PORTSMOUTH, N.H. 03801
603-431-2007

DEMCO

POKER FACES

POKER FACES

The Life and Work
of Professional Card Players

DAVID M. HAYANO

UNIVERSITY OF CALIFORNIA PRESS

BERKELEY   LOS ANGELES   LONDON

BICYCLE cards in the design of this book used with permission of the U.S. Playing Card Company

University of California Press
Berkeley and Los Angeles, California

University of California Press, Ltd.
London, England

Library of Congress Cataloging in Publication Data

Hayano, David M.
    Poker faces.

    Bibliography: p. 189
    Includes index.
    1. Gamblers.   2. Poker.   I. Title.
HV6713.H39   306'.4   81-11549
ISBN 0-520-04492-4   AACR2

Designed by Gayle Birrell and Michael Sheridan

Printed in the United States of America

1 2 3 4 5 6 7 8 9

And I only wrote half of what I saw . . .
— Marco Polo recalling his travels in
China, A. D. 1324

Contents

Preface

Gambling has found a permanent niche in American history and popular culture. Winning a jackpot, hitting it big with a small bet, succeeding in the face of insurmountable odds—these are all part of the American dream. Each day millions of people eagerly wager their money in lavish casinos, cardrooms, private home games, and off-track betting offices. Many others prefer to purchase lottery tickets from neighborhood stores or through the mail or bet with their friendly local bookie. Great universities like Harvard and Yale as well as churches, road works, buildings, and even armies have been funded in part by lotteries. More recently the widespread legalization of various types of gambling, while still incurring the opprobrium of some segments of society, has led to gradual commercialization, legitimation, and normalization of gambling. Of all the gambling games, poker, a distinctly American invention a century and a half old, is undoubtedly the most popular. And although poker may not yet be as American as apple pie, it has certainly become the standard Friday night after-dinner course in many homes.

About ten years ago, as a young anthropologist fresh out of grad school, I decided simultaneously to test my poker skills against those of the professional players of the legal cardrooms of California and Nevada and to conduct an anthropological study of my opponents. I was risking both money and time, but I had a hopeful vision, namely, that poker and ethnography could be compatible activities. (See Appendix A for more details.) Both required careful observation of misleading, disguised, and perplexing behavior. From a barrage of information and misinformation, both had to develop reasoned deductions, make decisions, and predict future behavior. Both poker and ethnography called for enormous patience and self-control. Only the respective pains and payoffs were different!

In addition to the millions of players who make poker their favorite hobby or leisure-time activity, there are some who play for a special purpose—to make a living. This book offers a contemporary view of this select few. My familiarity has been principally with middle-level professionals, those who attempt to grind out a few hundred or thousand dollars per day. Only several years ago this study of professional poker players might have been situated more appropriately in the sociology of deviance. Although the flavor of this approach can still be found throughout the book, I have chosen to emphasize those activities of the full-time poker player that make the game an occupation or a kind of profession. My posture reflects a change both in our society and in social science.

Recalling Marco Polo's understated but excited comment in the epigraph to this book, I too only wrote half of what I saw. The half of professional poker that I have not written about concerns the intricate technicalities of play, including the rules, the statistical foundation of card distributions, and game-specific strategies, concepts, calculations, and jargon, although some of the latter may be found in the glossary. This sort of knowledge is essential in the repertoire of the professional gambler, but since this is not a "how to play poker" book, a discussion of these topics would not be relevant here. Neither does this book examine in detail the economics of gambling, the connections between gambling and organized crime, or public issues relating to legislation and social control of gambling. These matters, as well as many other related ones, would carry me far beyond my original purpose.

As a poker player and ethnographer my interest lies in documenting the social mechanics of face-to-face confrontation. But poker, even at the highest competitive level, is not a spectator sport. The real action in poker is concealed. The seeming simplicity of a small table around which sits a handful of participants repetitively handling cards and chips masks not one but many complex hidden worlds. The observable movements of chips wagered and cards dealt do very little to reveal the genuine heart of the game as it is constructed from secret ploys, monumental deceptions, calculated strategies, and fervent beliefs. These deep, invisible structures are vital in understanding the ethnography of poker or in playing with any degree of skill. Poker is a game to experience and play rather than observe.

And therein lies the trap—for the casual player or wayward social scientist. Adapting a line from George Meredith, the nineteenth-century English scholar, I will merely conclude of poker that "It is in truth a most contagious game..."

Acknowledgments

I would like to thank the following publishing companies for permission to use these materials:

Hallnote Music Company for lyrics to *Deal* by Tom T. Hall (© Copyright 1975 by Hallnote Music Co.).

Owepar Music Company and Velvet Apple Music Company for lyrics to *Kentucky Gambler* by Dolly Parton (© Copyright 1973 by Owepar Music Company; assigned to Velvet Apple Music, 1980).

Warner Brothers Music for lyrics from the theme song to *Maverick* (© Copyright 1957 by Warner Brothers Music).

Writer's Night Music for lyrics to *The Gambler* by Don Schlitz (© Copyright 1977 by Writer's Night Music).

The Society for the Scientific Study of Social Problems for "The Professional Poker Player: Career Identification and the Problem of Respectability," *Social Problems* 24 (1977): 556-564, by David M. Hayano.

Sage Publications, Inc., for "Strategies for the Management of Luck and Action in an Urban Poker Parlor," *Urban Life* 6 (1978): 475-488, by David M. Hayano.

I owe special appreciation to Carl Klockars for his suggestions and help and to several anonymous reviewers for their incisive comments on earlier versions of this manuscript.

Rex Jones, a fellow poker player and anthropologist, more than anyone else stood along with me, each foot planted in a different world, and saw the possibilities of a productive synthesis.

Jack Miles, editor at the University of California Press, took a keen interest in my manuscript and treated it kindly, with a careful sense of sleekness and symmetry. Copy editor Amanda Clark Frost made the pages read immensely smoother.

I learned much about analyzing, studying, and playing poker from many different social and professional players. These friends, acquaintances, and opponents are too numerous to mention by name or initial, but they include many of the Rainbow and Horseshoe Club regulars in Gardena, California, who played from 1973 to 1979. (You know who you are!) I would especially like to single out Robert M. for his support.

And finally to Ruth, who saw that life and ethnography were one and the same to me and that the clickety-clack of chips and the soft shuffle of cards could be a calling for both.

Introduction:
"I Hate It.
No, I Love It!"

We do not what we ought;
What we ought not, we do;
And lean upon the thought
That chance will bring us through. *

In 1975 the Survey Research Center of the University of Michigan was asked
by the Commission on the Review of the National Policy Toward Gambling to
(1) study the extent of gambling in the United States, (2) estimate government
revenues that could be raised from various changes in gambling laws, and (3)
examine the potential social consequences of these changes.[1] A national sample of about 2,000 people was surveyed, and almost 300 of these respondents
were residents of Nevada. The results of the survey showed that more than
half (61 percent) of adult Americans had made a monetary bet in the previous
year. Most had placed bets on bingo, state lotteries, jai alai, horse and dog
tracks, or in casinos and off-track betting parlors. About a fifth of the bets
were illegal and made with a bookie or in an illicit casino.

*Matthew Arnold, *Empedocles on Etna* (1852), act 1, sc. 2, line 237.

Gambling and betting is widespread in most age, sex, regional, and population groups throughout the United States. The overall popularity of specific gambling games depends on availability, legal status, and gamblers' preferences. In states with legal lotteries, for example, almost half of the population purchased lottery tickets. In most states (excluding Nevada) gambling participation and the amount of betting increased with individual income. The estimated amount of money wagered on legal and illegal gambling in the United States in 1974 added up to a phenomenal total of $22.4 billion.

When legal gambling facilities are increased, gambling participation, including illegal gambling and betting among friends, also tends to rise. A majority of respondents, except in the southern states, were in favor of the legalization of at least one gambling activity, but there was little consensus on what this game should be. The favorites were bingo, horse or dog racing, and lotteries. In states where games were already legal, most respondents voted for their continuation. The commission also concluded that compulsive gambling would probably increase with the widespread legalization of gambling, since the figures from Nevada indicate a higher degree of social and compulsive gambling than in other states. As a general observation the commission summarizes: "Gambling is inevitable. No matter what is said or done by advocates or opponents of gambling in all its various forms, it is an activity that is practiced, or tacitly endorsed, by a substantial majority of Americans."[2]

Since this survey was conducted and the final report made available to the public, there is even stronger evidence that gambling participation has been increasing steadily as we can see by the popularity and legalization of various games. Forty-six states (the exceptions are Hawaii, Indiana, North Dakota, and Utah) now permit legalized gambling in one form or another, and each year more states create their own controlled lotteries. In November 1976 the voters of New Jersey approved a plan for Las Vegas-style casino gambling in Atlantic City. According to recent reports the success of New Jersey gambling, at least for the owners of the Resorts International hotel-casino, has been enormous. Gross earnings have run between $500,000 and $1.5 million dollars per day. In less than a year hotel-casinos have paid out $100 million in taxes.[3]

Every week millions of sports fans and bettors view rivalries between their favorite teams on television, and the predictions for these games are published in advance in local and national newspapers. Church and charity bingo games also attract millions of part-time social gamblers. In some states local nonprofit organizations are allowed to run slot machines and wheels of fortune, often in the guise of aiding charities, churches, or the cub scouts.[4] Despite occasional moral outbursts from the public, the propensity for gambling in the United States had led some reporters to consider gambling an integral part of the American way of life.[5] Television shows may be partly responsible for feeding this interest by providing "action" in gamblinglike games of luck and knowledge and by generating feverish levels of excitement for both contestants and viewers.[6] The effect of this "way of life" is that hotels and casinos in Nevada grow larger and continue to flourish, seemingly oblivious to national trends in inflation, recession, unemployment, and other serious social and economic problems. The total gross revenue from gambling in Nevada for the fiscal year 1976-1977 was $1.38 billion, of which the state received over $100 million in gambling taxes.[7]

Gambling is not only a preoccupation of Americans but also many European countries, such as Britain and West Germany, have completely legalized, regulated, and supervised public wagering in order to increase internal revenues. It is estimated that 94 percent of all Britons gamble occasionally, 40 percent regularly. In 1976 they bet over $15 billion on horses, lotteries, dog races, bingo, and all other kinds of casino gambling.[8]

A serious weakness in the commission's report which would point to an even greater degree of gambling participation than measured is its failure to investigate widespread gambling among card players. Card games, including poker, bridge, gin rummy, and pan, have historically been a favorite social and recreational activity for many Americans.[9] But it is poker, played in its various forms on kitchen tables and in casinos, which is America's most popular card game. An estimated 47 million people play poker regularly and they wager over $45 billion annually.[10] These figures pointing to the popularity of poker are impressive, but surprisingly little is known about the social organization of poker-playing and the motivations, strategies, and beliefs of its millions of regular participants. Even less information exists about full-time professional gamblers and poker players who are part of a vast gambling subculture and derive sizable gain from race tracks, casinos, and cardrooms. Judging by their estimated wagering capacity, social and professional gamblers play a significant role in the vast economy of unregistered cash transactions and may influence many individual lives as well as other facets and institutions of American society. For this reason alone, this massive but hitherto undisclosed subculture deserves serious scholarly attention.

POKER, CHANCE, AND SKILL

The idea that events can occur by chance dawned early in the history of mankind. One early object displaying concern for random or chance occurrence was the *astragalus,* a small cube made from the heel bone of a sheep. When this cube, forerunner of the modern die, was tossed in the air and landed on the ground, the side turned upward revealed a special message to the thrower. The random fall of objects was linked with early beliefs in divination, magic, religion, and the forecasting of future events. By the beginnings of the Chris-

3

tian era we find *astragali,* dice, throwing sticks, board games, and other games of chance. Whether for sport, fun, or serious purposes, the wagering of money or valuables on chance remains the basis of all gambling games.

The idea of the randomness of events, however, was not easily accepted everywhere. F. N. David writes, "With the advent of Christianity the concept of the random event of the pagan philosophers was finally rejected. According to Saint Augustine, for example, nothing happened by chance, everything being minutely controlled by the will of God. If events appear to occur at random, that is because of the ignorance of man and not the nature of events."[11]

The concept of random occurrences remained dormant in secular intellectual thought for many centuries. Not until the sixteenth century did men such as Ferrari, Tartaglia, Cardano (called the "gambling scholar"), and Galileo, followed a century later by scholars in France like de Méré, Fermat, and Pascal, give birth to the modern study of probability mathematics. Much of this renewed effort was stimulated by the desire to solve practical gambling problems.

Differences in structure of gambling games determine how risky each game actually is and whether a player can win in the long run. When comparing poker with other games and their casino setting, these differences in structure demonstrate why it is *possible* to win consistently at poker but more difficult, if not impossible, at most other gambling games.

First, games can be classified according to whether they pit *players against the house* or they are contests of *player against player*. Players are usually at a disadvantage from the start in games against the house because the house takes a percentage, called the vigorish or "vig," of each bet by not paying off bettors at the exact expected probabilities. It is as if a player agreed to a game of coin tossing with a bank at $1 per throw. Each time the player guessed heads or tails correctly, he would win $.99 or $.95 from the house. But each time he lost he would have to pay the house a full $1. Betting systematically, at least in casino craps, the player may almost approximate an even-odds situation, such as guessing heads or tails on the toss of a coin. In house-banked casino games the player does not actually bet for or against the house. He bets for or against the occurrence of events and the unshakable laws of probability. The house simply charges a banking fee for each bet.

Poker players play against each other. Deception, miscommunication, and the analysis of opponents' behavior are important facets of the game, as much or more than the knowledge of the mathematical probabilities for events. Cardrooms make their money in poker by either raking off a small amount of chips from each pot (usually from 5 to 15 percent) or taking a collection fee at regular intervals. In short, the cardroom is a rental agency that provides the neutral location, dealer (if necessary), and gaming apparatus for players.

Second, games vary according to the amount of *information* that can be ascertained about turns, moves, and players. In chess or backgammon, moves are plainly observable and each move influences the opponent's countermove. Such games are termed games of perfect, or complete, information. In poker, however, information about playing hands can only be gleaned from exposed cards (only in stud and Hold 'Em poker) and by watching others move, bet, and talk. No small amount of guesswork is involved. Poker is hence a game of imperfect, or incomplete, information. Players must form their own conclusions about what hands others players have, what betting decisions they may make, and what their behavior means.

Last, games can be plotted along the dimension *skill versus luck*. Games of total luck, such as craps, roulette, baccarat, keno, slot machines, bingo, the wheel of fortune, and lotteries, are governed completely by the laws of chance. Outcomes are neither controllable nor manipulable by bettors, although avid addicts of these games are likely to argue contrarily. On the other hand, chess is a game of pure strategy and skill; nothing is left to chance. Between the two extremes of luck and skill lie games such as poker and twenty-one (i.e., "blackjack") that combine elements of both. In neither of these games can the precise proportion of luck and skill be computed. That is why in many poker games, in short runs, the worst player at the table may end up with the chips and the best player may lose.

Winning consistently at games based on fixed house odds and total luck is highly unlikely. It would be unusual to find a full-time professional keno, roulette, or dice player (although there may be individuals who claim this status) because the house edge, anywhere from less than 1 percent to 20 percent, is sufficiently high and invariable to overcome short streaks in favor of the bettor. A player can, of course, win big once or even a few times, as do some slot machine winners and crapshooters, but this would not constitute professional gambling. In order to make a daily living a gambler must engage in games where skill can be exercised so that he or she can exert some degree of control over the behavior of other players and their betting decisions. The built-in element of risk is what gives all forms of gambling and poker their chancy quality. Uncertainty about future events — in poker, the deal of cards — always enters into play. So players devise strategies and maintain certain beliefs to account for what they cannot know in advance.

THE HIDDEN TRAPS

Poker certainly is fun. After ten hours of straight playing, nagging aches begin to attack your shoulders and neck and then spread downward, trailing the spine to your rump. After twenty hours the pains and numbness increase and spread throughout your entire body, especially your immobile feet and legs. Your eyes sting and tear from the smoke and the glare. When thirty or more hours have passed you are working solely on learned reflexes, and not very quick ones at that. Your alertness and attention span drop off rapidly. Only occasionally do you feel short bursts of energy (mainly after dragging in a big pot). But sooner or later it is inevitable: total exhaustion will set in.

Why all of this torture? Well, you either love to play the game or you are trying to get even. All of the winners have cashed out and departed hours or maybe even days ago. The passage of time—nongambling real time—is no longer a relevant measurement. Only the unpitied losers and day-and-night marathon "degenerates" are left to battle it out among themselves. Some will eventually get even and quit, others will give up before falling asleep or passing out, and still a few will cling until they are completely exhausted or completely broke—or both.

Imagine working at a task where your success or failure depends on a combination of the chancy occurrence of events and the ability to outguess and manipulate others. In this task the minimum condition for survival is the ability to secure and hold on to a playing stake of hard cash. Decisions must be made aggressively and quickly, sometimes in a matter of seconds, or else hundreds or thousands of dollars may be lost. Winning brings on a feeling of power and the sensation that the run of cards and the attack of opponents are well under control. But neither monetary gain nor success are permanent; they merely represent the peaks of the upswings in an ongoing series of bell-shaped fluctuations. When the player is losing, all of these feelings rapidly turn sour. Immediate adjustments must be made to these great swings of elation and depression that, like inseparable twins, accompany big wins and losses. These are the demanding and uncertain qualities of professional poker-playing.

Poker-playing is without doubt a difficult and erratic occupation. The dropout rate from "running bad" and "going busted" leaves many hopefuls in search of a more secure and profitable livelihood. Thousands may attempt to succeed, or simply survive from day to day, but only a few players ever reach the top of the status heap as measured by a large bankroll, skillful play, recognition of peers, and success in major tournaments.

In casinos, cardrooms, and private games throughout the world professional poker players of the highest caliber may win or lose thousands of dollars every day. In order to end up in the black at the close of a sitting, month, or year, each player must construct his own system of strategies and beliefs for selecting games, playing hands, making bets, managing a stake, analyzing opponents, recouping losses, raising money, quitting a game, and generating the momentum to win. But winning money is not necessarily the major problem; it is holding on to it that is difficult. The vicissitudes of chance and lapses in self-control may humble even the best players.

It is reported that Las Vegan Johnny Moss, a Texas-born pro from the age of nineteen, won $100,000 on some football bets in 1939.[12] With this fortune in hand he instructed his wife, Virgie, to shop around for a new house. Later that evening when she told him of the mansion she had found, it was too late. He had lost all the money. In 1950 Moss won the staggering sum of $10 million playing poker in Reno, Nevada. Because many people thereafter refused to play with him he turned to the dice tables and gradually lost all his winnings again. To survive as a professional gambler he borrowed a playing stake of half a million dollars in cash from his gambling friends. He eventually paid them back in $100,000 installments. Moss is neither typical nor unique among gamblers, but his example demonstrates what is needed to survive—in friends, money, and determination—in this risky livelihood.

Like ominous shadows, risk and hazard closely dog the footsteps of the professional poker player. Depression, frustration, and physical exhaustion wear away at his well-being and health while thieves and cheaters do more than cast covetous glances at his playing stake. But more than any other danger, the legitimate professional gambler must contend with his greatest occupational hazard—losing his entire bankroll, busting out, going Tap City. Professional gamblers devote much of their physical and mental energy to avoiding this end. For those who are skillful and fortunate enough to survive, the career of poker-playing can offer great personal and financial rewards.

But in the final accounting the balancing of credits and debits is not so easily reckoned. Full-time poker-playing is stressful, financially unstable, emotionally volatile, and sometimes physically dangerous. Every professional and regular player knows these traps well. Most have learned about them the hard way.

1
The Image and the Reality of Professional Poker

We needed money real bad at home and my daddy told me I had to stop work or stop gamblin'. And I said, "Daddy, if I don't work how can I get money to gamble?" And Daddy, he said, "Son, that's what gamblers got to figure out." So I quit work.

                               —Johnny Moss*

Playing cards originated in Asia, where they evolved from symbols and paraphernalia associated with ancient divinatory practices. During the thirteenth century cards were introduced, along with paper money and gunpowder, into Europe through India and the Middle East. Several centuries later the present-day four suits and court figures—kings, queens, and knaves—appeared in playing cards designed and used in France.[1]

The birth of poker is not well documented, although many scholars believe it to have been derived from *Âs Nâs*, a Persian card game played with twenty cards.[2] The French and Germans modified this game and called it *poque* or *Pochen*. When it reached the shores of America, most likely through the port

---

*Quoted in Jon Bradshaw, *Fast Company* (New York: Harpers Magazine Press, 1975), p. 153.

city of New Orleans in the early 1800s, its name became *pokah* because of the southern drawl. By around 1840 the fifty-two card deck, perhaps influenced by the English deck of the same size, replaced the original pack of twenty cards.

In the earliest version of poker each player was dealt five cards face down. Only one round of betting was allowed, and there was no additional draw of cards. The variations of poker that developed later substantially increased the amount of betting, action, and skill. During the 1860s the draw and an extra round of betting were introduced. Without the draw, poker was mainly a game of chance and bluffing, but the draw of cards favored a more strategic game. By 1875 straights and flushes were recognized as legitimate hands and the joker was played as a wild card.[3]

In the early and middle nineteenth century San Francisco was the undisputed gambling center of the West, among hundreds of boom towns from Dodge City and Denver to Virginia City, Nevada. Many large and prosperous gambling houses, such as the Bella Union and El Dorado in Portsmouth Square, were fed and fattened during the great Gold Rush by the wealth of the forty-niners. Around 1850 the most popular games included monte, faro, roulette, and chuck-a-luck. Poker had not yet caught on in public gambling houses because its action was considered too slow.[4] But by 1852 a gambling backlash began to develop, brought about by permanent city settlers who no longer considered gambling was a form of recreation that had to be offered as diversion to every itinerant miner, traveler, and visitor. Public sentiment turned against the gambling clubs and hotels, and in 1854 a California state law made gambling in and operating a gambling house a felony. Although this law was never strictly enforced, it ended the great era of public gambling in San Francisco. By the turn of the century nearly every western state and territory that formerly had thrived on wide-open gambling passed laws forbidding it in an attempt to clean up the West's wild and woolly frontier image.

During this same period, however, poker rapidly caught the attention of the public as the game spread from New Orleans and its fabled riverboat casinos to the smaller towns and cities in the East and West. As the steamboats plied the Mississippi during the nineteenth century, a lively commerce developed in many port cities, drawing together diverse people who shared an interest in acquiring wealth. Prior to the Civil War, many of these travelers made vast fortunes in cotton, tobacco, and land speculation. Along with wealthy businessmen, southern belles and aristocrats, and itinerant passengers who rode these rivers were others who sometimes posed as well-to-do scions, farmers, or preachers but who privately signaled among themselves that they were "professional gamblers." They were, in fact, skillful thieves and cheats. Herbert Asbury notes that by 1870

9

The entire country swarmed with itinerant Faro artists, *Monte* dealers, short card cheats, and Three-Card Monte swindlers, many of whom were notorious outlaws and gunmen as well while every town and hamlet, from Podunk-at-the-crossroads to cosmopolitan San Francisco, was infested by professional gamblers and harbored skinning-houses and occasional square games in numbers according to the population, the prosperity and gullibility of the suckers, and the venality of the politicians and office-holders. [5]

One of the most revealing memoirs of this period, George Devol's *Forty Years a Gambler on the Mississippi,* [6] describes vividly how the author conned and fleeced many unsuspecting travelers on the riverboats. Although gambling (and losing) at faro and poker was a large part of Devol's daily life, he made most of his money during his seventy-three years at a scam known as three-card monte. In this game the "mark" (victim) is shown an ace (or a pea under a shell) that is deftly manipulated with two other cards (or peas under shells) by a dealer. A confederate standing close by with a big bundle of money in his hand makes a bet and shows how "easy" it is to keep track of the ace and win. Anticipating a big score, the mark then places a big bet of his own. When he does, he cannot win. With the aid of confederates and marked cards, Devol survived for many years as a self-proclaimed "professional gambler." [7]

Cheating, premeditated and guileful, may have been the accepted modus operandi of most nineteenth-century gamblers. According to one report: "All riverboat gamblers were expert at cheating, and perhaps 99 percent of them, either occasionally or all the time, did cheat. One authority on the subject, who estimated that there were at least 2,000 gamblers on the Western waters in the mid-nineteenth century, could think of only four who were honest." [8]

Even at present the presumption that most, if not all, professional gamblers are in actuality wily con artists, cheats, or life's deserved losers still persists in historical texts, the popular media, and many social science writings. A large proportion of psychological studies of gambling and gamblers have been explicitly critical and moralistic and have focused primarily on the loser or compulsive bettor. [9] And almost uniformly sociologists have considered gambling a sordid aspect of "lower-class" subculture or an integral cog in the machinery of organized crime. [10] Professional gamblers are grouped with other kinds of social deviants who pose dangerous threats to the moral fiber of society. One example will suffice:

If there is a field of inquiry called "deviance," it is social deviants as here defined that would presumably constitute its core. Prostitutes, drug addicts, delinquents, criminals, jazz musicians, bohemians, gypsies, carnival workers, hobos, winos, show people, *full time gamblers,* beach dwellers, homosexuals, and the urban repentant poor—these would be included. These are the folk who are considered to be engaged in some kind of collective denial of the social order. They are perceived as failing to use available opportunity for advancement in the various approved runways of society; they show open disrespect for their betters; they lack piety; they represent failures in the motivational schemes of society.[11] (Emphasis mine.)

Largely overshadowed by this adverse publicity are legitimate, independent, skillful professional poker players. Within their own social world of cardrooms and casinos, many of them act as their own "moral entrepreneurs"[12] who push for respectability, social acceptance, and the correction of distorted occupational stereotypes. My point, of course, is not to convince the reader that most or all present-day professional gamblers are in fact respectable and honest in their dealings with others. (The other side of the coin is discussed more thoroughly in chapter 6.) Such a claim would be difficult to support. Rather, my interest lies in how individuals, professional poker players in this case, negotiate and resolve problems of social identity through their internalized attitudes and beliefs. Amarillo Slim Preston, for example, a nationally visible professional, offers this description:

I'm always being asked what it takes to be a professional poker player. Well, you must have a strong constitution and no nerves whatsoever. And you have to be an honest man. All the stock in trade that a gambler has is his word . . . In a room full of professional gamblers, we can walk off and leave all our chips on the table, even if we have to go back to the motel and change clothes, or leave the game to sleep for five or six hours. We don't worry a bit about somebody taking our chips. Now, go play in some of these private games with some of these goody two-shoes, and see how you come out if you leave your pile unattended for a minute. I've got two or three cigar boxes full of bad checks I've been given by businessmen, but I haven't got one from a professional gambler.[13]

To understand how personal and social images of gamblers are perpetuated, we need only look at the media, which exploits a few limited themes and exerts a powerful influence on current ideas about gambling and gamblers. These tired but attention-getting images will later be counterbalanced by a consideration of how the legitimate professional poker player evaluates his own work, for part of his symbolic strategy for survival requires a positive presentation of self and livelihood.

TARNISHED HEROES, TROUBLED LADIES

The occurrence of repetitive themes and character types offers valuable insight into how cultures, through their songs, rituals, dances, art, poetry, folktales, myths, and movies, embody stereotypes of people and what they do.[14] Film is an obvious channel that incorporates myths, concepts of self and society, and moral values. Generally, the media pays little attention to the role of the gambler, but this lack of interest also tells us something about public attitudes. There are no such genre or formula films for gamblers as for cowboys, gangsters, and monsters. Despite gambling's pervasiveness and popularity, social and professional gamblers have not received favorable attention. In one study high school students placed gamblers in the same category as murderers and gunmen.[15] In another survey, in response to the question "Who wants to be a professional gambler?" affirmative answers were given mostly by men who enjoyed taking risks in other activities. As a livelihood gambling ranked in the bottom half of a list of 131 occupations.[16] The dire message of community moralists, law enforcement agencies, the church, and of course our society's projective arts are probably responsible in part for these public attitudes. It is to portrayal of gamblers in film that I now turn.

At the end of *Belle Le Grand* (1950), Lucky John Kilton, a mine owner in Virginia City, faces a romantic dilemma involving two sisters. One sister is Belle Le Grand, who has given herself this "classier" French name; the other is Nan Henshaw, an opera singer. The two sisters grew up separately and as a result have considerably different interests and experiences. Belle, the older sister, who has just been released from prison, is the former wife of an ex-Mississippi riverboat gambler; she is a gambler and murderess herself. Kilton loves both sisters and must make a choice between them. Entranced with the more respectable, better educated sister, Kilton nevertheless recognizes the ineradicable social distinction between them: Nan is a sophisticated opera singer, while Belle, like Kilton, is a "weed." Struck by this sudden revelation, Kilton finally chooses the more compatible Belle as a mate.

Movie gamblers generally project a picture of deviance and alienation, of lonely, driven men and women who inhabit the shady side of society, often in intimate association with hustlers, junkies, murderers, con men, thieves, and other assorted villains. Film titles and plots sometimes blatantly express this unbreachable gap between gamblers and "respectable" society. *The Gambler and the Lady* (1952), for example, played on the inherent social differences between an American casino owner in London and Lady Susan Willens, his high society flame. In the end the broken gambler is killed by an old girl friend. A similar fate overtakes the unrepentant character in *Never Trust A Gambler* (1951) when, after being sought by the police for murder, he is gunned down on a lonely dockside.

12

A further portrayal of the gambler's inferior position in society and his questionable morality can be found in *The Gambler from Natchez* (1954). Chip Colby is an "honest gambler on the Mississippi" whose father, also a gambler, always wanted him to be a gentleman. Central to the story is Chip's romantic interest in a wealthy woman who is also attracted to him, until she discovers that he is a gambler and, worse yet, the son of a gambler. Despite good intentions Chip does not share her refined background. The tale of social dissimilarity closes predictably, for we are told that like prefers like, and Chip Colby ends up with the more earthy daughter of a French riverboat captain.

As in *Belle Le Grand,* the gambler-hero is united with the appropriate, that is, socially similar, person, but only after he has tasted and eventually rejected the high society woman or the southern aristocratic lady. Although the Old West or Mississippi riverboat gambler may be, underneath it all, a respectable fellow with a good heart, he resides in a socially contaminated world. He is guilty by association. He remains a solitary figure standing outside of the conventional institutions of society.

A recent television series presented an unaltered image of the gambler. An episode of *Phyllis* (January 1977), starring Cloris Leachman, depicted Buddy Desmond as a professional gambler who had served time for bookmaking. The inevitable distinctions between Phyllis and Desmond are not immediately apparent. She is attracted by his charm and agrees to date him. On their first meeting he takes her to the fights; on the second night they go to a football game. Phyllis is shocked by the discovery that he is a professional gambler and ex-con. "He lost $500 without batting an eye," she says with horror. Finally, he must drop her—the romance is doomed from the beginning—because he attributes his two-week losing streak and loss of $15,000 to her presence. Such romantic couplings between a gambler and a person of another (usually higher) class are never consummated in the movies. Thus, Tony Curtis as *Mister Cory* (1957), a Chicago poorboy-turned-wealthy-gambler, faces the same insurmountable pressure when he attempts to marry the daughter of a prominent businessman. Money alone cannot bring him class.

Gamblers Then and Now

Most films about gamblers take place in one of two time periods: in the Old West and Mississippi riverboat period from about 1820 to 1900, or in a modern setting, usually 1920 to the present, in an urban environment. Will Wright observes that a western setting has always appealed to filmmakers and moviegoers because of the mixture of adventure and diverse lifestyles: "There were farmers, cowboys, cavalrymen, miners, Indian fighters, gamblers, gun-fighters, and railroad builders, all contemporary with one another. Though these different types may have had little contact with each other, as a source of narrative inspiration the variety of livelihoods allows for clear-cut conflicts of interests and values."[17] Films set in the Old West, in contrast to films in a modern setting, attach more neutral values of social permissibility to gambling. Poker, dice, blackjack, faro, roulette, and other games of chance are included as a normal part of the setting. Every crowded saloon is filled with dance-hall girls and local characters who are drinking and playing poker as part of the colorful background for the major theme. Gambling is depicted as a routine social activity for ranchers, cowboys, riverboat travelers, and lawmen. This may not be a complete distortion of the historical record. According to one source:

> Almost everybody gambled in the Old West. Prospectors and dance-hall girls, cattle barons and cowpokes, clergymen and gunfighters all gathered around gaming tables to wager their newly won fortunes — or their last possessions — on the turn of a card or the spin of a wheel . . . Gambling was a Western mania, the only amusement that could match the heady, speculative atmosphere of frontier life itself.[18]

Gamblers are even occasionally the "good guys" in westerns.[19] By far the most popular role model of the likable rambler-gambler in the Old West was the star of the television series *Maverick* (which originally aired from 1957 to 1962). Featuring Bret and Bart Maverick (and later Beau, an English cousin), this series traced the fictional exploits of the two brothers who roamed the country living by their wits and their cards. While they were not beyond conning con men or stealing from unscrupulous ranchers and businessmen, when they did it was in a playful sense, with a marked emphasis on Old West morality and retribution. The Maverick brothers were basically good-hearted rascals who sought to rectify the wrongs committed against them and their friends by *real* con men and no-gooders.

Removed from the Old West, gambling is more likely to be considered an unnatural, grimy business. In films set in the contemporary era the most persistent plot dealing with gamblers concerns illicit activities involving organized crime, murder, or political corruption.[20] Gambling and its underworld forces are so pervasive that even legitimate businessmen, like casino owners, may find themselves battling evil influences and potential subversion. In the television series *Mr. Lucky* (1959-1960), the tuxedoed suave hero and owner of the *Fortuna,* a legal gambling ship, was constantly at odds with underworld thugs who sought to take over his operation. Honesty, then, is always temptingly corruptible because of the sinister social circles where modern urban movie gamblers congregate.

Several recent box-office hits, including *The Sting* (1973), *The Hustler*

(1961), *The Cincinnati Kid* (1965), and *The Gambler* (1974), have explored the subcultures of gambling and hustling and individual character types in greater depth than previous films. The last three, in particular, focus on the social background and motivations of losers in their struggle to become winners. One criticism has been that the accuracy of the dialogue and behavior of gamblers, compared with actual situations, may be way off the mark. Ned Polsky, for one, has commented on the out-of-date style of pool hustling and social milieu of *The Hustler*.[21] Similarly, glaring misconceptions of poker and poker players can be found in *The Cincinnati Kid*. "The Kid" (Steve McQueen) challenges aging Lancey Howard ("The Man," played by Edward G. Robinson) to the country's poker championship, and even though the Kid displays a lot of "heart" and is honest enough not to rig the game, he loses in the end in the final hand of five-card stud, his full house to Lancey's straight flush, a highly improbable outcome for a two-man contest.[22]

Both *The Cincinnati Kid* and *The Hustler* are cinematic studies of similar characters. The Kid and Fast Eddie Felson, the pool hustler, are both cocky winners at their own level who take on challenges of character and will against professional winners at their own game. In one case the winner is Lancey Howard; in the other it is Minnesota Fats. Both are dapper, impressive, and thoroughly professional in their psychological destruction of the two younger challengers. The differences between protagonist and antagonist build the dramatic tension and culminate in the final game to contrast good and evil, young and old, honest and dishonest.[23] As allegory, gambling represents matches of persistence and courage where ordinary poolroom hustlers and two-bit poker players can never win no matter how much confidence they talk into themselves. Minnesota Fats realizes this instantly. When he is losing badly in a game with Fast Eddie, he takes a break, washes his hands and face, and prepares himself psychologically for the next round. He *knows* the boisterous, overconfident Fast Eddie is a loser in the long run. Similarly, Lancey Howard shows no fear of the Kid, who has the requisite talent and poker experience but has not yet learned that winners cannot be beat at their own game.

Born to Lose

While gamblers are found in Westerns in every social setting and are flaunted as rogues, cheats, and outlaws, remarkably they are never compulsive gamblers. This sociopsychological type appears only in contemporary films, even though the idea of compulsive gambling is not new. To proffer one famous case, Dostoevski in his autobiographical *The Gambler* described in detail his passion for roulette.[24] The cinematic and public recognition of gamblers as compulsive, masochistic losers probably was stimulated by Freudian psychoanalytic theory and the popular writings of Edmund Bergler, who in 1936 first wrote of excessive gambling as a mental disease.[25] According to Bergler,

15

many gamblers are arrested at the anal stage of development and find maso-chistic pleasure in self-punishment; in brief, they have an unconscious desire to lose. This view of gambling as psychopathology became widespread among the general public and even among gamblers over the next several decades. Films repeatedly play on this theme of temptation and compulsion.

In *Lady Luck* (1946) the granddaughter of a habitual horse bettor com-plains that gambling is "in his blood, like insanity." And on a recent television episode of *Blansky's Beauties* (April 1977), the father of "Arkansas," one of the showgirls, arrives in Las Vegas for a visit and in minutes succumbs to "gambling fever." Thereafter he follows the road to trouble. First he loses $100, then $200, then $1,600 more borrowed from his daughter. He falls into debt to Big Leroy, a crooked gambler with a dice layout in his apartment, but fortunately Nancy Blansky comes to the rescue. After throwing away Big Leroy's crooked dice, she wins the man's money back in a legitimate dice game (how easy it is!) and father and daughter are happily reunited.

The Gambler (1974), starring James Caan as the hooked-and-in-debt col-lege professor, and Robert Altman's *California Split* (1974) also examine the downhill path to ruin and degradation as a result of excessive gambling.[26] In *The Gambler* Axel Freed (James Caan) loses $44,000 to the mob and his bookie in a private dice game. His only hope of paying his debts is to gamble more, for as a college professor (who assigns Dostoevski as required reading in his literature class) he earns only $1,500 per month. Freed borrows some cash from his reluctant mother, takes an impulsive flight to Las Vegas, and finds himself on a winning streak. He wins a bundle of money, but he cannot quit and he loses it all again. He is finally able to repay the long overdue debt to the mob by bribing one of his students, the star of the college basketball team, to play badly in a game. At the final buzzer the mob wins their bets and Freed is out of debt. But instead of enjoying life without danger, he faces risk again by walking alone into Harlem in search of a prostitute. In a dark, shabby room he manages to escape her cutthroat pimp in a fight, but not without first receiving a long knife wound across his cheek. In the final scene, as he looks in the mirror at the blood, an enigmatic smile crosses his face. Once again he has risked his life and won.

The two rowdy buddies of *California Split* go through a similar cycle of winning, losing, and finally triumphing. Or is it really triumph? Starting from Gardena poker cardrooms they take a quick jaunt to Las Vegas and win a bundle, but the inescapable existential question arises to plague them: What does it all mean? So even when movie gamblers do win, hesitation and doubt are usually not far behind to spoil the fun.

While the roles of gambling men in the movies have usually shown some degree of flexibility, from the rambling-gambling cowboy to the swank casino owner, women's roles in gambling films are much more constricted in time and depth. Lady gamblers, almost exclusively appearing in films set in the contemporary era, all bear the burden of a deep-seated psychological compulsion.[27] Barbara Stanwyck, a popular actress in the 1940s, starred in a number of gambling movies, including *Gambling Lady* (1934), *The Lady Eve* (1941), and *The Lady Gambles* (1949). In *The Lady Eve* she must delude her fiancé into believing that she is an English noblewoman rather than an experienced gambler if they are to continue their relationship. And in *The Lady Gambles* she is the classic innocent who succumbs to the glitter of the gambling casino. An ex-magazine reporter who visits Las Vegas with her reporter husband, she discovers the roulette tables and, almost in an hypnotic trance, gets hooked. In her own words, gambling is "exciting." But she soon begins to lose, falls into debt, and lies about the extent of her gambling losses to her husband and sister. An attempted partnership with the casino owner fails to work, and finally she is arrested for prostitution and ends up exhausted and ill in the hospital. There, in the hospital bed, it is revealed that her mother died while giving birth to her. This, obviously, has been the reason for her guilt and self-punishment all these years! On the verge of a suicidal leap from the hospital window she is stopped by her husband. As the camera pulls back on the embracing couple, there are indications that with loving support she might be able to return to normalcy.[28] For many women in the movies, gambling is an alluring vice, one that captivates and holds. Before the woman realizes it, she is changed into an unrecognizable, lying, gambling degenerate.

The media clearly have oversimplified and selectively narrowed the scope of real-life gambling behavior in both historical and contemporary plays of morality. In reel-life, heroes are tarnished by excess and social inferiority, and women must turn to prostitution in order to finance a vile habit. The message of the media seems to be that there are only limited types of gambling that are either immoral, illegal, or compulsive.

BACKGROUND TO A GAMBLING CAREER

Many professional poker players, particularly those aged fifty or older who now reside or play in Las Vegas, were born and raised in the South. A large number come from Texas.[29] In a rural, depression-haunted environment, gambling was a normal and expected part of growing up. For many it was a means of survival. Gambling offered the poor or unemployed with little formal education an opportunity to make quick, big money by applying their wits and skills in a game that could only be learned through long, hard experience. Johnny Moss recalls those hardships:

> There wasn't much easy money in Texas in them days and gamblin' was
> a way out. When I was a kid all the money I made I gave to my daddy

and he gave me back a quarter. Well, we needed it. But I never asked
people the price of nothin' as far back as I can remember. I just went in
and bought anything I wanted. We didn't have money and I decided to
get me some one way or the other. That's all, not for me, for my family.
I can get along on nothin'. But you got to take care of your obligations
win or lose. We needed money real bad at home and my daddy told me I
had to stop work or stop gamblin'. And I said, "Daddy, if I don't work
how can I get money to gamble?" And Daddy, he said, "Son, that's what
gamblers got to figure out." So I quit work. [30]

In the 1920s and 1930s poker pros, often as partners, played throughout
the circuit of backroom bars and mining and oil towns in the South, moving
from town to town making an adequate living from inexperienced workers
and local farmers. Poker was not the only important survival skill; golf and
pool-shooting were also valuable, practical money-making tools and included
in many high-wagering propositions. [31] High-rolling gamblers of this era, like
Nick the Greek Dandolas, Titanic Thompson, Bet-a-Million Gates, and Pitts-
burgh Phil, were notorious for the amount of money they wagered on a single
roll of the dice, the speed of a horse, or the turn of a card. They did not even
have to rely on contrived games as excuses to gamble. They wagered immense
sums on how far away a mountain was, which raindrop would slide down a
windowpane the fastest, which sugar cube a fly would land on first, and how
far a peanut could be thrown. [32]

Today only a few men maintain the life-style of the "traveling" pro. [33] Some
have deliberately remained on the road, seeking out private worldwide high-
stakes poker games sponsored by wealthy players who enjoy the prestige of
playing with (and losing to) high-status professionals. Others are career "road
hustlers" who are expert at cheating conventioneers and small-town locals at
fixed dice and card games. [34] In contrast to Old West and riverboat gamblers,
most professional gamblers today operate in a completely distinct social and
legal environment. The legalization of draw poker cardrooms in Gardena,
California, and gambling casinos in Nevada, both since the 1930s, has meant
that these businesses now have multimillion dollar investments to protect. It is
to their benefit to present favorable social images and offer cardroom security. These stable, sedentary cardrooms have produced a more heterogeneous
modern class of professional poker players. Members are drawn from almost
every segment of the socioeconomic, ethnic, religious, educational, and occupational ranks of American society. No longer are they typically poor, rural,
and southern.

Exposure to some form of recreational gambling or card-playing during
childhood or early adolescence lies in the background of most Gardena poker
pros. Starting in youth, poker and gambling, like chess to its avid followers,

eventually became a "passionate" game;[35] it swallowed up players' time and developed into a major interest in their lives. One lowball player, Joe T., remembers his background:

> I grew up back East. As far as I can remember my parents were always
> going to the track and having card games at home. They played
> everything. Gin, hearts, poker—you name it. In high school all the guys
> were always betting parlay cards or throwing dice somewhere. I probably
> gambled more in high school than anything else. Back then there used
> to be only one thing better I liked to do than play poker. I think they
> call it s-s-sex. But I like poker a lot better now. You know why? With sex,
> one shot and you're through. Here I can keep it up all day.

An early childhood experience with card-playing, though not an invariable prerequisite to later professional playing, nonetheless prepares the individual as a kind of informal, antecedent socialization. Unlike some deviant occupations, such as stripping and prostitution, which individuals may "drift" into one day because it is convenient,[36] professional poker-playing requires that the player at least acquire minimal playing skills and spend time learning and losing as an amateur. Professional poker players, however, do not undergo a uniform series of learning, recruitment, or training experiences. At some point, depending on their employment, financial status, and future goals, they decide almost entirely on their own when and if they are "professional."

Adolescent gambling is only one catalyst that produces intensified gambling involvement in adulthood. Another is work dissatisfaction. Most full-time players complain about their former jobs, pointing to the tedious work, hard physical labor, authoritarian atmosphere, low pay, incompatible colleagues, or the impossibility of "becoming someone" by "punching the clock." As adults, almost all Gardena pros performed nongambling work prior to turning to full-time poker-playing. Their work included such jobs as an acountant, engineer, plumber, bartender, insurance investigator, civil servant, businessman, writer, teacher, middle-level manager, postal worker, and unskilled trades of all kinds. Several players were laid off their jobs and started playing poker only as a temporary way of passing time and earning money before finally choosing it as a way of life. Says Ron T.:

> I used to be an accountant for an electronics firm. When I was working I
> used to play here a couple of times a week in the evenings after work.
> Then I got laid off and I started playing down here during the day. I was
> doing so good at it I figured, "Why should I look for a job now? I'll wait
> until I start losing." I never really did lose, so here I am. Anyway, I like
> to play cards.

Gradually the decision to seek an "honest" job in the "real world" becomes a memory of the past, something the gambler can no longer face because of the long period of unemployment, the lack of marketable skills, the adjustment problems of working at regular hours, and the increasing social and economic involvement with other gamblers. Most pros, regardless of their previous work, stated that full-time poker-playing offered more freedom to control their own time and money than any conventional job.

For the most part poker pros have self-socialized[37] themselves into full-time playing with little outside help and almost no deliberate anticipatory socialization. Once the choice is made, however, it does not mean that the life of poker is more fulfilling, fun, or easier than what they did before. One player who lost his job as a salesman when his company went bankrupt woefully summed up his situation:

> I thought it would be fun doing this for a while. You know, come and
> go any time you want to. But it's really a nightmare now. I'm here longer
> than when I had a job, and I don't even want to be here that much.
> When you get stuck you stay all day and night and don't make a damn
> buck. I'm still here from two days ago. I'm going to try to work my way
> out of this as soon as I can. Maybe I'll get back into business and not fuck
> around coming down here all the time. . . . See you here tomorrow.

TYPES OF PROFESSIONALS

As a sociological type the professional poker player is not easy to classify.[38] The diversity of working players is immense. I use the term *professional,* or *pro,* to refer to a poker player who derives all or a significant chunk of his income by playing poker as a sole or in some cases a subsidiary livelihood. In actual parlance this term is not heard very often; neither is *card shark* or *cardsharp.* One is more likely to hear *hustler, player, rounder,* or no special title at all. Because some of these more familiar labels carry judgmental or esoteric connotations, I have chosen to use the term *professional,* but not without reservations. Even though I have defined a professional primarily by the dimension of winning, actual players vary widely in degrees of poker skill and knowledge, career commitment and identification, moral sensitivity, and overall social involvement in cardroom life. There are, for example, elderly widowed women in the cardrooms who would like to win a mere $20 per day for rent and groceries. And a table away, one can find young, college-educated men "gambling it up" with daily bankrolls of thousands of dollars in the biggest games in town.

Given that this livelihood requires no special entrance examinations, standards of acceptance, formal training, or observable symbols of membership, it is difficult to state precisely what constitutes professional play. (I shall return to this point in the conclusion.) The boundaries of professional poker-playing cannot be established by definitional fiat; rather, they are constructed by self-images and situations. In this study I hope to imbue the notion of professional play with the essential characteristics of game and metagame skills and strategic methods that many of the best players discuss among themselves. I think that this can be done without elevating these players to some dubious, exalted status and making it appear that they are all dedicated craftsmen with highly tuned senses of judgment and morality who never lose. Such a characterization would be unrecognizable to them.

Four types of professional poker players can be distinguished in Gardena cardrooms. I base this typology on a close knowledge of thirty pros and lesser degrees of familiarity with forty-five more, both male and female. With few modifications, these types could be applicable to professional gamblers in other settings.

1. The *Worker Professional* includes men and women who work full-time, part-time, or sporadically and earn a substantial amount of money from gambling regularly on the side. The worker pro can be of almost any age. Obviously, not all people who have jobs and gamble frequently can be considered professionals. In fact, most part-time social gamblers are losers who must keep their jobs in order to support themselves and their costly recreation.

Many worker pros have frankly decided that playing poker as a permanent full-time occupation is more unpredictable and stressful than any conventional job. The unavoidable financial ups and downs are too difficult an adjustment to make, especially if the pro is supporting a family and must make regular monthly payments, such as on a mortgage or car. Some worker pros also admit that the idea of poker-playing as an occupation would not be acceptable to their spouses or relatives because of the stigma attached to poker as "work."[39] Even though some of these pros may play as many weekly hours as a full-time pro, they can still explain to their families that their frequent gambling is a mere hobby or form of relaxation from the pressures of their daily jobs. Familial influences, therefore, strongly affect the decision for many worker pros to remain at their regular jobs, no matter how successful they may be as players.

Some worker pros own private businesses or have flexible working hours where daily attendance is not necessary so that most spare time, including vacations, can be devoted to poker. Characteristically they arrive in the cardroom in the early afternoon and leave by the early evening. If they get "hot," they may stay later after rushing to the telephone booth to make check-in calls to home. Many of them play only during the week, leaving the weekend free for outside obligations. A few worker pros hold on to a variety of temporary jobs solely for the purpose of raising a gambling stake. They become construction laborers, bartenders, or on-and-off house-employed "shills." Once they acquire a stake and get "pumped up," they may quit their jobs and attempt to play poker on a full-time schedule. If they lose, they revert to work to support themselves and so initiate another cycle of working and playing. In Las Vegas many players take jobs as dealers, shills, or cab drivers when their private gambling is not successful.

Playing poker and gambling are an integral part of the worker pro's lifestyle. Winnings are a bonus, not "blood money" essential for social and financial survival. While gambling setbacks may occasionally force the worker pro to curtail the amount of poker-playing, or even quit for a while, he or she can still depend on a regular job as a continuing source of income. To the worker pro job security in predictable paychecks and the social appearance of legitimacy are more valued alternatives than attempting to live and work full-time in the poker cardroom.

2. The *Outside-supported Professional* does not work regularly but has a steady source of income from a pension, retirement or trust fund, savings account, unemployment or welfare check, investments, social security, alimony, or the beneficence of working relatives or a spouse. Like the worker pro, the outside-supported pro can adequately support himself without playing poker. Many retired men and women, nonworking housewives, and students fits into this category. They play in small-stakes games, usually during the day, trying to eke out a small profit. They consider poker-playing a form of recreation and a relief from boredom and loneliness rather than an aggressive, competitive contest of skill. Most of them are satisfied to cash out a modest profit over the week or month and not to lose or win big amounts in any one sitting.

Another type of outside-supported professional is the wealthy retiree, widow or widower, or divorced player with a large outside income. In playing style and money management strategies this player is completely different from the pension-dependent elderly person. Many men in this category are extremely competitive and play in the highest-stakes games. While they may play poker every day, most consider poker-playing as recreation, even if it is a full-time one, more than as a permanent money-making occupation. Since these players can "take it or leave it" financially, their attendance in the cardroom is not dependent on their poker successes.

3. The *Subsistence Professional* is usually a retiree or younger man who chooses not to work for others.[40] In order to survive this pro must play poker and win consistently. The subsistence pro is interested mainly in making a daily moderate income to support himself and to remain out of debt. He prefers to play in small- or medium-stakes games with the intention of winning no more than a hundred dollars at a time. Sometimes he sits down in five or more different games during the day and night and with each small win gets

up and cashes out. The subsistence pro does not choose to play in the most aggressive games or against the best players; he, in fact, avoids them. Poker is simply a convenient tool to earn quick, daily money. His major concern and strategy is to "last" financially, since for many of these players the cardroom, where they eat their meals, watch television, and meet with friends is their entire social and recreational life.

While some subsistence pros see poker-playing as a more or less permanent activity, others, particularly those who are unemployed and eager to work, think of poker only as a temporary involvement. Like the hopeful writer or actor, for example, the subsistence pro waits for a significant vocational interest to bloom outside of the club or for "something better to come along." Subsistence pros generally do not make any firm emotional, self-identificational, or social commitments to full-time poker-playing.

4. The *Career Professional* lives almost entirely on poker winnings. He usually plays in the biggest games available and actively seeks out other competitive opponents. The career pro has made a personal commitment to poker-playing as a full-time permanent occupation. His main goals are to win consistently, gain peer recognition, and continually sharpen his skills and knowledge. For the career pro, poker is far more than a tool to earn money. Poker-playing is a skillful trade that must be exercised with confidence and control at every opportunity. Unless he goes busted and is forced to accept other employment, he is not concerned with and does not want to worry about an outside job. Some of the more successful players, however, may earn additional income from outside investments that have been financed by poker winnings.

Table 1 summarizes the social characteristics of thirty male outside-supported, subsistence, and career pros. (I have omitted worker pros because they are an extremely heterogeneous group and their identities are harder to ascertain than the others.) Almost two-thirds of this sample of Gardena pros are unmarried or divorced. The majority white; minorities, in descending order, are Asians, blacks, and Latins. Playing poker is the favorite kind of gambling for almost all of these pros. Less than half attend the race track, the next most popular gambling activity, or bet on major sports events. In their physical appearance the pros do not uniformly fit the picture of the Runyon-esque dandified Broadway gambler, although some flaunt their winnings and high-rolling life-style with new clothing and expensive jewelry (gold watches and chains and diamond and gold rings are extremely popular). Other pros, even at high levels, display no sign of material interest. They dress in conventional leisure clothing, drive modest automobiles, and live in rented apartments in the greater Los Angeles area, many in or near Gardena.

As a group, outside-supported pros are older than the others and more than half are married. Subsistence pros are younger and almost all are single.

TABLE 1

CHARACTERISTICS OF THIRTY MALE PROFESSIONALS

Type of professional	N =	Age range	Mean age	Number married	Usual game stakes	Career identity	Upward mobility
Outside-supported	11	32-60	53	7	All ranges	None to moderate	None or little
Subsistence	8	32-45	38	1	Small to medium	Little to moderate	None or little
Career	11	26-43	32	3	Medium to high	Moderate to high	Little to much

Career pros form the youngest group and most are unmarried. The overall profile of the typical male Gardena poker professional reveals an unmarried, young to middle-aged (30-55) man whose formal education ended at high school or with two years or less of college. While gambling and poker playing were commonplace among peers and sometimes at home, none were themselves the children of professional gamblers. Most held one or more nongambling jobs and finally settled on poker-playing as an occupation not as a deliberate first-choice career but because of outside job dissatisfaction, a layoff, or early retirement. One of those reasons tied to a more than average interest in poker and initial success at part-time gambling cemented the pro's decision to try to make poker-playing a more permanent vocation.

From a small sample (N = 6) of full-time female players, five are either divorced or widowed. Their mean age is forty-eight. Most fall into the category of outside-supported or subsistence pros. Although some of these women may earn as much as or more than their male counterparts at the same level of play, female pros as a group do not demonstrate any significant degree of career identification or commitment. (Data from Las Vegas poker cardrooms may prove otherwise.) Gardena women, for example, do not plan to move to Las Vegas, play for increasingly higher stakes, or worry about the social acceptance of their cardroom activities. Like some of the men, most of the women played part-time poker during a period when they worked at outside jobs or when they were housewives. For the better female players poker-playing as a recreation increased in frequency as they won, and they then moved up to bigger games. When social relationships with spouses and growing children were weakened or severed, poker-playing changed into a nearly daily activity, a social and economic substitute for fading outside relationships. The women never considered poker a first occupational choice. It is rather an alternative precipitated by social and economic conditions outside of the cardroom. When women pros begin to lose heavily, unlike men they are more likely to curtail the frequency of their play or drop to a smaller game than attempt to build a completely new bankroll by seeking an outside job or borrowing extensively from other players in the cardroom.

These four types of professional poker players are ideal types in the Weberian sense.[41] These are primarily descriptive categories based on the actual characteristics of many different players; as such, they are not intended to be definitive, mutually exclusive categories. This typology then must be recognized as highly flexible as it applies to specific players.[42] Whether a player fits into one category or another is dependent on his perceptions of self, his success, and his gambling aspirations. Many winners would deny that poker is anything more than a game of chance or a temporary pastime and would scoff at any mention of professionalism. Some long-time cardroom habitués, however, make highly vocal claims of their professional status. Many players do not fit into any single type, and some fall into two or more types simultaneously or sequentially. A player may resemble a money-conscious subsistence pro in the morning game and if he loses risk more than he usually does with the career pros in the night game. Any one player may slide from one type to another or out of the entire typology as his winnings move up and down or as outside pressures influence his allocation of time, energy, and money.

I estimate the total number of subsistence and career pros in Gardena cardrooms to be around one hundred *at any one time.*[43] It is more difficult to calculate the exact number of outside-supported and worker pros. They do not have to gamble as often as subsistence and career pros, and their profits above other sources of income cannot be measured precisely. In Las Vegas cardrooms at least several hundred career professionals can be found in action. Like those in Gardena, their range of wealth, skill, and identification with poker varies considerably. Additional poker pros can be found in other California cardrooms and in Lake Tahoe and Reno, Nevada. I cannot guess the number of professionals who play in private home games throughout the country, even though many of them probably overlap as casino and cardroom players. I must emphasize that the estimate for Gardena or any other place does *not* refer to the same players over time. The cardrooms can support only a small percentage of winners, and not all winners are professionals. Because of the hazards of daily poker-playing and heavy losses, many pros go busted and are forced to survive precariously or drop out of the system entirely. In their place a new crop of unemployed men, housewives, or retired workers attempts to step in, not as personal substitutes for one specific dropout but as competitors-at-large. They remain until other players force them out of the chain of survival.

DOING FACE-WORK

Remaining in the game, especially for the career pro, demands more than financial and temporal investments. Maintaining a high degree of career identification for the professional poker player means espousing a new self-image and definition of routines and tasks, what Erving Goffman calls face-work:

> The term *face* may be defined as the positive social value a person effectively claims for himself by the line others assume he has taken during a particular contact. Fact is an image of self delineated in terms of approved social attributes — albeit an image that others may share, as when a person makes a good showing for his profession or religion by making a good showing for himself . . . By *face-work* I mean to designate the actions taken by a person to make whatever he is doing consistent with face. Face-work seems to counteract "incidents" — that is, events whose effective symbolic implications threaten face.[44]

26

The need for face-work varies immensely among different professional types and according to stakes, sex, and age. Many low-level pros, for whom the cardroom is their only social existence, care little about their image either outside or inside of the cardroom. As one observes the publicly recognized high-stakes career pros in the higher echelons of the hierarchy, the display of positive face-work increases proportionately. Women pros, who occupy mainly the middle and lower ranges of the hierarchy and are not career oriented, do not seem particularly committed to any sort of occupational identification and thus make no attempts at face-work. Even if they make an adequate subsistence by playing poker, they can easily detach themselves from the "serious" life of career playing.

While many outsiders consider poker-playing a kind of deviant work, the values of this occupation in wealth, success, and material comforts are not all that different from those in conventional occupations. Gale Miller observes in his study of "odd jobs": "Although deviant workers differ from others with respect to the stigma that is attached to their work and themselves, the negative public image of these persons only complicates their work lives—it does not make their work categorically different from that of others."[45] Miller adds that "an adequate understanding of deviant work in contemporary society must involve a consideration of the ways in which such work skills and rationales are distributed and made available."[46]

In order for deviant workers to negotiate greater respectability for their occupations, routine tasks may take on newly significant motives and presume to serve important societal needs, as when prostitutes or taxi-dancers assert that they are providing a necessary service to the public.[47] Following this line some professional duplicate bridge players define their play as "education."[48] Several public and closet professional gamblers do the same by referring to themselves as "actuarial advisors" or "speculators."[49] Dismissing the idea that poker is a mere game or recreation, some Gardena poker pros make frequent comparisons between poker-playing and other kinds of nongambling work. Rick H. explained:

Most people think that poker is a game. It isn't, man. It's work. You have to work at it like anything else and you get the payoffs. You can't just sit down and play. I go and think about the players and the game for a while and draw up a game plan. I don't like to play long hours because I'm concentrating and figuring the odds all the time. Hell, I work less hours a month than a doctor, and I can take vacations any time I want to. This is what I want to do. This is my career.

Career pros speak of poker-playing as a time-consuming yet generally rewarding life-style. They frequently play for long hours—even days—at a time, but they do not consider themselves compulsive gamblers, nor do they want to be treated as such. The compulsive gambler, it is explained, is a poor player and a consistent loser who does not possess the psychological makeup for skillful, controlled play. Several pros, however, publicly admitted that they were "sick" because they preferred playing cards to anything else: "I see these guys down here more than my wife and kids. I've sure been screwed a lot, but never been kissed. Sure I'm sick to play here. What do you think if you sit here all day and night?" This kind of self-diagnosis is a partial acknowledgment that gambling is not "normal" work. The diagnosis may also be the social actor's affirmation of the stigma on full-time gambling. Doing face-work, then, the gambler may present not only positive social images, although they seem to be the most important ones, but he may sometimes choose faces that set him apart and make him different, faces that shock outsiders. He may deliberately adopt stigmatized characteristics, parade them, and label himself as undesirable, useless, or deviant.[50]

The current professional poker player's image extends far beyond the walls of the once isolated cardrooms and backrooms of bars. Therefore, one writer on gambling notes

it becomes important that these winners portray the proper image to the public. There's no reason why these super-players shouldn't endorse products and give testimonials, just like other winning personalities. They can go on to bring fame to the game of poker through public exposure in the various media.[51]

Professionals playing poker at this high level have become increasingly concerned with public acceptance and public assurance that cardroom games are on the level and players honorable. In short, respectability and legitimacy are the primary goals of most face-work. Once vast sums of money are won and lost, gambling activities seem to draw the favorable curiosity of the public. Media coverage enhances occupational respectability and carries an obviously materialistic message. A player who displays tall stacks of black one-hundred-dollar chips is a person to be envied no matter what his line of work. The occupational image of the professional poker player is improving in position relative to images in other deviant occupations to which poker has been compared. The apparent reasons are the rapture of the public media, the huge sums of money at stake, and players' louder, positive images of self and work.

2
Social Organization of the Cardroom

Poker is America's most favorite game. Seventy million
adults play cards and about 47 million Americans prefer
poker. Poker is as American as baseball and hot dogs. Many
of our most famous Presidents were poker enthusiasts. Poker
contains a greater amount of skill than bridge, or any other
card game, according to authority John Scarne. *

Card playing, like all gambling, has never been without its vehement critics. Responding to public pressure, the California legislature in 1891 passed a law specifically prohibiting gambling and the playing of stud poker in poker houses. A strange quirk in the law, however, exempted draw poker from this ruling.[1] Explaining this law in 1911, Harold Sigel Webb, the attorney general of California, ruled that draw poker was a game of *skill* because no cards were dealt face up as they were in stud. Draw poker was therefore not gambling and could not be stopped by antigambling laws. This decision opened the way for the operation of numerous public, legal draw poker clubs throughout California. At present over 400 cardrooms (the estimates vary) are scattered over the entire state in 176 different communities. The cardrooms range in

*From a Gardena cardroom brochure.

appearance from converted storefronts with one or two tables to Gardena's carpeted and chandeliered "poker palaces."

Modern five-card draw poker was about fifty years old by the time the flat, fertile land of the Gardena valley, fifteen miles south of downtown Los Angeles, was being settled by fruit and vegetable farmers. By 1930 the newly incorporated city of Gardena had grown to a population of 3,000. Six years later its residents legalized the operation of draw poker within the city limits.

The economy of the city of Gardena, with a population now of over 50,000, is built on numerous nurseries, industries, manufacturing plants, and, of course, the city's six large public poker cardrooms (the Rainbow, Monterey, Horseshoe, Normandie, El Dorado, and Gardena). Combined, the cardrooms can seat over 1,500 poker players at one time, making the cardrooms the greatest concentration of draw poker clubs in the world.[2] Because of the presence of these cardrooms in this residential suburb (80 percent of Gardena's residents are homeowners), the clubs must continually respond to criticism that equates poker and gambling with other vices. In order to live in peace with antigambling forces, such as the church, some city politicians and lawmakers, and the local chapter of Gamblers Anonymous, the cardrooms defend themselves as respectable, legitimate businesses that offer inexpensive meals for local businessmen, jobs for many city residents, and low property taxes for Gardena homeowners.[3]

That legal poker cardrooms exist in Gardena is not well publicized. Many people in the Los Angeles area have neither heard of Gardena (often mispronounced "Gardenia") nor its poker clubs; others believe, erroneously, that twenty-one and other casino games are played illicitly in miniature Las Vegas-style casinos. The cardrooms would like to promote a positive public image because they must remain on good terms with community leaders and politicians and can be voted out of operation by city residents.[4] Billboards and advertisements, for example, emphasize dining facilities and conviviality. One poster reads, "Get a Great Deal on Dining." Another noticeable billboard at a major intersection indicates: "Turn right. There's food and fine entertainment. Meet and enjoy friends." The "entertainment" presumably is a bashful reference to poker-playing, for the cardrooms do not feature stage performers of any kind.

All Gardena poker cardrooms are relatively modest single-story buildings that stand next to large, adjacent parking lots. Personalized license plates ("I Bet," "Wheel," and "Gimme Two") in the parking lots clearly reveal the preoccupations of the cars' owners. Each cardroom houses a restaurant, lounge, and television room, but since alcoholic beverages cannot be served on the premises neighborhood bars do a lively business. Players can buy drinks in these bars with cash or cardroom chips.

Neon lights in the shape of a pointing arrow flash the name of each club on its exterior wall, and a smaller wooden sign signals whether the place is open or closed. Cardrooms are open freely to the adult public (adults over 21) twenty-four hours a day, although each cardroom is closed one day in the middle of the week. On any one day at least four cardrooms are open, and all are in operation from Friday morning to Tuesday morning. A poker player can find action every hour and every day of the year except Christmas.

American Legion and VFW posts hold the operating licenses of three of the clubs.[5] This practice began in 1945 when Gardena began to help returning servicemen by allowing them to hold card club licenses out of which they received regular fees. The clubs themselves are owned by numerous individuals, each of whom holds "points," or shares in the club.

While clocks are distinctly absent in Las Vegas casinos, time is a constant reminder in Gardena poker cardrooms.[6] No windows indicate whether it is day or night, but strategically placed clocks on the wall indicate the hour and half hour by a red-lighted bulb. When the red light on the face of the clocks turns on, *time,* the required fee for playing, must be paid. Depending on the stakes of the game, fees vary from $1 to $10 per half hour. There are no other taxes, membership costs, or pot rake-offs. The gross revenue for all six clubs exceeds $30 million per year. In 1980 the city of Gardena was allocated approximately $4 million in annual taxes and license fees, or about 25 percent of its total operating budget.[7]

Because of the importance of playing on *time,* of paying to play, Gardena poker can best be described as a no-nonsense, speedy affair. In some games as many as forty to sixty hands are dealt per hour; this amounts to one complete game every minute or minute and a half. Shuffling, cutting, dealing, and the mechanics of opening, betting, and drawing cards are performed smoothly in a matter of seconds. In contrast with the staged scenes of poker games in popular novels and films, commercial cardroom players never make long-winded speeches about calling, raising, or folding because other players would not allow them, not wanting to hear yet another "poker story." Nor can players run to the bank or sell their houses for more money while involved in a hand, for the law prohibits playing with any money that is not on the table. The social and physical ambiance of Gardena cardrooms is completely structured for serious poker-playing, and there are fewer distractions than in cardrooms elsewhere. In Las Vegas hotels, for example, cardrooms are usually allocated a small side area away from the main casino floor and its dice, twenty-one, and roulette tables and slot machines. Even so, a player sitting in a Las Vegas poker game must contend with clanging slot machines, noisy acts in the front lounge, gawking tourists walking between the casino and the elevators, and the general hubbub produced by hundreds of other casino gamblers on the move.

Spatially, the Gardena cardrooms consist of the *floor,* the rectangular or

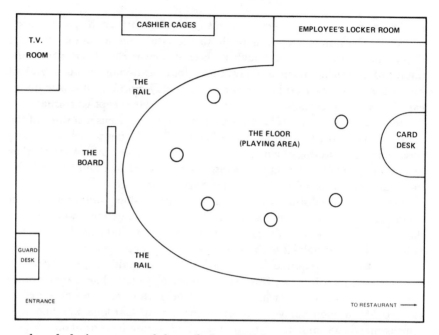

oval card playing area, and the *rail,* the adjoining section where spectators or "railbirds" watch and incoming players wait. The wooden rail is not only a physical partition; it is a symbolic separation where busted, desperate gamblers play vicariously and wait for willing moneylenders. By law each cardroom holds a maximum of thirty-five tables, seating eight players to a table, and is divided about equally into tables for high-draw and lowball poker, although the latter game seems to be fractionally more popular with customers.[8] Tables in each half vary according to the stakes of the game. Game stakes, set by law, are classified according to the required amount of the bet before the draw and after the draw. The standard stakes are: $1-2, $2-4, $3-6, $5-10, $10-20, $15-30, $20-40, $30-60, $40-80, $60-120, $80-160, and $100-200. In order to sit down in a chosen game, the player must purchase an initial *buy-in* of at least ten times the opening bet, that is, $10 worth of chips in a $1-2 game or $400 in the $40-80. All bets and raises, unlimited in number, must be made in these exact increments, unless a player is "all-in" (has only part of the bet remaining in front of him).

TEMPORAL ORGANIZATION

Like the demarcating barriers of the floor and rail and the games of varying prices, the temporal organization of the cardroom also divides and brings together a diverse assortment of competitors. It is difficult to determine with

32

precision the beginning and ending of some games that go on all day and night and are fed by a constant supply of new players as big winners and losers leave the game. A brief outline of twenty-four hours inside the cardroom will show how much of its activities and player traffic is regulated by the organization of life in outside society.

8 A.M. to 12 noon. The early daytime players walk into a quiet cardroom that is no more than a third or quarter full. The blackboard (the waiting list) begins to fill up with players' initials, and while waiting they eat breakfast, drink coffee at empty tables, read the newspaper, or study the racing form. Some tables have never broken up and have continued with four or five players throughout the night. As midmorning approaches new games at every stakes level begin. By noon 50 to 75 percent of the tables have a game in progress. Arriving players wait on the rail or in the restaurant, which is cluttered with nonplaying lunchtime diners.

Noon to 6 P.M. Most tables in all stakes are "solid" with the early morning players, afternoon regulars, and part-time gamblers who have come directly from their jobs. By the evening many housewives, day workers, businessmen, and elderly patrons leave for home. The early morning players, after eight to ten hours of poker, also leave, and the cardroom begins to thin out before the evening rush hour.

6 P.M. to 12 midnight. This is the busiest period in the cardroom. Most of the tables are "going" with games, and the rail is bustling with waiting players and diners. Additional players arrive after a day at the racetrack, evening sporting events, or dinner elsewhere. In the late evening the graveyard shift of gamblers, who have slept all day, finally strolls in. As midnight approaches the last of the remaining day players leave, as do those who work at day jobs and winners who have played since the afternoon. More games break up and new tables are consolidated from the old ones. By midnight seats are available in most games and arriving participants can usually sit down with no delay.

Midnight to 8 A.M. Although many games are made up of less than eight players and are likely to break up at any time, some of the liveliest poker action takes place during these hours, stimulated mainly by losers who are losing badly; this is called being "hot and stuck." The rail is empty and the television room is closed for the night. Only half at most of the card tables are in action, and no new games are begun. There are no initials on the blackboard, and new players are instructed to see the floorman for a seat. The remaining players are those who are attempting to get even from the day or afternoon and the late-night shift who are wide awake and planning to settle down to card-playing for the entire night. Only a few new players arrive after evening work or recreation. Some high-stakes players walk in after leaving busted games in other cardrooms. During the early morning rush hour, some players who had been losing too much to leave finally bolt out the door and

33

drive directly to their day jobs. The full-time gamblers, the unemployed and retired, and those who stubbornly persist in getting even continue to play and do not worry about the time as much as they do about their visible playing stakes. Hours after sunrise, the day shift of employees and new early morning players arrive to begin another day in the nonstop cycle of poker-playing.

Attendance in the cardrooms fluctuates not only during a twenty-four-hour cycle but during longer periods—the week, month, and year—when it predictably increases and decreases according to the occurrence of outside celebrations, holidays, and important sporting events. Many cardroom players avidly watch and bet on major baseball, football, basketball, and boxing matches and leave the tables noticeably depleted. Generally, Friday evening is the most crowded playing time, Sunday and Monday evenings the least. Each month the early weeks and weekends are busier than those at the end of the month when many busted players must wait for first-of-the-month paychecks. On national holidays and vacations around Christmas and New Year's, attendance increases and the cardroom is congested with waiting players. Playing dips slightly after these end-of-year holidays and reaches its lowest point in June, the summer vacation season for many working regulars.

In addition to these broad temporal and social fluctuations in play, social commitments outside of the cardrooms also affect frequency and duration of play. For a smaller field of professionals and cardroom hangers-on, however, every day—holiday or payday—is a gambling day. Outside events take a distant second place to playing poker. Dedicated regulars will be at the cardroom on New Year's Eve, on Monday mornings, at the beginning and end of each month, in heavy rain and fog and in the baking heat of summer, and at almost any other time when they are not sleeping. Vacations are not missed. One player said that he cut short a camping trip with his family after a few days because he got "horny" for poker. These gamblers, the solid core of the cardroom, must adapt to the outside society's temporal life only inasmuch as it regulates who and how many other players will appear in their well-worn territory to give them a gamble.

CARDROOM EMPLOYEES

When tables are filled it is the task of the *boardman* to record the initials of waiting players on a large, visible blackboard divided into high and low sections and by game stakes. The "board" indicates which games are going and which ones are yet to begin as players' initials are added to the waiting list. Above the chattering voices and the clacking chips, the monotonous drone of the *floorman* can be heard reading initials from the board and designating games available for immediate seating. The floorman, who organizes games in a specific section of the cardroom, has more contact with players than any other employee. A floorman with long experience knows the initials of several hundred players, their favorite game and stakes, and their success record. Although some floormen may have a passing interest in poker and gambling, not many of them are regular players. All, however, are knowledgeable about the house rules and regulations of cardroom poker.[9]

The floorman-customer relationship, though decidedly advantageous to the former, is bonded by the reciprocal exchange of favors and tips. After a big win many regular customers throw the floorman a chip, accompanied by the invitation "Buy yourself a drink." Regulars also indirectly tip the floorman by "taking out" chips for new decks of cards, which players in high-stakes games can request every several hours. When the new deck is brought to the table, an ante or two is taken from each pot until $10-30 is collected. From this amount the floorman receives the largest share and gives the boardman, section porter, and the cardroom manager a "toke." The floorman may reciprocate the goodwill of the players by "looking away" and charging them less than the actual collection fees for the game they are playing at high-stakes tables, or sometimes by taking no collection at all if the game is four-handed or less.[10]

High-stakes and low-stakes poker sections are supervised by a separate floorman or floormen. Veteran floormen oversee the big games, while trainees look after the small tables. One of the floorman's main duties is to ensure that each table is composed of at least seven players, because paying customers, especially in small-stakes games, frequently complain about playing in "short" games. The floorman also understands that waiting players on the rail represent lost revenue to the club, so he must be decisive about starting new games and be able to recognize which initials on the board are "live," that is, represent actual players who will not turn down the game, and which ones are "dead." In addition, the floorman arbitrates disputes concerning technicalities of play, changes decks when requested, monitors seat changes, and directs the novice floormen and chipgirls in his section of the floor.

Chipgirls (only recently including some males) are uniformly clothed in white blouses and dark pants or skirts and wear a heavy, compartmentalized apron that is loaded with cardroom chips. They convert players' cash into "checks" (cardroom chips), take half-hourly collection fees, and act as waitresses, serving food and beverages to the players. Symbiotic relationships, like those of the floorman and customer, frequently develop between cardroom regulars and established chipgirls. Although the practice is not condoned by the house, chipgirls allow some well-known daily players to buy chips without paying immediately in cash (this is called "playing out of the apron"). Players reciprocate such favors with handsome tips.

The only other significant cardroom employee who is in contact with players regularly is the house-employed *prop* (proposition player)[11] or "shill," the latter term more familiar in Las Vegas casinos. But Gardena props, unlike Las Vegas shills who roll dice at empty crap tables and decorate the baccarat pit to give the impression of action and to attract customers, are salaried by the house (at about $90-150 per day) and must play poker and pay *time* with their own money. They do not merely pretend to gamble; they are actual players. Props are overwhelmingly male, equally divided between single and married men, and each cardroom employs from six to twelve of them in staggered shifts. The prop's most important role is to fill in seats at tables that are short of outside customers. At the request of the floorman, props must change tables and games as they are needed in different sections of the club.

The *club manager* orchestrates the entire crew of cardroom employees during his working shift. He usually sits behind a protected center card desk or in his office, although he sometimes wanders around the club, remaining inconspicuously in the background along with higher level managers and pointholders. Most managers appear as stylish businessmen in conservative suits, white shirts, and ties. Ambitious floormen are sometimes trained for these positions. The official policy of management regarding players is that the poker cardroom is first and foremost a business that derives its income from renting seats to willing patrons. The club manager is therefore not particularly interested in who wins or loses, how much a player wins or loses, or the concomitant social and psychological repercussions. To the manager, professional poker players, if they are even identifiable, are merely reliable daily customers. The manager's primary attention focuses on how many seats are occupied by satisfied, returning players. He prefers to see long games where players do not go busted too quickly and make complaints about the other players or the cardroom. Cardrooms compete among themselves to see which one can fill the most tables and produce the largest annual gross earnings. Gardena cardrooms and their pointholders and employees have been instrumental in defeating legal measures to open cardrooms in nearby communities in order to restrict competition.[12]

Filling out the personnel of the cardroom are other employees — porters, restaurant waitresses, busboys, checkgirls, cashiers, guards, parking lot attendants, telephone operators, and card desk bookkeepers — with whom the player's interactions are normally minimal. All employees, however, serve as part of the necessary backdrop, functioning silently and efficiently against the daily table dramas of winning and losing.

SOCIAL CONTROL IN THE CARDROOM

Any person who upsets the economic, legal, or social functioning of the cardroom may be ejected, temporarily or permanently, depending on the decision of the cardroom manager. Undesirables include obnoxious drunks, brawlers, obvious cheats and thieves, and those who persistently cause aggravation to the players and employees. Because the cardrooms earn their income from the number of players they attract, they also bar entrepreneurs or hustlers who steer regulars into poker games in motel rooms or private homes within Gardena city limits. As a nearly self-sufficient society, the cardrooms prefer to solve problems of social control within their domain by their own rules and systems of enforcement. Except in rare cases, they do not seek help from the local police. By calling on outside support they are in effect advertising that poker-playing and cardrooms create trouble and require supervision. This is an image they do not want to display in a sometimes critical community.

Almost all social controls at the card table are directed toward maintaining a fast-moving game. Everything else is unwanted distraction. The responsibility for conducting a fast game, in the absence of house dealers, lies mainly, and equally, with the players themselves. A boisterous player who assumes too much authority and control on his own may be addressed derogatorily as the "table captain." The few who feel that their behavior is beyond reproach and must have the game played their own way may also be reprimanded for acting like prima donnas. When a loser complained of an easy-paced, slow game, an observer quickly raised his voice in protest:

Man, you are way out of line! You ought to see yourself when you're winning. You're jerking off and telling jokes and holding up the game to your own speed. When you're losing you're the first one to want to speed it up and play fast. You ought to play with a mirror in front of your face so you can see what you're doing.

Peer group criticism at the card table is the major sanctioning agent for social control and for regulating improper behavior and adhering to general cardroom norms. Some personal idiosyncrasies can be overlooked as long as a player looks like he might have a lot of money to lose and does not slow down the game. As exceptions, "loose" drunks are allowed their moments of kinetic instability and poker novices their retarded pace, as long as they do not carry it too far. To losers who are anxious to play and get even, slow games, when not enough hands are dealt, are particularly frustrating. A loser will usually demand to "play fast" and find support from others. Playing fast means helping to do menial clearing work like pushing chips to the winners and throwing in discards to the next dealer. It is also an appeal to curtail "bullshit" like excessive table talk, holding on to winning hands as a semipermanent prize, and deliberately, joyfully acting out deceptive moves in the few seconds after the hand is officially over. With well-timed remarks and cooperation, a disrupted game will normally speed up until the next social breakdown. Most of the time informal face-to-face sanctions imposed on players by other players are sufficient to maintain social control.

Two serious kinds of interruptions—violent physical altercations and card-playing arguments—require appeal to higher authority. At the first clamor of raised voices, the floorman will run toward the antagonists and attempt to quell the disturbance. If he and his compatriots are unable to keep angry players apart, the security guards will intervene. Usually their presence alone, if a fight has not yet broken out, will suffice to return players to their normal state.

As much as fisticuffs interrupt the flow of play, they are not a significant threat to the social order of the cardroom. Lesser card-playing disputes, which often concern improprieties, misinterpretations or ignorance of the technicalities of play, and ambiguities of body and hand movements, occur more frequently and are more difficult to resolve. A rap of the knuckles on the table may indicate indecision but can be interpreted by another player as a pass and concession of the pot; the dealer may hesitate when dealing cards to himself and his hand may be declared dead; or a player may pull some hidden money from under an ashtray when he has a good hand and wants to raise the pot. Incidents like these challenge the rules of cardroom play and the tenuous foundations of over-the-table social relationships every day. Most of the time players do not attempt to make decisions on their own because their arguments would remain unsolved. They would rather rely on an official decision rendered by the floorman or manager. Whenever a cardroom authority is called, the game is halted, the cards and chips are left in place, and the troublesome hand is recounted. When a particularly difficult problem over a technicality arises, the players request the cardroom manager, the ultimate authority, rather than the floorman.

It is not to any player's advantage to continually balk at slight improprieties and seek out petty decisions: this would violate the most important cardroom norm, speedy play. Players usually slavishly obey the general rules and etiquette of cardroom poker without supervision and suppression. Sometimes they even make up their own rules for the game as long as everyone at the table agrees. Late at night I have played in some games where the cards were dealt counterclockwise, each player held six cards, two jokers were put in the deck, deuces were wild, or the betting limits were increased beyond legal standards. All these agreements, of course, are illegal by cardroom and city regulations and will be stopped immediately by the floorman or manager if discovered.

Gardena poker play follows forty-one general house rules (see appendix B). In all the cardrooms I have observed, regular players and floormen generally overlook or selectively enforce at least fifteen of these rules.[13] Cardroom managers, however, rarely deviate from literal interpretation of the book's rules. Let us examine three of these written rules to see how the quality of enforcement reveals organizational flexibility for different types of players at different levels of play.

Rule 3: Players may not ante for other players. In many high-stakes games friends routinely ante each other whenever one wins a pot. I have never heard of objections to this practice in a big game, probably because the antes represent such a small amount relative to the size of the bets. Anteing is more a ritual token of involvement than a sum that makes a difference between winning or losing. In small games, however, the ante is usually closer to the size of the bets and players are more fastidious about correct anteing procedures.[14]

Rule 30: All chips must be kept on the table. When money is placed on the table, chips must be requested. Gamblers in big games often keep and protect large bills under their stack of cardroom chips. It is understood, of course, that this money "plays" if it is needed for a bet. Players also deliberately change chips back into cash if the stacks in front of them might draw unwanted attention from onlookers. Money and chips change form and go on and off the table with regularity. But in small games, where players usually do not sit down with more than four or five times the required buy-in, frequent arguments arise when a player is caught "squirreling away" a quarter chip or a dollar bill in his pocket. For regulars in these games would like a chance to win all the chips they can force another player to buy. In contrast, many pros and high-rollers carry with them or have access to ten to a hundred times the minimal buy-in. Greater cash flow means that the rules pertaining to the immediate purchase of chips and the exchange of money will be more relaxed.

Rule 32: No playing behind. This rule means that a player can only make bets with chips that are stacked in front of him. He cannot play with promised money. This rule is strictly enforced in small-stakes games. In big games, however, many regulars do not always like to purchase chips or pull money out of their pockets when losing or "down to the cloth" (having only a few chips left). In this condition they often declare themselves to be "playing behind," "playing open," or "covering all bets." Such a declaration saves the player the trouble of buying chips immediately and give him a sense of greater control over vanishing money. Regulars, pros, and friends will trust one another to make good such bets. But if a cardroom stranger or known (and hungry) loser should make a similar promise, the floorman will be called in to make sure that he purchases chips before the next hand is dealt.

Twelve other cardroom rules are likewise selectively enforced. Regulars and trustworthy patrons are given greater interpretive leverage than strangers and small players who can be controlled more easily by citing specific rules and appealing to higher cardroom authorities. In high-stakes games that draw together a denser concentration of professionals and friendly regulars, rules are more lax and their interpretation becomes an issue only when an irritated player complains, such as when one commented: "I've seen more bullshit and wheeling and dealing go on in some of these games than you can believe. If some of those players were playing somewhere else they would have been

39

barred or shot dead. It's a wonder any new players ever sit in the game with the reputation it's got. People talk about it all the time, about the fooling around and crap. Play right for a change."

As in many other bureaucratic and hierarchical social systems, rules in the cardroom are enforced differentially from top to bottom. Friendship, money, and reputation can nurture advantageous cardroom flexibility. As John Lukacs has concluded, "Poker is a game of a thousand unwritten rules... there are a thousand different ways in which poker can be played *legally* but *not quite correctly,* where its rules are strictly observed but its human relationships are not."[15]

THE PLAYERS: INITIAL SOCIAL CATEGORIES

Gardena's six poker parlors attract over a quarter of a million players annually.[16] Some writers in the popular press have chosen to publicize the clubs and their patrons in an ungenerous light. One writer commented that the many elderly players in one club reminded him of "recruiting posters for Forest Lawn,"[17] while another described Gardena as a "repository for exhausted lives."[18] Sometimes the players themselves perpetuate these portrayals. When one player wished aloud, "There should be a home for degenerate lowball players to go when they get old," another added quickly, "There is. You're here."

Indeed there is a noticeable proportion of elderly players in the cardrooms. But poker-playing seems to be a secondary interest; most of them lose and expect to lose. Their main concern seems to be to pass the time in small-stakes games, meet with friends, watch television, and eat moderately priced meals. In this respect, generally maligned and neglected social institutions such as bus depots, racetracks, and cardrooms may fulfill beneficial social functions that have gone unrecognized.[19] Referring to elderly gamblers in Las Vegas, a psychologist has concluded that

> we find that millions of small gamblers, men and women, with families
> and without, often find that gambling provides them with the
> opportunity to participate in the decision-making process that is often
> denied them in factory, office, or home. It offers them the opportunity
> to win and experience the joy that comes with winning, and it offers
> momentary hope. Seldom venturing more than they can afford, they are
> for the moment able to escape the humdrum of their daily existences
> and experience the peak emotion of total involvement.[20]

From a survey and estimate of about 1,500 players in Gardena, Jones[21] calculates that 46 percent of the men and 74 percent of the women are over 60 years of age. These figures, however, could be misleading and would show greater variation if other factors were taken into account, namely, the specific club, the time of day, and, most important, the stakes of the game. The elderly tend to concentrate in two or three clubs that offer a higher proportion of small-stakes games. Few players over 60-65 are regular players in big games. Most of the older players also tend to be day and early evening players who avoid late-night hours and all-night play. The cardrooms thus show a clear-cut stratification by age that a casual observer would not discern if he or she did not properly sample by time and cardroom area.

At the extreme end of this critical spectrum sit outraged moralists such as Walter Wagner, a publicist for Gamblers Anonymous, who states that in Gardena lives are forever being destroyed by the gambling "plague," and that house-employed props coldly extract their income from the gullible public. Many of Wagner's assertions are hasty and undocumented. For example: "I'd estimate that the clubs cash at least 10 percent of the Social Security checks in Southern California. [And] more than 50 percent of the people who play at Gardena are Jews. And, of course, they're all losers."[22] A sour Gardena poker loser expresses his special pique against women: "All are old, fat, wear heavy makeup and too much perfume, complain about everything in general and the pretty waitresses in particular, and each has enough money to open her own branch of the Bank of America."[23]

The spare attention and haphazard observations of journalists and writers, intolerant moralists, and the few students of gambling show a paucity of reliable data about the cardrooms. The many distortions and self-serving stereotypes remain unchallenged because most observations are based on little or no participation in the cardrooms, coupled with a vague understanding of the social dynamics of poker-playing. A closer, "inside" examination of the thousands of poker players reveals that their own social categories, which for the most part go beyond "first impressions," govern the underlying pattern of whom players are and are not likely to compete against.

Players are categorized initially by themselves and by club employees according to (1) frequency of play, (2) game preference (high or low poker), (3) usual game stakes (small, medium, or big), and (4) regular time of play. Tony J., for example, plays in the cardrooms every afternoon about 2 P.M. in a $10-20 lowball game. Any deviation from his normal pattern will prompt questions. If he sits down to play high draw, someone will comment that he is on "the wrong side of the room." If he plays in a smaller game, a player will remark that he is probably busted. These demarcations are socially significant, for they circumscribe personal relationships; two men may play in the same club for ten years, only twenty feet apart, one in a high-stakes draw game, the other in a small-stakes lowball game, yet they may never recognize or interact with each other. These initial categories are also partial reflectors

41

of proxemics and status. High-stakes tables are usually placed deliberately in the center or back of the cardroom away from the rail where they are free from onlookers and receive better service; their players are generally accorded some degree of curiosity and respect by small-stakes players.

Categorized by frequency of play, cardroom customers can be regulars (including full-time professionals) or occasionals. Similar to racetrack regulars observed by Scott,[24] regulars in Gardena consider poker-playing their favorite type of gambling and social recreation. Gambling in one form or another is a significant and time-consuming part of everyday life to many cardroom regulars. While sitting at the poker table, a regular may be waiting to hear the racing results from Santa Anita or Hollywood Park, planning football or basketball bets, or contemplating a quick weekend trip to Las Vegas. Most regulars work at an outside job or are supported by some other source, and while many of them may win consistently (but not enough to give up their jobs), the majority of them are losers who admittedly come to play and make daily or weekly "donations." Regulars include working businessmen who play exclusively in the afternoon, nonworking housewives who are supported by their husbands, elderly retirees, wealthy widows, students, and steady workers of all kinds. For these players the frequency and severity of losses strongly determine the weekly and monthly rate of poker-playing. When they win they appear in the cardrooms more often and stay longer than usual. When they lose their attendance tapers off, and they may become occasionals or not step inside the cardroom again for months. With a renewed stake, most dedicated regulars eventually make it back to the cardrooms.

Occasionals play in the cardroom less often than regulars, and to them daily poker-playing or gambling is not vitally important as a social or recreational outlet. Playing poker may be a night off from their families and other social responsibilities or a once-a-month outing. Like regulars, occasionals come from all segments of the population at large. While many former regulars may be occasionals who have had to reduce the intensity of poker-playing because of losses, other occasionals who "run good" become daily regulars as long as they continue to win. For many individual players the status of regular or occasional shifts with wins and losses.

A preference for high or lowball poker also separates the players. In fact, many cardroom players know how to play only one type of poker and are not interested in learning other varieties. These two major varieties of poker and their respective followers are talked about within the cardrooms as distinctly different. Players often comment that high draw is a slow game, while lowball, because of its structure of "blind" bets and raises, is an action game. Regulars and occasionals can be found in both types of games, but most players show a marked preference for one game over the other.

Players also can be grouped according to preferred game stakes. Such deci-

42

sions are not totally independent of how much gambling money the player can raise and what he or she is willing to risk. Once regulars reach a certain level of action, they tend to remain at those stakes or work upward to bigger limits. Most players do not like dropping down to lower levels. It is as if a psychological plateau had been conquered, and to step down would be a disgraceful fall. Many players, of course, never work up because of their limited financial condition or the acclimatization to other regulars in a particular game.

Players are also known as day or night customers. A regular night player in a game at noon might be asked why he is in so early, or a day player seen after midnight will be assumed to be "stuck" (losing). One regular player contrasted day and night games and explained why he preferred the latter: "The day shift is too tight. There's no action in them games. At night they're all stuck and loosened up. I'd rather play at night any time. That's when you can really make the money 'cause of all the gambling going on." A few players and many pros straddle both shifts by playing for several hours, leaving the game to go home and rest or eat, and returning for one or more sessions throughout the day and night. Other players cannot avoid marathon sessions at the table. Once stuck they play for days and nights at a time in a stubborn attempt to get even or "even worse," as they frequently complain.

Added to the frequency and hours of play and the variety of games and stakes that regulate players' interactions, many cardroom participants harbor stereotypical ideas about the poker-playing capabilities (or lack thereof) of players in certain minority groups. These ideas, dubious as they may seem, serve in metagame strategies for selecting and avoiding opponents and games. Drawing players from a wide cross section of Los Angeles, Gardena cardrooms attract players of many different ethnic groups who give the game its United Nations flavor. The poker-playing stereotypes of ethnic groups that I have heard in the clubs generally echo wider notions about ethnic character.

Females are the most maligned group, even though they constitute only 10 to 30 percent of all players. For the cardroom is stratified by sex as well as by age. Most female players can be found in small- or medium-stakes games. (Pan, also a legal card game, is notorious as a "ladies' game.") Male card players, as the majority in cardrooms, often refer to poker as a "man's game."[25] Some say they prefer to play at a quiet table without "broads," and they chastise weak male players for not betting their hands "like a man." Female regulars, if they are accepted, are dubbed "one of the boys." These attitudes are common in competitive situations. Experiments have shown that when men and women compete at the same task, the success of women is more often attributed to luck than skill, while for men the opposite holds.[26] Similarly, in the cardroom many winning women players are criticized for being mindless "ticket holders," "human card racks," or plain lucky players in a public undervaluation of their capabilities. A male regular once described Nancy T., a female daytime player, as "unconscious":

> She doesn't have to think. She just waits there and the cards run all over her. If she had to think about playing cards she'd be busted in a week. If I held half her cards I'd make twice as much as she does because she doesn't know how to get the "max" out of her hands. All she knows how to do is bet those "no brainers." I tell you she's just totally unconscious, just unconscious.

Players also delineate further social networks in cardrooms where they do not play regularly in terms of different, usually inferior, moral, financial, and opportunistic standards. Regulars classify cardrooms according to the existence of an on-going high-stakes game, what type of game it is, and what players are likely to participate. Regulars have a tendency to play exclusively in one particular cardroom, avoiding others, and these players often speak of the other places as rife with cheats and partners. One outspoken critic on the rail severely attacked the playing choice of a fellow player: "Why do you want to play at that club down the street? Those lowball games they have are all bad. I think everyone who's barred from here ends up playing there because the management is hurting for players. They'll let anything go on as long as you pay the collection."

A player's overall attendance and participation in the cardroom varies then according to a wide range of factors, many of them related to his perception of what constitutes good playing conditions. Players promptly offer positive and negative opinions about the various cardrooms' attitudes toward customers, the service of the chipgirls and porters, the lighting, the food in the restaurants, the capabilities and friendliness of the floormen and managers, and the success the player has experienced. Other conditions include the presence or absence of specific players and the type of poker that is offered. One cardroom is known for its daily California draw blind game, another for its high-low, and a third for its high-stakes lowball tables. All of these personal preferences, prejudices, and stereotypes dictate where most players, including professionals, ultimately decide to play and with whom they come into contact.

The social world of the regular and professional consists of about ten to twenty-five other players with whom he plays nearly every day. Although fellow players may have known each other for years, this does not mean that personal rivalries and jealousies over the table are abated; in fact, daily play tends to stimulate new tensions and exacerbate old wounds. A regular makes less frequent contacts with an additional twenty-five to fifty other players. Beyond that, he is familiar with at least several hundred others by sight and from past games. The loose networks of social interaction in the cardrooms

44

are spun and patterned by the who, what, where, and when of games and by the frequency of play. From the potential pool of thousands of Gardena regulars and occasionals, each player develops his own set of relationships, including those individuals he relies on and excluding those he meticulously avoids. Throughout the year these relationships split up, shift, and recombine; depending primarily on wins or losses, players move silently in and out of numerous social networks in various games and cardrooms.

Each cardroom—indeed each separate table—can be considered a unique social unit with a characteristic texture. This character is brought about by the random conjoining of different individuals who attract and repel each other, by their strategies for subsistence, and by their personal styles of expression. From this jumbled social diversity the regular and professional poker player must devise a more specific social order, one that goes beyond initial groupings and stereotypes, one that is more relevant to the daily battles at hand. In a word the player must categorize the gaming style of each of his varied opponents.

SECONDARY CATEGORIES:
LABELING PLAYING STYLES

Cardroom identities are so pervasive that players are often skeptical that a regular works at an outside job or cultivates other interests besides cards. A prop mentioned to me that he used to sell real estate, and not slowing down his deal a fellow player quipped, "Yeah, he sold his house to stay in action."

Entering a cardroom one passes through a "symbolic door"[27] whereupon outside society's rules and tedium no longer seem important. Inside, the tone of face-to-face interaction is regulated by its own peculiar sets of rules. Once past this cardroom door, the normally accepted hierarchy of status may be turned completely upside down. Within the cardroom it is regularity of attendance, personal reputation, skillful play, and wealth that stratifies players. Doctors and lawyers may become known suckers, unwitting victims of the poker skills of college students, plumbers, or housewives. Admiration among peers may come from a brilliant play, a successful bluff, or an amazing comeback when almost any player may bask temporarily in poker glory. Part of the change from outside role identity to that of poker player thus requires that some sort of precise social classification be established in order to make exploitation and gain more than a chance affair.

Over the poker table initial categories such as regular or day player, although they demarcate broad social identities, are shallow surface labels. These designations are not the most important ones in an ongoing game. Knowing whether a person works at an outside job, is an electrician or a student, or is a day or night player is not important in a poker interaction. In fact, players seem to show little interest in the outside-of-the-cardroom lives of other players. Unlike other bounded social gatherings that seem to force participants to identify themselves through the handy institutionalization of ritual greetings and small talk, no such norm for interaction exists in the cardroom.

The most important perception in a poker game is a player's categorization of his competitors and their poker behavior, specifically their style of play. Labels for playing styles regulate the quality and quantity of game interactions between competing players and lie at the heart of the conception of poker as a practical exercise in sociosymbolic reading. In a way, the actual hands that are determined by the fall of cards are only the catalyst for interaction. It is the mixture of diverse players, sometimes more so than the aces and deuces, that determines the flow of the game. Experienced players react against, adjust to, and devise strategies for each player almost regardless of the cards. One type of player will loosen up every game he sits down in, while another will create a somber, attentive mood among participants and the pall will destroy any action.

Numerous sociological studies have shown that people in service occupations deftly categorize their customers at a glance and confirm these impressions shortly thereafter by observation of obvious physical and social traits: cabdrivers size up their fares, cocktail waitresses distinguish between good and bad tippers, and milkmen seek out relationships with particular customers.[28] Social labeling is thus an aid to monetary or social gain. So, too, poker players have devised a system of labeling to organize and categorize the complete spectrum of opponents. For the astute, experienced player, gaming styles are fairly easy to discern. In the space of a few hands an experienced player can determine with some degree of confidence another player's skills and general style by observing the type of hands played, the table position, the incidence of bets, checks, bluffs, or raises.

Susan Boyd, in a study of poker clubs in Missoula, Montana,[29] has broadly grouped poker players as "tighties" and "loosies," the former being conservative, give-nothing-away players while the latter are more likely to play weaker hands, more hands, attempt frequent bluffs, and occasionally throw their money away. As the two most important labels for poker-playing styles, "tight" and "loose" cut across all other initial social categories such as age, sex, game stakes, playing frequency, playing time, and preferred variety of poker. A tightie may be a 75-year-old woman in a small lowball game or a 22-year-old man playing at an expensive draw table.

Regional differences in labeling may occur within the wider poker-playing population, but most terms are understandable on first hearing. In Gardena a *rock* is equivalent to a Montana tightie. A rock plays mainly according to statistical percentages, makes very few bluffs, rarely loses money on poor hands, and generates little action in the game. In actual table demeanor many rocks resemble the archetypal, immobile poker player who gives little away in money or information about himself. Because rocks play tight and cause others to tighten up by restricting the amount of betting and raising, they are often publicly criticized for their playing style or merely for their presence and intention to play in a game. As one rock approached a table, Mike H., who was losing badly, warned him: "Don't sit down here. Go over to that other game—that's rocky mountain, more your style. We're all hot and stuck and gambling here. If you sat down I'd never get even 'cause you'd 'nut everybody up.'" Mike also requested the boardman to rewrite the name Rick (another tight player) as Rock on the board. Laughing, he added that when the floorman called down the name Rock for an open seat "about fifty people looked up like it was them." When Mike saw Rick walk to the table he loudly asked the floorman if he had seen "a large granite truck in the parking lot." And whenever Rick played a hand his action was met with mouse-like squeaking noises as a critical reference to his tight, "squeaky" play. This kind of joking and name-calling, whether it is intended seriously or not, is frequent and more or less accepted as part of table interaction. When a loose player or loser sits down, the regulars become more attentive; they straighten their posture and offer each other collusive smiles. But rocks are greeted with deliberate audible groans and complaints.

Like rocks, *hit and run* players provide little action in the game, but for a different reason. After each small win or loss they get up from the game and quit. Their major strategy for cardroom survival is to play a tight, conservative game and move from table to table and club to club, making no financial or social commitments to any one game. Most players would much rather compete against an *action player*, a raising and betting loose player who is not afraid to gamble. In the long run most action players probably do not win,[30] but in short sessions they may be successful in beating the odds and making the course of play difficult for the tight players. One rock, a regular lowball player, admitted:

> I don't really like to see Jerry T. in the game. He makes me nervous with all that action. He puts in so many bets and gambles on his hand that he intimidates a lot of people. When he's in the pot I usually get out of his way. I don't want my whole buy-in burned up playing one hand. I come here to spend a couple of hours and enjoy myself, not to be a cutthroat.

Extremely loose, action-provoking players, called *berserkos* or *desperados,* take many improbable risks in their betting and raising, and by doing so they force others to do the same. One player explained his reasons for his play: "I come down here for action. I don't care whether I win or lose. I have no respect for money. I just want to gamble. If I didn't want to gamble and wanted just to stay even, I wouldn't have walked in here. You're even when you walk in the door." Often these players can build a small playing stake into hundreds or thousands of dollars within an hour, or they can lose three or four times as much as a tighter player would in the same amount of time. These ultra-action players invariably generate a high-pitched, electric atmosphere of gambling and can loosen up the tighter players with their betting and bluffing. Although they are usually consistent losers, they are thought to be dangerous just because they totally lack respect for money and can bust many players with their aggressive, risky style of play.

When an overloose and weak betting style is combined with a poor knowledge of poker, the result is a consistent loser, a *turkey, pigeon, live one,* or *juicy* player. Many players of this type are also *calling stations* who must see and call the final hand of every pot in which they are involved. Players often say that a calling station "sleeps good at night" because he does not have to worry about whether he was bluffed. Losers may also be incompetent money managers, that is, *sickies* or *degenerates,* who "blow back" large profits and never leave the table.

The cardroom categories also contain the *angle shooter,* who takes advantage of every possible mistake that is made, particularly by naive players and occasonals. Angle shooters must be distinguished from the more innocent table jokers who make the same deceptive plays, but only for a laugh. The serious angle shooter makes many misinterpretable "moves": he pretends to throw his hand away before it is his turn to act, he discards one card when he is actually drawing three, and he reaches for his chips or prematurely spreads his hand to forestall a bet by another player. One was said to have "more moves than a belly dancer." Other angle shooters continually stretch the boundaries of legality and propriety. They "buy short" (less than the required amount), "go South" with chips (sneak them off the table), or spend long breaks in the bar while their seat is "locked up," preventing another player from sitting in it.

The characteristics and labels for individuals and their playing styles tend to be fairly stable. Players seem to demonstrate consistent patterns of poker behavior throughout their lives, although almost everyone at some time shows temporary fluctuations: an action player may cut back on his betting and play like a rock; a losing rock who chases hand after hand may become a calling station; or with a modest win a complete live one may begin to hit and run. Deliberate, calculated changes are most likely to be made by experienced players and professionals who successfully mix their modes of play and self-presentation from tight to loose, from giving no action to too much action, depending on the competition and pitch of the game. These *tough* and *strong* players, who are difficult to beat and whose play cannot be easily categorized, are treated with a good deal of respect while at the table. As the main user and constructor of game-relevant labels, the professional poker player himself must, if at all possible, deliberately dodge any predictable tags.

3
Controlling Luck and Managing Action

Patience, and shuffle the cards. *

The fast poker played in the cardrooms of Gardena and Las Vegas makes the game on the surface seem an entertaining pastime, but at every step unseen, active calculations make the play a most serious matter. Strategies for luck and action are some of the most critical factors that separate winners from losers and losers from their money.[1]

Poker has been called a game of imperfect information because players must plan strategies and make decisions in the dark; they do not always know what their opponents have planned or what the wisest and most profitable course may be. Lack of information about other players, whether in table games or daily social interaction, is a handicap that successful competitors must overcome. Hence:

*Miguel de Cervantes, *Don Quixote,* II, 23.

Every game includes an information game in which each player seeks to uncover the real identity, the actual intentions, and the secret stratagems employed by the other. The condition of imperfect information renders all social games problematic. Indeed, uncertainty of outcomes is a feature of games that provides the players with anxious concern over strategic decisions and zestful incentive for action when the game is on.[2]

The *metagame strategies* of poker pros proceed on the assumption that gaining information about other players by deliberate and careful observation and gaining information about the situation by perceiving luck-related contingencies is imperative for cardroom survival.

Games fall under the general sociological rubric "strategic interaction." These interactions are characterized by deceit, stealth, and discordant messages about the self in situations of "mutual fatefulness."[3] Gambling games, however, pose a special typological problem for students of strategic interaction. Gambling games are not quite like recreational board games played for enjoyment and relaxation; nor are they miniature models of normal social interactions. This is because of the nature of the opponent. Opponents in Goffman's strategic games are treacherous adversaries—like spies, criminals, and corrupt politicians—found in tactical arenas of social life. But in some gambling games, including poker, that combine elements of both luck and skill, players are faced with real opponents on the one hand and the more intangible forces of luck or chance on the other. Players must prepare themselves for both. The behavior and strategies of poker players therefore do not appear to be wholly explainable by the assumptions of actor rationality found in many decision-making models and by the mathematical theory of games. Neither accounts for such a formidable and troublesome opponent as luck or chance. If this argument is stretched, we may include a third "opponent" recognized by most gamblers: the player himself. He is engaged in a constant battle with his inner forces as to play or not to play.[4]

Playing strategies are a fundamental part of most games of mixed luck and skill. Studies have shown that subjects in gambling games prefer to exercise at least some amount of skill, rather than to rely completely on luck, in order to intervene and affect the outcome of events. Male subjects, more so than females, prefer games of skill over games of chance, persist at them longer, and have greater expectancies of success.[5] Furthermore, the gambler's "subjective probability" has been shown to be more important in decisions than actual mathematical probabilities.[6] His decisions, which often must be made quickly and under duress, are normally based on simplification and expediency rather than optimization. Experimental studies of risk-taking suggest that "all decisions and predictions are guided or governed, implicitly if not explicitly, by what we imagine luck and unluck might bring and not merely by cold-blooded 'objective' calculations."[7]

My interest in the strategies of the professional poker player was initially piqued by the writings of several researchers attempting to discover the elusive qualities separating gamblers who win from those who lose.[8] Unfortunately, those studies as well as many "how to play poker" books and "winning secrets" revealed by professionals offered little systematic understanding of when, how, and why different types of game and metagame strategies are used. Players resort to metagame strategies mainly to alter the allocation of their resources, such as time, effort, and money, and to reverse the state of losing. In doing this they direct their at-the-table attention both to the control of luck and the management of action, the latter referring to interpersonal conduct. But before any player settles on one or more strategies he must first consciously evaluate both his monetary resources and the run of cards.

HOW'RE THEY RUNNING?

Strategies are attempted solutions to practical troubles. Goffman expresses it this way:

> Individuals typically make observations of their situation in order to assess what is relevantly happening around them and what is likely to occur. Once this is done, they often go on to exercise another capacity of human intelligence, that of making a choice from among a set of possible lines of response. Here some sort of maximization of gain will often be involved, often under conditions of uncertainty or risk.[9]

Survival for the professional poker player means striving to win in every sitting. But because of the chance factor in gambling games, as well as the gambler's own variable playing performance, he cannot win 100 percent of the time. In a series of games the gambler may at various points be roughly even, winning, or losing. By counting chips and money at frequent intervals the professional gambler formulates a subjective measure of "how things are running." This evaluation is usually an approximation between the ideal state of total winning and the worst conception of his own ability. It is in periods of loss that metagame strategies are most likely to be invoked and a player's gaming experiences reexamined. The major proposition may thus be stated: The more the gambler deviates from the ideal condition of winning and perceives the severity of loss, the more he will adopt specific metagame strategies to change his losing state to a winning one.

Regulars and professionals who are most familiar with the different clubs, games, and stakes are the players most likely to find losing troublesome, for they must return to the clubs day after day and offer excuses when they are absent. Moreover, veteran gamblers, having experienced many up and down periods, also believe that conditions may change for the better as a result of some kind of strategic action. The poker player's definition of the situation is concerned specifically with "how things are running" at any given moment. For people who gamble every day, "How're they running?" is virtually a standard greeting. Cards run, horses run, and dice run—that is, they all move and can be wagered on. Furthermore, the question asks how a player stands psychologically and financially in relationship to his current betting action.

The question "How're they running?" usually elicits one of three answers. A player may say that he is (1) *running good* or *hot,* (2) so-so or *holding his own,* or (3) *running bad* or *on tilt.* Winning or losing is rarely a permanent condition among regulars; it is always relative to the outcome of past games and to how much one is winning or losing. The most important gauge by which regulars judge themselves, and subsequently decide to change the way things are running, is their location in a cycle of winning or losing and the length of time they have been there. The only situation that does not require prolonged worry is when a player runs good for a long period of time. Every other situation demands a new course of action.

Full-time poker-playing is a continuous, timeless activity. Many regulars regard daily poker-playing as one long game, interrupted only by periods of sleep. Many regulars eat their daily meals from movable trays positioned directly at their side so they do not have to leave the table or miss a hand. These players mark the passage of time not by clock hours alone but by how well they are doing. By stacking and counting chips at frequent checkpoints— when they win a big pot, when they lose one, in lulls in the game when bored, and when ready to quit—they monitor their progress in single games and over longer periods. (Often, in the heat of a game, the chips move so fast that players lose them before they are even brought to the table. Some regulars forget the number of checks they have written and must have the floorman ask the cashier how much they are "in.") Except for single sittings, regulars and pros who play every day are rarely "even"; they are usually either winning, losing, or in a state of flux.

Running bad or on tilt is disastrous for a professional because losing a stake and composure at the same time directly threatens the player's present and future quality of play. Being on tilt refers to (1) the degree and length of time in a losing period, which may run from one crucial hand in a game to a period of months or years, and (2) the degree of monetary loss relative to a player's total stake. More important, being on tilt is *always* accompanied by visible moods such as anger, depression, hostility, or anxiety when a player changes from calm to erratic behavior and loses his patience and composure.

In this tilted state many players express loud, pessimistic attitudes toward poker, gambling, and the cardrooms. A normally controlled player, having lost his patience, may adopt a self-destructive style of play like a berserko or sickie. Or he may threaten never to return to the cardroom. (The usual line, never believed, is "If I ever get even, you'll never see me here again!") Tablemates will comment that he has "popped his cork" and make popping noises whenever he plays a hand, or they joke insultingly about his need for "a new asshole" after being punctured up the backside so many times.

All that is needed to send a player on tilt is to have one good hand "cracked." Players often complain that they went on tilt and their fortunes changed suddenly and irreversibly because of "unbelievable" circumstances:

> You can't believe what happened to me yesterday. I was in this game and was up a couple of hundred. I got kings full pat, and this complete dummy behind me draws three cards to a pair of fives. A pair of fives! What do you think he made? Four fives! After that I was on tilt for the rest of the night. It was all downhill and I couldn't do nothin'.

After being outdrawn on several such hands, one pro stated sardonically that he was planning to write a book that would be more famous than Ripley's "Believe It or Not." His book, for poker players, was to be titled "I Don't Believe It."

A player on the losing end of a pot is said to take a *tough beat* or *bad beat* when opponents make statistically improbable draws, which are referred to as "Gardena miracles." Players who seem to make them frequently and win big pots are jealously called "miracle workers." One regular who made a full house drawing three cards to a pair[10] announced, when called, that he had made a "Kathryn Kuhlman special" (a reference to the late television faith healer and believer in miracles). Before he turned the hand over, the losing player in the pot threw his cards away. He knew exactly what the winner had made.

Repeated tough beats drive even the steadiest players on tilt and force them to change their normal style of play. Regulars often sarcastically request the floorman to bring "crying towels" for the losers when complaints are heard. But losers and tilted players do more than just feel bad. In a huff, some players rip up the cards, throw their chips in the air, and storm angrily out of the club. The most notorious example of tilted behavior—a story told by many regulars and now part of local folklore—took place on January 12, 1965, when a losing small-stakes lowball player fired a shotgun into three cardrooms. He killed one player and wounded twenty-seven more in his mad attack.[11] Witnesses who had played with him blamed his violence on his losses.

Routine Work: Monitoring Other Players

Recognizing "how they're running" refers not only to the player's own situation but to his opponents'. Regulars and pros who play against one another nearly every day can identify winners and losers, even over several months or a year. Part of the daily gossip in the cardroom consists of reporting the "line-up" of the previous night's game: who won or lost what amount of money, whether people who were stuck "bailed out," and how long the games lasted. This gossip is not mere talk; it is valuable information about the psychological and financial condition of opponents. In addition to this daily news, other telltale clues identify a regular or pro who is running bad. Erratic attendance in the cardroom, a smaller than usual daily bankroll, borrowing money from others, hitting and running, and changing cardrooms or playing for smaller stakes are indications that a player is not winning. Professional gamblers realize that their own survival means keeping abreast of the playing histories of others so that they can modify their own tactics when necessary.

Opponents who are running bad may be played harder and bluffed more often, especially if they display timidity and act as if they are playing with "tight" or "scared" money. Experienced players are keenly aware of the changes in playing styles and emotions that accompany winning and losing and take full advantage of their observations by running over or running away from particular opponents. As I sat down in a game, Don S. gave me this advice: "You know Bill J.? Well, he's hot and stuck and playing on his case money. He's playing like a complete, scared turkey. All you have to do is rattle your chips and he'll run out of the pot. Just play solid hands against him though and don't get him pumped up because you'll never get it back until he loosens up."

Accurate deductions about another player's success can usually be made by walking by his table and observing his overall demeanor and the number of his chips relative to other players. Sitting behind many neat stacks of chips, winners exude confidence and enjoyment in the game. Losers, in contrast, appear irritable and depressed; they do not possess as many chips (unless they have bought a lot to bolster their confidence), and they may have changed games or seats several times. Absences from the cardroom for more than several days pose a problem of character maintenance for regulars who run bad. Before leaving the city for a vacation, many regulars and pros deliberately announce their plans at the table so that they will not be gossiped about on their return. One pro complained:

Every time I leave town for a few days the word gets out that I'm busted. That's what they'd like to think. I went to Mexico once and heard someone say that they saw me in L.A. That's the kind of petty bullshit I can't stand! What it is, is that they'd like to think that I was busted so that they could have something bad to say about me.

Such cues and daily cardroom gossip enable regulars to keep current on the poker biographies and playing styles of many of their opponents. Several pros, in fact, keep notebooks and file cards on the characteristics of several hundred players. They compile additional records on their own daily wins and losses, hours in play, average profit or losses by the hour, the amount of collection fees paid, and money loaned and borrowed. They discuss these notes with friends and sometimes use the information to form friendly competitions to see who can win the most money. Much of the spare time of pros, whether on the rail or at home, is spend in such practical activities as note-taking or in wishful thinking. They dream about making "monster" (huge) wins and winning for days and days without a loss. They also read poker books, think about and analyze past games and successful play, and study gambling and sports publications. Some players spend much of their time studying statistical charts of poker hands and thinking up problem situations.

These routine activities—home study, game plans, statistical calculations, meticulous record-keeping, and regular cardroom hours—are all intended to improve the player's repertoire of skills and knowledge. Poker-playing, then, gives some players the impression of the potential for personal growth and a satisfying feeling of personal accomplishment. Played properly, poker is often said to be a science rather than a mere game. Analyzing the patterns of "how they're running" contributes to a store of usable, practical information.

THE POWER OF WORDS AND ACTION: INTIMIDATING AND MANIPULATING OPPONENTS

Much of the playful and serious character of game interaction derives from manipulating talk and game-related symbols.[12] Some players are even known as specialists at "talking" a good game—deceiving, intimidating, and cajoling novices into making bad judgments and costly playing errors. Indeed, lies and insults (up to a certain level) are a standard form of poker table interaction. Verbal duels and one-liners, while sometimes delivered in jest, also serve as potential warnings and not-so-subtle criticisms of another player's action:

God, are you rocky! They even named a movie after you. If I played your discards I'd probably make a million bucks.

You're so rocky you probably shit bricks.

I've played with tight players, but you're tighter than a nun's cunt.

Players openly call one another rocks, pigeons, donkeys, and other pejorative terms and publicly insult opponents' actions and playing competence. Anthropologists have found that in many societies verbal abuse or "ritual insults"[13] accompany situations of play, perhaps to ease tension and express aggression in relatively harmless form. Insults in poker games may fulfill these same functions, and they may also have the intended or unintended effect of changing, destroying, or weakening opponents, thereby making them more likely to commit errors or begin "steaming." Raking in the chips the winner tells the loser to "get a job" or threatens to send him and other "poker bums" back on the freeway forever. These gabby methods of intimidation are highly effective in many instances, especially against players who are easily flustered.[14]

Another reason for obnoxious or aggressive actions is to loosen up tight players or drive them out of the game. Rocks and ultraconservative players who give little action are the most obvious targets of abuse. Sometimes the battles of intimidation and name-calling reach comical proportions, as in this incident, pitting an impatient loser against two rocks:

M. T., who was losing heavily and steadily, was called, pot after pot, by two players who played a tight, conservative game. Repeatedly M. T. would bet his hand, get called, and lose the pot. After several identical outcomes, in frustration he took out a pen and wrote "No Action" on the green felt tablecloth with arrows pointing in the direction of the two players. Following that, he kept shouting "N. A., N. A." (for No Action) every time either of them was in a pot. He tried to convince the rest of the table that they did not deserve any play because they were too rocky. The other players were laughing too hard to pay any attention.

Almost no player escapes verbal abuse. Winners with good playing reputations are sometimes singled out as targets for the barbs thrown by needlers, or "needle artists," particularly when the former have blown back a lot of chips or are losing to the worst players in the game:

I see the elephant's been in town. [Meaning: You used to have a lot of chips but they look like they've been stomped on by a large animal, and now you don't have any.]

Look here! The carrots are eating the rabbits. Marge [a chipgirl], bring this here boy a *turkey* sandwich and a glass of water. This fish needs plenty to drink.

Winners also needle losers whom they do not like by giving them "instructions" on how they should have played a losing hand, no matter how they played it, or asking them irrelevant questions such as what cards they caught on the draw.

Players in aggressive games express much of their table talk in the idioms of power and dominance. They threaten to "punish" or "take care of" others. To punish another player means to beat him out of future pots or to "burn up" his money by excessive raising. Among some of the more vibrant players, splashing chips and money around, presenting an aggressive front, and talking a game indeed act as effective symbols of power. These players can "buy" pots by frightening and intimidating opponents who are too confused to defend themselves.

Intimidation, threats, and needles can arise out of unpremeditated spite or can be carefully constructed ploys to change the playing style of another—to make a good player bad, a bad player worse. These aggressive attacks, however, are not applied indiscriminately. There is an unwritten rule among regulars that obvious live ones, wealthy losers, and cardroom strangers should never be criticized publicly or made to feel bad about their poor play and the extent of their losses. Losers or "feeders" should by all means be kept in the game. Warning several regulars about their irritating conduct at the table, a pro said: "You guys better tone down on all your yelling and fooling around during the game. You're going to lose all the feeders, and then who're you going to be left with? Just yourselves jerkin' off as usual. Whose going to support you then?"

Another unwritten rule stipulates that losers should never be "educated," that is, given poker lessons over the table on how and what kinds of hands should be played. When a bad player does win a pot, regardless of how poorly he played the hand, he is aided by regulars who push him the chips and congratulate him on his hand. Meanwhile, to each other, the regulars exchange collusive glances whose meaning signifies that they have a live one in their midst. When a loser leaves the table, a lesson in cardroom group alignment can be learned. Regulars resume their insider talk free of censorship and hidden meanings. Once the loser has left the cardroom, he is the butt of many jokes. When a medical doctor, after dropping several thousand dollars, finally gave up and left the game at five in the morning, a winner asked rhetorically, "How would you like to be operated on by him today?" When a gas station owner left broke, another player commented, "It's all right. He'll be back. Tomorrow he'll just raise the price of gas to $10 a gallon and won't accept credit cards."

Not all professional poker players are slanderous and scurrilous. Many pros and winners are calm, silent players who survive in the cardroom without needles, insults, or fights. The intensity and type of verbalization seems completely a matter of personal style. And I repeat that most spiteful table talk is usually packaged with humor. All experienced poker players know that unfortunate circumstances and going busted are not the exclusive province of unskilled losers. To wit, they know that the cards and words may turn against *them* at any time.

Angle Shooters, Slow-rollers, and Miscallers

An angle shooter bends the rules of the game to his own advantage. He will attempt to save money on a call, for example, by forcing a showdown with no bet or making a player accidentally spread his hand too quickly. In one case I saw:

> M. E. and another player, H. H., were in the same pot. H. H. bet $20 on his hand. When it was M. E.'s turn to call, he threw $40 to another player he owed money to. The chips fell just outside the edge of the betting area. H. H., of course, thought that M. E. had raised, and having a strong hand he re-raised. An argument ensued and the floorman was called in to make a decision. He judged that M. E.'s $40 did not constitute a raise, but he awarded H. H. the pot. H. H. was so irate at losing M. E.'s extra $40 "raise" that he grabbed his chips and left the game.

Most players agree that pulling angles or shots of this kind damages the flow of the game. Pros often caution players not to angle or drive big losers out of the game, because one loser in the game could mean thousands of dollars per year to the winners.

Another kind of ethically marginal ploy that some players use to humiliate or "jerk off" opponents is the *slow-roll*. This means spreading one's own hand, the obvious winner, last on the table after the other player thinks he has won and begins to pull in the chips. In its deliberate version this is pure psychological warfare. An example:

> Tom, the slow-roller, called Mary's bet for $20. Mary then declared her hand to be two pair. Feigning a depressed tone of voice, Tom asked "How big?" At that point Mary quickly laid down her seemingly unbeatable two pair, two aces and two kings. As she was scooping in the chips, Tom waited a second, coughed, said "Excuse me," and turned over three threes, the winning hand.

Miscalling a hand[15] is another tactic some players use to gain momentary pleasure and deflate the steady composure of an opponent. Miscalls occur often at the same time as slow-rolling. A player may call his hand (before showing it) as "two pair," which could mean four of a kind; "no pair" could be a straight; "aces" could be three of them rather than two. When the loser thinks he has the hand beat he turns over his hand only to find that the winner has miscalled his hand, and since "cards speak," the miscaller wins.

The intended effect of angle-shooting, slow-rolling, and miscalls, these devastating combinations of table talk and devious action, is to give a competitor the short-lived satisfaction of having the best hand and then destroy his morale by showing him a better hand or by contesting the pot. Most cardroom players do not usually practice these ploys, but they do occur when one player takes a dislike to another or feels that in some way he has been the victim of one of these tactics and wants to even the score. Sometimes these disruptive improprieties are acceptable — even entertaining — when they take place between friendly players who know each other well and want to "play" with each other. Swift repartees are included:

Player A (speaking loudly about player C): You know why he jerks off the game and himself all of the time?

Player B: Yeah. Because he didn't have any toys to play with when he was a kid.

Player A: I knew he couldn't win the hand with three jacks. He's always been a jack-off.

In words and action players create games of one-upmanship to see who can get the last laugh. Of course there are limits to these tricks, for they can anger other players and drive perplexed newcomers out of the game. One regular who observed two friendly slow-rollers viciously try to outdo each other concluded: "Boy, those guys are really mindfuckers. They just don't want to beat you and take your money. That's not enough. They want to destroy your head."

Active, aggressive, high-stakes poker-playing as practiced by experienced regulars and professionals involves many strategies for self-presentation and manipulation of the behavior of others. The game is never a leave-it-to-chance affair. The direct result of these contests of interpersonal power is to change the action of the game and the opponent's mood and — with luck — his financial condition. Players intimidate, angle, insult, and deceive others in order to put them on tilt and "open them up" while at the same time give themselves a psychological advantage. But occasionally even the most stable player may lose his composure after several setbacks or after being needled once too often in a game. If he changes to a less controlled, looser style of play, then he becomes the live one, the one who is "good for the game." He becomes a victim of the game of intimidation he may so successfully play on another day.

59

CONTROL OF LUCK

Most poker books, statisticians, and professional gamblers vehemently protest the existence of luck (a term that is defined in many ways) and the idea that it is a factor in winning or losing.[16] Mike C., a Gardena pro since 1971, offered this hesitant opinion of the concept:

> I think my wisest course is to discount the notion of luck. But in the framework of this game-playing situation, it may be that the laws of average are really dictated . . . I don't know. This existence seems very peculiar to me. People who deny that the laws of probability exist are generally very unintelligent. So although I have some skepticism, it's on a different level than the person on the street. Their skepticism is based on ignorance. Mine is based on philosophical bewilderment. The laws of probability are the only thing I can perceive of as being real. In the absence of other information I am wisest to stick firmly to them. But I may be totally wrong. I may wake up with a totally different explanation that I'm not aware of.

In referring to luck, I am speaking of the belief in a general agent that affects or explains the fall of cards in detectable patterns, that is, statistical runs and frequencies. For even seemingly random events, such as the distribution of cards,[17] tend to generate patterns that card players rank according to game rules, values, and meanings. A study of poker players in cardrooms in San Jose, California, found that consistent winners and players who broke even considered luck only half the game; it could not be relied on all of the time.[18] But regular losers blamed the outcome of the game on chance and ultimately explained losses by reference to "bad luck." Some players in Gardena feel that winners possess an internal, almost magical quality that can be acquired by touching them, buying their "lucky" chips, or sitting in their seats when they leave.

My observations indicate that most poker players believe, or at least *behave* as if that intangible, luck, partially if decisively explains the distribution of cards and players' successes or failures. Luck is often described in terms of a law of conservation: it can be used up, run out, wasted, and negatively affected by pessimism. The power of luck is a highly sought-after prize in the cardroom, and many players admit frankly that they would rather "be lucky than good."

Two types of cardroom luck can be distinguished. *Self-directed luck* refers to strategies that are used to improve a player's own unfortunate situation. Most poker players rely on this type of luck at one time or another because they tend to think of their own welfare first. *Other-directed luck,* usually in the form of bad luck, is that cast on others to change their playing fortunes. According to most players, this latter type of luck is thought to be more "irrational" or "magical" than the first kind. Thus, luck, when it is courted and called up by poker players, is most likely to be self-directed and for personal gain. A belief in luck in a small sample of female players in Gardena did not tend to make the players take more risks than skeptical subjects.[19] But among professionals, either type of luck has a bad name, presumably because of its unscientific, imprecise, and irrational connotations and its preeminence over skill in the minds of many players.

The ultimate occurrence of luck in poker is called a *rush*. This is the unpredictable, coveted time when a player experiences an unstoppable winning streak, lasting anywhere from several minutes to hours. A rush validates the idea that luck can grant any player an unexpected windfall. Players wait for and "play out" their rushes; they play in nearly every hand while they are "in heat." In a broader sense, a poker rush can be compared to a push or momentum, as the latter term is used in sports: "The key element distinguishing momentum from its comparatively dull counterparts is the *intensity* of play achieved: the tension, excitement, and outstanding quality of execution which surpasses a certain minimum level and remains at this height for a definite duration."[20] Unpredictable bonuses, rushes come and go and are neither explainable nor controllable. They are talked about as a kind of unbridled, miraculous run of cards. A rush usually produces positive results— players get even or make quick profits. But "downhill rushes" are just as intense, and painfully so, and a player may lose on every hand for hours.

Poker players do not sit passively and wait for rushes. They attempt to control "normal" luck by using physical objects and strategies to change their *timing* in order to hold winning hands at the right time and place. Timing is usually described as "good" or "off":

You can't believe that turkey's timing. He was winning on everything— pairs, busted hands, all kinds of shit. It's a miracle when your timing's that good.

Yesterday I got killed on everything. You know, it's not a matter of how many cards you hold, but the timing. What good is it if you have a full house and everybody's looking out the window? Every good hand I had got cracked, or I just dragged the ante. My timing's been off for about a week now.

Belief in lucky objects varies greatly among players. Favored objects are key chains, coins, chips, jewelry, and special articles of clothing. Associated with this reliance on special objects is the belief in lucky seat numbers, days of the week, and playing times and locations. Such use of lucky objects has been observed among crapshooters and baseball players, giving credence to the hypothesis of Bronislaw Malinowski that ritual magic is most likely to be found in situations of uncertainty.[21] A retest of this hypothesis among American and Irish students measured the frequency of the use of magic in six different activities with varying levels of uncertainty: gambling, dangerous events, exams, sports, face-to-face interaction, and illness. For Americans the highest incidence of the use of magic occurred with gambling.[22]

Even those professional gamblers who are contemptuous of superstitious behavior in general may find themselves courting luck in a game situation. Ken Uston, the world's most publicized professional twenty-one player, admitted after several losing sessions:

> The next morning before leaving to play, I put on some Old Spice
> after-shave lotion. My next session was a dramatic winner. For the next
> several weeks I doused myself with this lotion without fail before playing.
> If I went out the door, and remembered that I'd forgotten the
> after-shave lotion, I'd return for it. Sure, we're scientists, but I guess
> certain superstitions creep in periodically.[23]

Many professional poker players who have great respect for skillful play regard the use of magical or lucky objects as poor means to success, as examples of "practical magic"[24] invoked by fools and losers. Some Gardena regulars, however, take these measures quite seriously. One player, with his eyes rolling and head angled toward the ceiling, murmurs droning spells and waves his hands in circular motions over the table and his cards before each deal. This special technique is intended to give him winning hands (self-directed magic) while directing losing hands to his opponents (other-directed magic). Experienced players view this sort of behavior with obvious disdain, for in their opinion a player who actually holds these beliefs must be a sure loser if he must resort to desperation tactics in order to win.

Calling on magic and other more mundane strategies — whether effective or ineffective, founded in myth or science — nevertheless has the effect of reducing anxiety about the outcome. Such strategies, therefore, whether brought forth by a skeptical winner or a true believer, cannot be dismissed as irrelevant.

"Who Left This Lucky Seat?"

More than personal charms, the most common cardroom tactics to change luck consist of various *immediate, short-term,* and *long-term* moves. Most players rely on group-shared, rather than idiosyncratic, strategies and beliefs, for in situations of uncertainty, security can be found in reliance on "normal" beliefs. Many of the examples adduced below can be found in almost every poker setting.

Immediate moves concern the next hand to be dealt and indicate that a player's luck is beginning to run bad. Deliberate shuffles and cuts, for example, accompanied by muttering to the cards, are moves meant to direct good hands to the player concerned. These directions often accompany requests to the "poker god" to ensure that the player will not lose again on a second-best hand. While such beliefs and actions may not always be serious, they can be seen as preparatory procedures for more intensive strategies, especially if the cards, with impertinent disregard, continue to run bad.

Most players take short-term and long-term moves far more seriously than frivolous table magic or reliance on lucky objects. Major *short-term controls,* which are intended to arrest a small losing streak, involve requesting the floorman to change the deck of cards, taking a different seat at the table[25] (especially a winner's vacated seat), or moving to a new game, table, or even club. In Las Vegas cardrooms many poker players believe that certain dealers are either lucky or unlucky for them. They praise lucky dealers and tip them generously, but when an unlucky dealer sits down on his or her shift, the player may leave the table or punish the dealer by not tipping, or by tipping only grudgingly after winning a pot.

Innocuous strategies for the control of luck, such as changing decks or seats, may in fact affect the distribution of cards, but only for one hand or a short period of time. This is nonetheless long enough for the believing poker player to verify that his chosen strategy is the correct one. An example demonstrates:

> J. K., who was losing $1,200 in a game, moved over to a seat number 4
> from seat number 1. The second hand dealt to him was a pat flush.
> He won a huge pot over a pat straight and three of a kind. Scooping in
> the chips, he yelled out, "Who left this lucky seat? It's the seat. It's gotta
> be the seat, because I haven't changed any!"

Over the table, players habitually argue about the comparative efficacy of seat versus player.

The use of short-term controls within brief periods relates directly to the degree of monetary loss and "tiltedness." The greater the loss and anxiety, the more players try to control their losing state by employing luck-control strategies. Winners, however, do nothing to change the conditions and reasons for winning, whatever they may be. The player's assumption is that luck, or any other responsible agent, must be held constant so that winning will continue. As a result, it is quite unusual to see a player in the middle of a winning streak request a change of cards, move to a different seat, or get up from the table for a break. Winning gamblers do not explore new possibilities; they are content to use old, reliable methods. It is the losers who seek out new games and places where they can win.

When a losing player talks of really running bad, the implementation of *long-term controls* for luck usually follows. Drastic measures may be taken, such as playing in a different cardroom, changing from high to low poker or vice versa, or gambling for higher or lower stakes. Tommy M. used all three methods at once and explained why: "I used to play $5-10 draw at the Monterey, but the cards ran out and I blew back a lot of money. I went on tilt and now I play $10 blind at the Horseshoe, and I'm doing a lot better. When the cards run out, you gotta change."

The ultimate long-term control for consistent losing is to quit playing temporarily—for several days, weeks, months, or even years—in hopes that the cards will change over time. A player may even cease playing altogether.

Luck-control strategies act like a thermostat to alter bad runs of cards and return a deviating situation to equilibrium. Gardena regulars and professionals who play every day rely automatically on a combination of immediate, short-term, and long-term moves in order to maintain a viable playing stake. These strategies allow the gambler to perceive a relationship between changes in his behavior and concomitant results, and thereby believe that luck and the run of cards can be controlled to some degree. Creating favorable situations for the strategic player means making the chancy world of poker less chancy. Ironically, a player is considered skillful if he can attract good luck and use it to profitable ends.

THE MANAGEMENT OF ACTION

The slang term *action* had its beginnings in the gambling world.[26] To poker players action is a concept that refers not only to location of play but also to players and games as a potential source of income. More specifically, action points to the pace of a game and the betting styles of the players. Some games and players provide little or no action, and it is difficult to win significant amounts of money. But in games with "good" or "a lot of" action, players raise, bet, and bluff, money changes hands at every turn of the cards, and the intense degree of play commands everyone's attention. Even losing players may commend the quality of a game with good action, for they can appreciate the play for its own sake. They also know that they might be able to get even when the action is good.

Regulars and professionals usually abide by a familiar poker saying: You've got to give action to get action. By this they mean that a loose player who creates more betting action will receive more play than a tight player. One common example of overgenerous action occurs in some lowball games when two players, knowing that each will be drawing a card, agree to raise each other five or ten times before the draw. After the draw, they will also agree that the first player will "bet blind" (not look at his drawn card) and the second one will "raise blind" (without seeing his card). This is what poker players mean when someone "gives action" and likes to gamble. Tight players, who bet only on cinch hands, are not likely to accept this kind of proposition.

The term *gambling* has two connotations. The more general lay usage refers to monetary risk-taking while the poker pro uses the term to mean a game-specific style of betting and playing. In the lay sense, every poker player gambles and is a gambler. But in the poker player's narrower meaning, gaming styles vary considerably and not everyone gambles to the same extent. Some gamblers take greater risks, bet and raise more on incomplete hands, and play "fast" (this alludes not only to the speed of play but also to its intense quality). Rocky, tight players are never called gamblers.

In order to receive the right amount of action in calls and bets, a professional must be able to change the pace of his betting and present the image of a player who gives action and gambles and thus deserves action in return. Some simply announce that they will start gambling and leave it to their opponents to guess whether this talk is truthful or meaningless table banter. Doyle Brunson, former World Series of Poker winner, makes the point that poker is a game of self-presentation and action management explicitly:

> Poker is a game of deception. You want to confuse the players you're giving action to. Like if you're up against a loose, liberal player, well, you give him more of a gamble than you would a guy who's sitting there playin' tight. You get into a pot with this guy and you better have the "nuts" most of the time when you stay for the last two cards. But even with a tight player you might change your pace. You might splash around, give the impression you're playing more liberal than you are, like you might give him a loose call once in a while, because what you want to do is loosen him up if you can.[27]

Players who seldom bluff, who rarely run a "play," or never challenge bad hands are not likely to receive full monetary value from their hands. Knowing this, regulars and pros often put on the image of a person who gambles, makes risky bets, bluffs frequently, or is nothing but an incompetent player, especially to newcomers in the game who do not know them. Over the long run, most poker players would probably agree with these two assertions: (1) the best hand will usually win the pot (in other words, bluffing most of the time is not a winning strategy), and (2) a playing style that is *slightly* on the tight side will probably ensure survival longer than one on the loose side.

These two assertions generate an important, persistent conflict in self-presentation for all professionals. Endless table talk, deceptive moves, and dramatic presentations are devoted to the specific task of "talking loose and playing tight." In Gardena one of the most notable examples of this kind of player is Crazy Mike Caro, who describes his image-making in terms of its monetary payoffs:

> I think that players call me a lot more than they should. I think they put
> justifications for their calls in the knowledge of the plays that they've
> won twenty minutes ago. They tend to overappraise things. They don't
> react just right. They call me too much, plain and simple. It's the
> illusion of catching me on a lot of bluffs because it's emphasized in their
> mind, because my act is so bizarre. I think I've always had a good
> recognition of commercialism in proportion to gain as far as poker is
> concerned: how much I advertise my hands in relation to how much
> profit I'll make. I think I've always had a good feel for that. I think what
> happened is I started doing that and found some very creative plays that
> seemed to work well, and expanded that, and then felt very at home
> adding verbalizations and exaggerated actions to that in order to get
> a very wild and bizarre image. I've become almost addicted. I'd deny
> any emotion, you know. Now I've come to a realization that I have such
> a bizarre image anyway that it might be helpful therapy to act my
> feelings. If I'm angry I exaggerate it probably a hundred times. If I'm
> euphoric I exaggerate that a hundred times. I think that this helps me
> psychologically. An outpouring of emotion is like psychodrama to me.
> At the same time it's therapeutic and I think it has money returns.

On different occasions Crazy Mike would discard cards at random (or pretend to), give away "bonus" chips to losing players, deliberately play with six cards (a dead hand), raise and bluff with absolutely no chance of winning, play a portable tape recorder indicating whether he would pass or raise, and challenge other players to "death matches" in which the loser must kill himself.

Another pro, Bob C., explained how he "advertises":

> I sometimes play a complete bust and end up losing the pot. When I do,
> I make sure I throw the cards face up so that everybody can see them,
> and I laught it off as if it were a fun game to play loose and bluff. If
> I get one rock to change his ways it'll be worth it. But you can't advertise
> too often though because you'll go busted yourself.

Some pros are deliberate theatrical advertisers who flaunt their "busts" (useless hands) by turning them face up on the table under the nose of a player who threw away the best hand. When advertisers do hold a strong hand, they usually receive full value from it in calls and overcalls, because players do not like to be reminded that they made a bad laydown. The cardroom claim is "It pays to advertise."

One ambiguous feature of the rules of poker specifically encourages deceptive self-presentation and advertisement. No specific cardroom rule dictates what a player should do when he bets and his hand is not called. Table etiquette suggests that the bettor either throw in his discards face down or turn his hand up and show everyone (i.e., "Show one, show all"). These two suggestions, as judicious as they seem, are not always followed. Many experienced players use their cards to create an image, such as the image of a profuse bluffer or a tight nonbluffer. Pros work the table game of show-and-tell in both ways. They fan their cards in front of players whom they would like to bluff, showing them only solid hands until the right time. Or to increase the calls from tight players, they intentionally show them every bluff.

Exposing cards occurs in the split seconds when an indecisive opponent is deciding to call or after he gives up and passes. For an opponent who may call and obviously holds the losing hand, the advertiser may begin laying down his cards slowly one by one while adding a distracting narrative. First he turns up a four of diamonds ("Well, I think I have a straight"), then a ten of hearts ("No, it must be two pair"), and next an ace of clubs ("Now I don't know what I have"). Exasperated, the confused player calls, and the winner reveals two more aces. If the confused player should pass too often, that is, if he does not call enough hands, he will be bombarded with half-shown hands and misleading talk until he finally starts to loosen up and call. Then the pro will show him the best hand, for the price of a call, of course.

To change the pace of a slow game a player may announce that he is ready to gamble. Coming from a rock, this kind of proclamation is usually met with laughter and sarcasm. Players know that rocks do not gamble, and when they say they will, it means obviously that they are betting with the best hand and are not really taking a chance at all. Rocks who do not normally raise with good hands and whose betting habits are cautious are harshly criticized with the insult "You'll never be arrested for gambling." They, in turn, defend their mode of play rather than succumb to table criticism: "I have to play here everyday. There's no point in me gambling because I'm not going to break the bank anyway. You guys who want to gamble ought to go to Vegas or pitch pennies out in the parking lot. We'll see who'll end up on the rail first — you or me."

It is to the advantage of pros to keep wealthy live ones in the game because they generate action and make the game more attractive to waiting players. When the action and play-making is particularly stimulating, a winner may jokingly request the floorman to "put a rope around this game." In order to prevent a loose player or a big loser from "escaping" (winning and leaving), tablemates may lend the player money, offer verbal expressions of sympathy when he complains about losing on good hands, and avoid publicly insulting him. Sorry, frustrated faces appear when the pros have been beaten by a recognized underdog who has escaped with the chips, for they are left with themselves to play, and they know better than to try to fool one another with the same distractions.

Picking Spots

Unless an occasional poker player is attentive, he is unlikely to develop an immediate, correct categorization of other cardroom players. Most beginning and occasional players tend to be ego-centered. They devote undue attention to their own cards rather than carefully observing other players and following the action in the game. This is a critical oversight, for many pros assert that playing players is at least equally important as playing one's own hands.[28] Since pros derive much of their income from knowing when to raise, call, bluff, and throw in their hands, their categories for players must be updated continually. As players win or lose they sometimes dramatically change their style of play. As one pro told me: "Larry J. used to be loose as a goose. After he almost went busted a year ago, he tightened up like a clam. You've got to play him different. To get action you've got to give action, and he ain't seein' nothin' but the nuts from me from now on."

Pros will often pass on the characteristics of unfamiliar patrons to one another as a new player is about to sit down in a game:

I passed this big rock factory on the way to the club, and there he was, this big boulder, sitting in the middle of it.

Get him stuck and on tilt, and he'll be on the freeway in an hour.

He's tighter than two coats of paint.

These terse, categorical comments are sufficient for most pros to get the message and regulate the amount of action given the new player.

Labeling individual players and their playing styles is routine daily work for pros. They also classify whole tables and games by similar considerations of tightness or looseness, action or no action. On the basis of these evaluations a pro generally *picks his spot* when confronted with several different games. This means that he will carefully size up various tables and judge which is the best one, that is, the table with the worst players and the most money, and which games are the ones he wants to avoid. One player, for example, looks for a table with men wearing beards, crosses, and tattoos because such players might be superstitious, or he chooses a table with an attractive woman who may distract the male players.[29]

A tableful of loose action players, live ones, and wealthy losers—the ideal game—is referred to as a *juicy* game, or a *cherry* or *strawberry* patch. Such games are highly profitable for regulars and pros and easy to beat. Standing on the rail, regulars will instruct the floorman or boardman to put them up only for a specific table, or, once seated in another game, they will request to be on the waiting list for a change to the better game. Nonplaying employees, particularly floormen, also make these evaluations. Good games are made up of a high proportion of strangers, loose players, and customers who usually play a different or smaller game. Bad games are seen to have the same, predictable faces of daily, rocky regulars.

One way for a pro to pick a spot is to scrutinize the list of initials on the blackboard as soon as he enters the club and before he sits down. A glance at the list of initials determines how many and which specific players are waiting and how long each specific game in progress is likely to last without breaking up. A *full board* with many initials indicates that plenty of players are waiting and the game will not dissolve prematurely. A *live board* indicates that the initials represent actual players rather than props or people who have long since gone home. *No board* at all, no initials listed, means that the ongoing game will be short of players for a while and may dissolve at any time. A quick board analysis is part of a pro's daily survey of games. For most of them do not like to get stuck in a high-stakes game with no backup players and little chance of getting even. Tom L., a prop, gave me this advice:

> Don't get stuck in that $20-raise blind game. If you do and there's no board you're going to be sitting there talking to yourself. There's no way to beat that kind of game unless you hit and run 'cause you can't get even in the $10 game. If you're not doing anything, just sit in a small game for a while and wait until it fills up with the live ones. There's no point in playing with Hal, Art, Jimmy, and Red 'cause they're not going to give nothin' away.

Deciding where and when to play, a regular or pro must consider his own daily resources. If he is "short" and does not have his usual stake, he may select a small-stakes conservative game rather than an action-dominated big game. If, however, his bankroll is built up, he may want to "take a shot" in the biggest possible game for maximum returns.

In addition to picking spots by player-labeling information and the size of playing stakes, other considerations such as the time of day, week, or month are also relevant. Many pros consider weekends and the first days of the month excellent times for playing. Sid L. said: "The first of the month is the juiciest time of all. All the businessmen come in and blow away their paychecks like nothing. Show me a lineup like that and I'll be there."

Picking spots is a general strategy for regulars and pros who have had adequate time and experience to categorize and label others. Normally, it gives them the assurance that they will be one of the best players at an easy table. But in many high-stakes games, there is usually only one ongoing game, and the live ones are eliminated rapidly, leaving only strong competition. When picking spots is not possible, the only choice left for daily gamblers may be the toughest game — but the only game — in town. For some pros this alternative also serves its purpose. Instead of deliberately selecting easy games and opponents, they choose to play against the strongest players in the club and revel in the competition, the high stakes, and the incomparable action. Explained one pro: "Yeah, I pick my spots. I pick the strongest competition available. I like the competition. I enjoy it. I genuinely believe that I can beat any competition, and I like trying to do it."

A player who has not had a chance to pick his spot and who is stuck in a game that is too slow or too tight will raise the stakes or change the game's betting structure to create more action. In other words, if everyone agrees, a bad game can be transformed into a good game. High-stakes games can be made *raise blind* games, which forces tight players to loosen up and bet more without seeing their cards. In some lowball games, players will *kill* the pot by raising blind before the cards are dealt, thereby doubling the stakes; or they may play *winner-leave-it-in,* which requires that the winner of the last pot leave in twice the amount of the normal blind bet and double the stakes. Many of these action-escalation tactics take place in the early morning hours in the cardroom when losing players decide that they would like a better shot and take a bigger gamble at getting even for the day.

Some wealthy action players and inveterate gamblers find that no poker game, no matter how easy or flustered its opponents, provides enough action. Such players may offer one another *side bets* or *propositions* in order to generate more betting and a faster flow of money. Side bets may be made on which player is dealt the lowest spade card, Pinochle cards (the jack of diamonds and the queen of spades), or various combinations of colors (suits) and numbers. Side-betting usually takes place only in high-stakes games and only among certain action-craving players who may wager anywhere from $20 to $100 or more on each hand. The poker game, then, can become a mere side spectacle to the major proposition bets. In one game an action player who was not even playing was able to gamble to his heart's content by standing behind a seated player and betting on his hand against another player's hand for the "low spade" at $500 per hand. Now that's action!

4
Winners Talk

You've got to know when to hold 'em, know when to fold 'em
Know when to walk away, and know when to run.
You never count your money when you're sittin' at the table,
There'll be time enough for countin', when the dealin's done. *

Without restless housewives, weekend good-timers, drunks, live ones, millions of amateur players, and self-destructive gamblers, there would be no professional poker players. Without gambling losers, winners could not survive. Sometimes the differences between professional and amateur, winner and loser are indistinguishable, for no gambler ever sits comfortably on one side only. At other times the distinctiveness of the two groups is obvious. Unfortunately, in the social sciences there are more theories that focus on the behavior of losers in life, especially in gambling, than winners. An attempt to explain this academic bias would itself require a separate study. And so we are left with a puzzle: What are the special personal characteristics that differentiate winners from losers?

The Gambler, words and music by Don Schlitz. © Copyright 1977, published by Writer's Night Music. Reprinted with permission.

The most common traits[1] that gambling winners are presumed to possess are (1) mental alertness and concentration on the task at hand, (2) strong self-discipline, (3) a great desire to win, (4) tremendous self-confidence, (5) the ability to surprise, (6) an excellent knowledge of the probability of events, (7) a more than average analytical mind, and (8) the ability to judge other individuals correctly. In addition to these I suggest that the major factor that gives professionals and winners a significant edge at poker is their knowledge of valuable game and metagame strategies. The first relates directly to a practiced familiarity with the game, its technicalities, and its mathematical foundations. The second, equally important to winning, concerns involvement in and competency within the subcultural, symbolic interactional activities. These latter competencies refer to a player's degree of comfort within gambling environments and his practical knowledge of the subculture's players, argot, beliefs, and routines. A player can only acquire this expertise by direct experience, by spending thousands of hours playing in and thinking about various games.

I estimate that on any one night 20 to 25 percent of poker players in a given cardroom will end up winning. Over time, however, the winners will not always be the same players. The poker player with less than average skills can probably expect to win 15 to 25 percent of the time (roughly once out of every four to eight plays) simply because of chance alone, as long as he does not "blow back" his profits and as long as he quits when he is ahead. Winning at this modest rate, of course, will eventually lead to poker losses over an extended period of time. The slightly more skillful amateur can probably increase his winning rate to 40 or 60 percent, but to show a profit this too will probably not be high enough. Most professional poker players agree that a winning rate of 60 to 80 percent, far above the level of chance, is required to earn a modest to substantial profit (providing monetary wins are at least equal to losses). I do not know of any professional who can claim a winning rate of more than eighty percent, even though some pros may have had long winning streaks of thirty to sixty plays. Winning at poker is thus a matter of gaining edges in percentage points over opponents in day-to-day games and in each individual hand.

Understandably, most pros hate losing, for repeated losses of large sums of money may mean finding a nongambling job or becoming indebted to others. One player commented: "I get a sick feeling any time I'm stuck more than a couple of hundred dollars. I've been playing for years and I still can't get used to the idea of losing. I do anything I can to get my money back. Man, I hate losing. That's not what it's all about." These feelings and the distasteful options keep many players from maintaining their self-control and preserving their status as able, intelligent players.

72

CAREER GAINS AND COSTS

A fourteen-year-old girl wrote to *Gambling Times,* a popular monthly magazine, to ask "what requirements (if any) there are to become a professional gambler and what advantages and disadvantages there are being a professional gambler."

The magazine replied:

> A professional gambler is his or her own boss, makes his or her own hours, and can be a "free spirit." Professional gamblers can make places like Las Vegas and other exciting wide-open cities their home base. The disadvantages are irregular hours; playing cards or other games for long periods of time in smoky, stuffy and noisy places; and dealing with people who might not be the most wellbred in the world, and especially dealing with losers who can be angry, mean, and at sometimes, vicious . . . Then the gambler must have a talent or instinct for the game; skill that surpasses his opponents. Finally, he must be bold and have guts and be aggressive — the killer instinct is important.[2]

This reply is frank but understated. The personal investment in poker-playing for professionals is immense. Many pros play almost every day, averaging far more than forty hours per week inside the cardroom and 2,500-3,000 hours per year. The poker cardroom is not only the location where the pro makes a living but also the place where players eat, relax, meet friends, and receive telephone calls. Little time is actually left for developing non-gambling interests outside of the clubs. Depending on frequency of play and game stakes, career pros may earn from $5,000 to $45,000 per year, the mean being around $15,000.[3] This mean, though, is deceptive. Some players may wallow in the gravy of $40,000 year while others barely manage to keep afloat above the poverty level. These figures were derived from a nonrandom sample of the same thirty professionals (excluding worker pros) referred to in table 1. Only a few players kept detailed daily records of their play. One pro's record book showed that he netted $24,000 in 1976, making $29 per hour in the $10-20 game and $46 per hour in the $15-30. Others players did not keep daily notes and were either hazy about figures or reluctant to discuss precise gains and losses.

Since these figures were estimated in 1976, the legal betting limits of Gardena poker have increased tenfold. The highest game then used to be $20-20. The limit was increased to $40-80, and it is now $100-200. The average wins and losses for small- and medium-stakes players will remain unchanged by the new limits. But for wealthy regulars and career pros the increase in betting limits has substantially raised the average amount of daily, weekly, and yearly wins and losses for players who play near or at the upper limit. One regular high-stakes pro criticized the change of stakes, which was favored by many players:

> You remember when we all played $20? Nobody really got hurt too much. I mean you could lose a thousand or two, but so what. With the big limits, it's a bad thing. Now they want your arms and legs. All those players'll like the action and get used to the stakes, but most of them don't have the real money to back 'em. They're going to be busted faster than you can blink an eye. They think that they can take a shot in the big game for a few thousand, but I tell you, I wouldn't sit in that game for less than $30,000. Next thing you know they'll be on the rail trying to borrow from you and me. All I know is that there's going to be a lot of houses sold this summer.

The more a player wins and the higher limits he plays for will not always produce greater profits. Big players have a tendency to borrow more, take greater monetary risks, and lose proportionately more than small players. Clearing $15,000 in a year may mean winning $30,000 and losing $15,000 in the same period of time. For most working nongamblers, a regularly issued paycheck is taken for granted. But full-time gamblers must be prepared for vast irregularities in income. A player may lose for four solid months and then in a weekend recoup those losses and show a profit of $10,000. Full-time players must carefully manage their money to adjust to any outside emergencies, especially during periods when no money flows in. When they win a substantial amount they buy clothing and other necessities, usually in cash, and may pay six months' rent in advance. When losing they cut back on all purchases and use their money only for poker. The full-time poker player may sometimes have great sums of money and at other times none at all.

Occasionally poker pros themselves perpetuate the image of the good life of quick and easy money, especially after a big win. But the time and effort that is necessary to make a modest living month by month or year after year does not always substantiate this ostentation. Succinctly summing up the difficulty, an often-heard cardroom saying laments, "It's a hard way to make an easy living."

Despite the ceaseless day and night action and unlimited stakes, Las Vegas poker pros do only slightly better than Gardena pros. Ian Anderson observes that "Fewer than ten players really cream it—making over $100,000 yearly. Most big-time players are in and out of the money. When broke they hang on the rail bordering the poker pit and put the arm on the regulars for a stake."[4]

Frank Wallace guesses that the net average earning for all poker pros in Las Vegas is only about $12,000 per year.[5]

The instability of full-time poker means that players may show drastic swings in their overall yearly income because of the games they select and when they play. It may take a year for a player to net $25,000, and in the next four months — or four days — he may lose it all. (I have seen this happen more than once.) Those who can grind out an average annual income of $15,000 are only a small minority among professionals and gamblers as a whole. The slippery monetary gains of professional poker-playing are won laboriously, earned irregularly, and tough to keep.

The financial costs of full-time poker-playing, along with table losses, are an additional drain on a poker pro's bankroll. Pros in casinos and cardrooms must pay dearly to play: Gardena games and high-stakes Las Vegas games charge collection fees; pot rake-offs are common in most small Las Vegas games. These fees must be paid immediately, they cannot be negotiated, and they are often increased. Hand after hand and hour after hour they add up to a stupendous amount for both the house and the individual player. Depending on the stakes of the game, the yearly fee for individual poker pros in Las Vegas ranges between $15,000 and $30,000.[6] In addition, a pro who has won a sizable pot in a casino game traditionally tips the dealer a small fee, usually about the size of the ante.

As an example of the steep costs of full-time poker-playing, consider a medium- to high-stakes Gardena player who sits at the table for 3,000 hours per year and pays $5 in collection fees every half hour. His contribution to the house adds up to $30,000, not including gratuities to the club personnel. Many players and pros avoid paying such fees by waiting until the collection light is off before sitting down and by leaving just before it flashes on. A few pros who can successfully control their playing times play as few hours as possible and leave as soon as they have won a psychologically satisfying limit or have lost their daily limit. Others employ a different system, playing as many hours as possible and regarding their livelihood as a kind of hourly wage work. Whatever a player's preference, the costs of full-time poker playing add up to a considerable amount: from 30 to 100 percent of a player's profits may be paid to the house. Win or lose, of course, the costs to play must be paid on time. One of the players' most uncontested observations is "The house is the only winner."

A sensitive matter with respect to a gambler's income is not how much he earns but whether he reports the income to state and federal internal revenue services. By law all gambling winnings are taxable and must be reported. Gambling losses can be deducted with proof only if the amount does not exceed winnings.[7] If, for example, a player wins $20,000 in a year but loses

$30,000, for tax purposes he is "even" and cannot write off the additional loss of $10,000. Full-time poker players adjust to paying or not paying taxes in two ways. First, a player may keep complete records of wins, losses, and expenses, such as house playing fees, declare himself a professional gambler, and pay taxes on all or some of his winnings. In so doing he openly advertises his occupation and pays his dues. Second, a player may choose not to report his mode of livelihood or his winnings, for not even the players themselves know exactly how much another wins or loses in the cardrooms in a single sitting or over longer periods. A player who appears to be winning may still be suffering from last week's extraordinary loss; or he may look like a winner with several thousand dollars worth of chips in front of him, but he may have bought many times that amount. A losing player could be systematically removing chips from the table in each game he plays. So for players who do not keep records, precise money flows are unknowable. If a player does not declare his occupation as gambler, he can easily claim to be unemployed or self-employed, or he can appear on the payroll of an actual business. Other secretive gamblers may turn into nonpersons with no identification papers or proof that they exist as certifiable citizens.

CAREER CONTINGENCIES

Examining the longitudinal dimension of professional poker-playing reveals much about card-playing as a career. We must first place this occupation in its appropriate social context. Structurally, professional poker-playing contains many hierarchical levels that are demarcated physically and symbolically in the cardroom by game stakes. One can find paupers making their final bets, life-time indebted losers, and millionaires within a chip's throw of one another. From scraping for quarter chips, it is possible (but difficult) for a player to work upward and eventually gamble for any possible amount. This vertical movement is what concerns me in this discussion of career contingencies.

Here a delicate empirical distinction must be made between players who *attempt* to make a living playing poker and those who *actually* do so. It is not easy to tell the two apart. Both groups are identical in some respects in that they appear to possess an available source of cash and they play every day in the same games. But the player attempting to make a living may be risking his entire stake in one night or he may be deeply in debt to others. Some gamblers in this category play in an indebted condition for years, or for their entire lifetime as poker players, and never repay their debts completely. In practice, then, it is possible to be a full-time big poker player and personally be broke but living in relative luxury. A player can do this because on winning days he pays off some debts and bills — no player at this level loses all of the time — and on losing days he can borrow more money. In this price range $50 dinners and $10 cigars make little financial difference to the player's total wealth (or lack of it), and yet this lavish spending displays the accepted symbols of success. Such players are full-time professional gamblers who have made the card-rooms a permanent habitat, but they are not winning gamblers overall.

The data in table 2 follow the outcomes of the same thirty players who were listed in table 1. Four years later, in 1979, the long-term effects of poker-playing are evident. The most significant finding is that half of the players tapped out at least once, and most have either quit poker or begun to build a new bankroll by working and part-time playing. Even among the pros who have remained at the same or higher stakes, at least half of them went busted one or more times during the period 1975-1979. To presume that they played steadily at the same level would be a mistake: they have simply bounced back quicker than the others. Some were able to reach their regular level only after borrowing and making a comeback or by quitting poker, working full-time, and then returning to the game. Career pros, as would be expected, show the most staying power and immunity to downward movement. They can persistently seek action at big stakes by borrowing money on their reputation or they find backers to wholly or partially finance them. Reaching a high level of play and remaining there cannot be accomplished without making many friends and enemies and without owing or being owed favors.

Very few players like to step down to smaller games and occasional play after being on top. Outside-supported pros use this option more than the other two types. When they do step down, it is usually because they must protect a diminishing bankroll. Pros often complain about the lack of excitement and inferior action in small games:

It's impossible for me to play in the $10 game now. It's so boring and slow most of the time that I feel like falling asleep between hands. And the players are so stupid they wouldn't know what to do with a hand if their life depended on it. I sat in one game and couldn't believe the action. No one ever bet. It was check, check. It's driving me crazy being there.

Five out of six women remained as regular players at their usual stakes, although all of them too experienced shaky stretches when they played occasionally or quit for several months. Replacements for the pros who went busted and quit, disappeared, or died often came from the ranks. Several working players with whom I played every day for several years eventually quit their jobs when their poker winnings increased and they began to play full-time in 1977. Others worked their way up from smaller games, and a few new outsiders stepped into the big games immediately.

TABLE 2

THIRTY PROS FOUR YEARS LATER
(from 1975 to 1979)

	In same or higher stakes	In smaller game	Plays occasionally; may work on side	Quit	Whereabouts unknown (presumed not playing)	Deceased
Outside-supported pros (N = 11)	3	2	3	2	0	1
Subsistence pros (N = 8)	2	0	4	1	1	0
Career pros (N = 11)	6	0	4	1	0	0
Totals (N = 30)	11	2	11	4	1	1

What happens to pros over the age of sixty? As the saying goes, "They don't die, they end up on the rail." There, with little possibility of work, older pros play in the small games and harbor few aspirations of moving up. Some have entered full-time poker-playing from part-time playing relatively recently because of retirement; others function as outside-supported pros who have managed to save enough money for both a living and playing stake. In Las Vegas a few older players reach the pinnacle of their occupation by playing, winning, and eventually taking on less physically demanding activities like investing in businesses, managing cardrooms, or writing poker books. Few other significant career options are available for older players. This limitation of intraoccupational viability and growth is characteristic of many so-called deviant occupations.[8]

Players who can sustain the life of a full-time pro for over a year or two without seeking outside means of support are undoubtedly in the minority. Some last only several months. To survive five or more years in the cardrooms requires extraordinary patience, skill, and a hefty, fluid bankroll. There is a permanent core of no more than thirty to fifty players, and even fewer pros of any type, who have lasted in the cardroom for more than twenty years. Working, nonprofessional regulars are probably the most resilient group of all players. Many work solely to gamble and play poker, and they lose consistently year after year. But unlike pros they can bank on their jobs to support them when they gamble and lose.

The long hours, fierce competition, labor of all-night playing, irregular and unpredictable profits, and high costs ultimately exact their toll from all groups of players, amateur or pro. Upward mobility and wealth are the exceptions; downward mobility, losses, and many temporary absences or even permanent detachment from the cardroom is more the rule. This is why full-time professionals sometimes become working regulars or occasionals; regulars turn into twice-a-year occasionals; and many occasionals, after a week's flurry of nonstop poker, vanish from the cardroom forever.

Three Case Studies

These three personal profiles show the causal relationship between a player's volatile swings of fortune at the poker table and his vulnerable status as a professional. These brief studies are not meant to be typical but are offered as illustrative examples from the cases I observed. Case A concerns the upwardly mobile pro, case B the steady, stationary player, and case C the gambler who slips downward.

Case A. Bill M., a lean, clean-cut man now in his early thirties, started playing in the Gardena cardrooms in 1971 after dropping out of college (where he majored in business administration). It did not take Bill long to adjust to the small-stakes cardroom games because he had played poker since his teenage days. Determined to take the game seriously, he read all the poker books he could find and experimented with various hands and situations to determine which were profitable and which were not. Within six months he outplayed almost every regular in the small games, and his modest initial bankroll grew rapidly. Rather than spend time in middle-level games, he jumped immediately into the $10-20. By 1972 Bill was a regular night player in the high-stakes games.

During the first two months of 1972 Bill won over $15,000. With the cash he purchased a new sports car and moved into a bigger apartment in a beach city a short drive from Gardena. Shortly thereafter he started to lose, first gradually, then regularly. For the next several months he only won once or twice out of six nights' play per week. His bankroll dwindled, but rather than drop down to a small game that he said he could not "handle psychologically," he decided to lay off for a while and play less often. He had always entertained thoughts that he might supplement his income by writing. This would also take up much of the free time he had when not playing poker. By the end of 1972 Bill, who at first could be categorized as a career professional, was an occasional cardroom visitor. Sometimes he played only once or twice per month, arriving in the cardroom at unpredictable times and usually with a small bankroll. Many players like Bill might have quit at this point, but Bill thought he would give his playing future another chance. He sincerely believed that he was one of the best players in the cardroom.

Through several months of erratic attendance he again built up his bankroll by playing in the big games and hitting and running. When he lost, it was not more than $500-800. As his winnings picked up, he played more often and he spent less time on his writing and hobbies outside of the cardroom. Gradually he gained back his former status as a high-stakes regular. As of 1979 Bill was still a Gardena regular, and as long as he wins enough of a profit to support himself and his expensive tastes in jewelry and cars he will continue to see poker as a reliable way to make a living. He finds it increasingly likely that he may someday move to Las Vegas and tackle some of the bigger games and competition. Before such a move he plans to study thoroughly each type of poker game and again experiment with various hands and plays. With complete confidence in his abilities and his knowledge of poker, even during losing periods, Bill knows he can always make "some kind of money" in the cardroom.

Case B. Harold D., born in 1932, played poker and other cards "as soon as he stood up." Now approaching fifty, he is a short, slightly overweight man. During high school and especially during his years in the army (he enlisted immediately after graduation), Harold learned much about competitive poker-playing. In the army, he says, it was "all poker and dice." After leaving the service he entered a junior college on the GI bill, taking courses in the humanities and arts but with no clear idea of his future goals. While attend-

80

ing college, he worked part-time in a photography studio where he met his future wife. Their childless marriage lasted only a year.

Hal discovered the Gardena cardrooms in 1963 after his divorce. At first he "lost his shirt" every time he played, but he gradually picked up pointers on the cardroom style of play from other regulars. He has not read any books on how to play poker, claiming, "I'm too old to memorize the numbers." Yet since 1963 he has managed to survive as a full-time subsistence professional.

Other players describe him as "steady" and "controlled." His even temperament is one of his most useful cardroom assets. Hal has few interests outside of the cardrooms; he does not even watch sporting events or gamble on any other game, and he rarely takes a trip to Las Vegas. By his own admission he would like only to play in the $10-20 games and "pull down" several hundred dollars a day. He does not want to play in the bigger games or challenge stiffer competition. Hal has deliberately chosen not to attempt to be upwardly mobile. "I like these easy games," he says. "There's too many hotshots and gamblers in the big games."

Since 1974, when I first played with Hal, he has occasionally "run bad," like almost every other player. But rather than chase his losses in the bigger games, Hal plays on a daily stake of no more than $300 and does not keep money in the player's bank or borrow money from cardroom friends. Hal never flaunts the fact that he is a steady, winning player, and he stays on friendly terms with almost everyone. Some do not even mind losing to him because he is a "gentleman."

Hal judges his prospects of finding a job outside of the cardrooms, if he must, as dismal. "Who would want to hire a broken-down card player?" he asks. The idea of remarriage does not interest him. "I'm married to the cards," he boasts, and "I hope they don't divorce me." Hal foresees that he will last a long time as a player and then perhaps "die of a heart attack at the table."

Case C. Like many cardroom regulars, Jerry A. discovered that he had a better than average chance of winning in the small games if he played a bit on the tight side and controlled his losses. A bespectacled, graying man in his early forties who speaks with a slight accent, he says that as a child he learned how to play poker and other card games in his homeland in the Middle East. In 1967 he arrived in this country as an aerospace engineer with his wife and two children. After eating lunch one day with his fellow workers in a cardroom restaurant, he looked over the games and decided to play for fun after work.

First he played only on weekends in the small games. When his profits increased he moved up to the bigger games. With a casual but relaxed style of play, he was fairly successful and was "holding his own." By 1973 he had quit his job and was working part-time as a draftsman for an independent engineering firm near Gardena. He was also playing poker every evening. He pre-

81

ferred the evening and night hours and usually ambled into the club around 8 or 9 P.M. decked out in new and expensive clothing. He once showed me a brand new gold watch he had bought himself as a Christmas present.

Jerry was an average and not very competitive player. He rarely bluffed or played hands that had little chance of holding up. He made an adequate side income for several years as a working professional. In 1976 he was divorced and admits that the years of late-night card playing had something to do with the breakup of his marriage. As a bachelor again, Jerry played cards almost every day during 1976, quit his part-time job, and tried to move up to the bigger games.

Burdened with outside expenses, including child support and new car payments, Jerry started to play for higher stakes and he began to lose more frequently. On his downward slide, his attendance in the cardroom was not as predictable as it had been during the previous three years. Sometimes on losing nights he borrowed money from cardroom friends and usually managed to pay them back a little at a time. When those sources dried up, and not wanting to play in the small games in his regular club, Jerry changed cardrooms. Optimistically, he said, "I thought it'd be better here with a different batch of faces who don't know me."

By the early months of 1977 Jerry's visits to the new cardroom were also erratic and he no longer displayed a new wardrobe every day. With no outside job he was playing at a subsistence level in small games and was attempting to pay his bills, loans from cardroom acquaintances, and rebuild his bankroll. He won for about four months before finally going busted. Several months later I heard that he had borrowed more money from several other players and had changed cardrooms again. After that, in the summer of 1977 he dropped out completely and no one knew where he was. (In 1979 I saw Jerry at a movie theater in Los Angeles. He said he had remarried, was working as a clothing salesman, and played poker in Gardena "maybe once a month.")

THE STATUS PYRAMID AND TOURNAMENT PLAY

Among the millions of poker players in cardrooms and casinos, in smoky backroom bars and men's fraternal clubs, and in thousands of dens and living rooms, the reputations of the best players grow as these players consistently end up with the money. Most of the time news of small victories does not penetrate beyond the winner's small circle of poker friends. A few players in these diverse settings, however, deliberately seek out high-priced games and stiffer competition. The cardrooms of Las Vegas represent the top challenge to the hopefuls who dream of turning their small stakes into hundreds of thousands of dollars. Las Vegas is the social, financial, and symbolic center of all high-stakes poker-playing. Good poker players with ambitions and plans of upward mobility often view playing on the periphery as unrewarding or just plain boring. Hence the move to Las Vegas, the poker testing grounds, where players finally face the truth about their abilities.

Many Las Vegas games resemble "fastest gun in the West" contests, where newcomers literally attempt to "outdraw" the established pros and tournament winners in order to enhance their own reputations and bankrolls. As one Las Vegas pro observes, these challenges are not easy:

> I've seen 'em come and go by the busload. They come to town, play
> tight, and win a while. But it ain't like home. Here the games go
> twenty-four hours. They play too much, play in bad games. They don't
> pick their spots like the locals. No, these hotshots got to be in action
> every day. They go against tough competition, play long hours, and
> drink like fish . . . Next thing you know, *they* are throwing the party . . .
> Yeah, I seen it all. Seen 'em come and go. We eat 'em for breakfast,
> them local champs.[9]

Professional poker players throughout the country, or even in Las Vegas alone, do not fall into a universally accepted hierarchy. But within the gambling and poker-playing subculture players at each level rank themselves and others primarily by word of mouth on a number of traits. Poker players first separate themselves from other gamblers and generally hold themselves and their own skills in higher esteem. (They may also include the successful twenty-one card counter in their class.) Most have an easy time finding weaknesses in other players and strengths in themselves, and they will publicly state their views. The constant disagreement about the ranking and abilities of individual players only underscores the high level of ego and self-confidence that professional poker players must display in order to survive at all. Poker is not a game in which the meek inherit the chips.

The most important factors that determine a player's reputation and relative rank are the size of his personal playing bankroll (accumulated by poker winnings) and his style, skill, and knowledge of the game. Poker players make distinctions as to how much a player knows about a particular game and the style and "heart" with which he plays. These are quite distinct traits. Assessing one Las Vegas tournament player, an observer on the rail pointed out:

> He probably knows more about the game than anybody else. He's got the
> mathematics of the game down pat. But he's got no balls. He's got a
> heart this big [measures a half inch with his fingers]. If he doesn't have
> the nuts he's not going to be in the hand, and most of the time you
> can run him out with a big bet. You see all those crying calls he made
> with the best hand? No balls and no heart.

83

Pride and ego are also included as part of the stakes. Full-time gamblers do not like to admit defeat and walk away from the table broke. As Mickey C. analyzed the situation:

> You know why most of these players go busted? It's not because they
> don't know how to play. That's not it. It's because of their egos. They've
> got to show everybody and themselves that they're the world's greatest.
> I just sit back and play my game, and they can make all the moves
> and talk they want. In twenty years I've seen hundreds of these flashes in
> the pan. Give them the trophies. I'll take the money.

Poker winnings and personal reputations tend to increase mutually, and as they do, these successful qualities are linked to superior intelligence and cleverness. But not all winners and pros are well liked or admired. Some younger pros are openly critical of older, conservative players whom they describe as unimaginative, predictable, and mathematically incompetent. Many of the young players cite knowledge of statistics, game theory, and psychology as part of the newer "scientific" and "theoretical" aspects of poker in which older pros are only "intuitively" competent,[10] which condescendingly connotes an inferior skill. Contrasting a younger scientific player with an older, presumably unscientific one, a pro in his early thirties stated: "The player who knows his mathematics, psychology, and can read and intimidate others is what I mean by a scientific player. That player is just overkill against some of the older players. It's not even close even though the older players have 100,000 hours at the table."

Many older pros who have lasted years in the cardroom are skeptical about the staying power of the younger pros, who argue loudly over the table about the "theoretical" aspects of the game and the "correct" play of each hand. One older pro retorted: "I've been here long enough to see every type come and go, like those computer whiz kids and brain surgeons. I've been here twenty-five years. I'll outlast them and every other college professor who comes down here."

Because of the number of available games ranging from nickel ante to no-limit poker, Las Vegas cardrooms, more so than California cardrooms, attract players who would like to play "big" and be associated with the local subculture of players. While Las Vegas offers any game of any size to willing players, Las Vegas locals also believe that the kinds of poker they play—mainly varieties of five-, six-, or seven-card stud and Hold 'Em—are inherently more complex, more action-stimulating, and more skillful than other types of poker, particularly five-card draw, which many consider old fashioned. Some pros consider Hold 'Em poker, played for no-limit or table stakes, the Cadillac of poker games.[11]

Professional poker players can thus be ranked internally by many factors, from the courage they display to the type of games they play. Poker players also rank themselves hierarchically by game stakes. Broadly, all poker players, including professionals, fit into a three-level pyramid or hierarchy. Ranking players by the criterion of game stakes may appear to be objective, but it can be misleading. Wealthy players may choose to play in small games while adventurous newcomers with relatively less capital may decide to "take a shot" in the big games. And in some high-priced games one can find many player types: pros with nearly unlimited credit and bankrolls, pros who are deeply in debt and must play for big stakes, pros who are backed by sponsors, and a fresh supply of working regulars and tourists. Game stakes, then, are not a completely accurate measure of an individual player's personal wealth.

There are fewer players at the top of the financial pyramid than at the bottom. The upper tier consists mainly of career professionals and wealthy regulars who play for stakes of $100 and higher up to no-limit. In these games daily wins and losses may run into the tens and hundreds of thousands of dollars. Poker-playing at this level is a potentially destructive system because of vast monetary losses that usually can only be made up by more gambling. Within this upper level there is a distinction between those players who normally seek out the biggest games available and those who play in the next to the biggest games. Millions of dollars may change hands in some games at this level of play.

The middle level of the hierarchy of players, which ranges from $10 to $100 limit, probably supports most of the pros of all types and attracts thousands of outside amateurs. Many tables in Las Vegas and Gardena cardrooms fall into this price range. Players in this category show extremes of winning and losing. Some in the lower end risk a hundred dollars while others in the upper end bet ten thousand dollars or more. Middle-level players, of course, with smaller bankrolls, do not have as much flexibility in game choice as upper-level players who can play in any game they choose.

The lowest and largest level of the pyramid consists of small players in the betting range $1-10. Most cardroom tables are in this range to accommodate the many recreational players. Wins and losses at this level vary from less than a hundred to over one thousand dollars. Career pros here tend to be either starting a climb upward or down from a setback, but these are the usual playing stakes for many subsistence and outside-supported pros.

Upper-level players differ from lower-level ones not only in the amount of money risked; the former are generally much more skillful. Of course, there are superb, skillful players in all three levels of the stakes pyramid, but the middle and highest strata hosts and develops a higher proportion of such capable players. Their skills include card sense and the ability to control and symbolically use large sums of money or stacks of chips to manipulate opponents. It is probable that successful poker play at the various levels demands facility with the same general skills, but each level emphasizes different capabilities.

The Payoffs of Poker Tournaments

For years there was no way to determine which poker player was the best in the world at his particular game. Recently, to amend this condition and as a step toward the ratification of a public ranking of players, tournament play has become increasingly popular and rewarding for both professionals and amateurs. But there is criticism of the results. Many players frankly express their doubts that winning a tournament is a valid measure of skill or produces an objective, incontestable ranking of players. One entrant dismally remarked that "the luck factor increases about three times in tournament play." In a tournament each player purchases the same amount of chips, and the game stakes are increased every few hours or as players are eliminated. These qualifications are, of course, quite different from normal cardroom play where the stakes remain the same and players buy as many chips as they want. Despite these constraints, one reason why tournament play has become more attractive to players is that with a large number of entrants and combined purse, a relatively small investment can generate a huge return. A $1,000 entry fee may return $20,000; a $10,000 buy-in may bring a quarter of a million dollars. Tournament play also stimulates betting among spectators and immense action in side games. When tournament players are eliminated but remain eager to win back their buy-in, side games often develop and upstage tournament play with limits exceeding those in the tournament.

The *World Series of Poker* was conceived by Jimmy the Greek Snyder,[12] a Las Vegas oddsmaker (not to be confused with Nick the Greek, a now deceased high-rolling gambler), and Benny and Jack Binion, owners of the Horseshoe hotel-casino in downtown Las Vegas. In 1970 this group decided to bring together the top poker players in the world. By a vote of his peers, Johnny Moss, a long-time pro from Texas, was acknowledged the winner. Since 1971 the World Series of Poker tournament has been conducted with a "freeze-out" policy, which means that all entrants buy the same amount of chips and they play until one person ends up with them all. That player is declared the winner. In 1971 Johnny Moss won the first official title again. Every year thereafter the main poker event—table stakes Hold 'Em requiring a $10,000 buy-in per player—has grown larger and more profitable for the winner.[13] In 1980 the total prize money exceeded half a million dollars of which the winner received 50 percent ($365,000); second through fifth place won 20, 15, 10, and 5 percent, respectively.

Besides the major Hold 'Em event, the World Series of Poker, which now runs annually for about four weeks in April and May, features a dozen other games with varying entrance fees. [14] In 1978 the world's first California-style, five-card draw poker contest was added, and because draw poker is not played regularly in Las Vegas only seven entrants competed; six of them were from Gardena cardrooms or had played there in the past. [15] The World Series of Poker seems also to have spawned other publicized poker tournaments in Las Vegas, including *Amarillo Slim's Poker Classic* (begun in 1979) and several large money championships in twenty-one, backgammon, and gin rummy hosted by large hotel-casinos on the "Strip."

Both the centralization of a worldwide poker hierarchy and television and newspaper publicity have helped give the professional poker player celebrity status and a greater sense of historical continuity. In May 1979 a Poker Hall of Fame was instituted in Binion's Horseshoe hotel-casino in downtown Las Vegas. The first seven members elected include Edmond G. Hoyle (1677-1769), J. B. (Wild Bill) Hickok (1845-1876), Nick the Greek Dandolas (1883-1966), Felton (Corky) McCorquodale (1904-1968), Sid Wyman (1910-1978), J. H. (Red) Winn, and Johnny Moss. [16]

Tournament poker play, marathon games, and winning players have also been the subject of a number of recent novels. [17] These gains are a departure from the traditional, tawdry image of the poker player, and the personal identity of many players has been affected. One professional poker player says:

> When I meet a person who doesn't know anything about gambling and poker, I expect them to be impressed. I expect them to be positive. I think that professional gamblers are pretty much idolized by a great number of people. I think that most people would love to be able to admit that they could give up work and play poker. It's not an undesirable profession. When I'm at parties there's a lot of curiosity and interest about what I do.

Some writers have even compared the winnings of tournament poker players with the salaries of professional athletes. The implication is that poker resembles a competitive sport. As such, the Hold 'Em competition of the World Series of Poker appears annually on CBS-TV's *Sports Spectacular* with celebrity interviews and play-by-play commentaries. The title of the tournament, itself, suggests a sports play-off of international magnitude. While the increased attention of tournament play has generated a wide public audience and tremendous payoffs for the winners, it has also created additional worries for the players. As Clifford Geertz describes so precisely for the Balinese cockfight, [18] it is not the cocks alone that are fighting, it is the men who own them and wager on them.

So it is with poker tournaments. Men risk money, reputation, and the hopes of bettors and backers on the rail. Players and nonplayers alike negotiate with one another to buy or sell a piece of the action (this, in itself, is a measure of peer-group recognition); they discuss the merits of the informal "line" (odds) on each player and make side bets on who will be eliminated first. In some tournaments an entrant may have five or more side bets on other contenders or a small piece of their action. A player may not even have to purchase the buy-in to a tournament with his own money. Shares, as it were, may be split up between playing friends, nonplaying friends, and backers.

Of the social risks one tournament contestant said: "You don't know what winning this tournament would do to my reputation in town. I'd get all kinds of offers all over the place to play for any stakes I wanted to. It's real important for me to show that I won't freeze up or anything like that, and that I've got what it takes." "Having what it takes" is not easy. One observer of tournament play described the tension that emanates from the table:

> Tournament playing is rough. You have to get used to the idea that a
> player will bet thousands of dollars without even a single pair of cards.
> You play for keeps, and you have to be able to deal with the terror of
> losing all that you have. There is no clemency, only the survival of the
> fittest. Show any sort of vulnerability and you are immediately
> annihilated. The eyes remain cold and stern, the hands steady. When the
> fingers get moist from the tension, you discreetly wipe them on a napkin
> resting on your lap. You camouflage any indication that the game is
> getting to you, even in the end, when the game finally *does* get you.[19]

The occupation of professional poker playing is moving rapidly from underground subcultural secrecy to public legitimacy. Those who play in the highest-stakes games and who win the major tournaments often refer to themselves and others as "superstars" or "top-ranked" or "world class" players, thereby wearing newly acquired social titles that obscure their historically unconventional image. These semantic enhancements, as well as the vast sums of money they win, make them in their own eyes comparable to high-paid professionals in other occupations and to "show biz" personalities.

Not all professional poker players, however, seek out difficult tournament competition or care to risk reputation and bankroll on what Erving Goffman calls "character contests."[20] Some are content to grind out a modest living without public notoriety and the challenges of tournament play. But for both the quarter-and-dollar gambler and the recognized superstars of poker, successfully sustaining a livelihood year after year presents as many obstacles as rewards.

CAREER TENSIONS

The professional poker player lives with ineradicable ambiguities, contradictions, and strains.[21] What players say and do,[22] what they think and do not think about poker and their cardroom lives frequently gush forth in comments at the table and on the rail. These persistent strains derive from the uncertainty and, most of all, from the social, psychological, and financial instabilities in the pro's life. At least three major tensions are apparent.

1. *Individual Survival versus Interpersonal Support and Cooperation.* Surviving in high-pressure professional poker-playing depends almost entirely on the skill of the player acting on his own as decision-maker. Each pro must play his own hand. But making a more inclusive life out of cardroom poker-playing demands constant association with others. It means sitting at a table for weeks, months, and years with the same loyal regiment of regulars and the occasional influx of "new blood." From these numerous social interactions, friendships arise and small cliques form through mutual card-playing admiration and the reciprocal exchange of money and favors.

In high-stakes games where huge sums of money are won and lost, the pro must win enough to "make the nut" (pay the daily bills) and keep a stake intact but avoid being brutal to friends across the table. The pro must balance individualistic survivorship interests and more personal, cooperative tendencies, which all gamblers occasionally seek. A professional cannot be too friendly or entangled with others without risking his capacity to win; yet he cannot be too detached from his playing peers, for someday his own financial and social survival in the cardroom may rest on their generosity in lending him money and looking out for his interests. Pros must reconcile hard play and soft play and must tactfully weigh social as well as financial gains and losses.

2. *Self-control versus Self-destruction.* Professional poker-playing is an exacting test of personal comportment. Self-control, especially stifling emotions when defeated, tired, or angry, is essential in order to survive. But self-destructive behavior can be set off easily when a player is repeatedly outdrawn or outplayed by another. In defeat, the player may then begin to "steam," go "on tilt," attempt to buy every pot with aggressive betting, or pick out special opponents to beat and destroy, often in unfavorable game conditions. Almost every poker player I have observed has at one time or another lost some degree of self-control, if only for several minutes. Some, of course, are notorious "steamers" and are prone to "opening up" more than others. Being "opened up" feeds on itself and often creates a chain reaction that results in further losses, lack of composure, and finally self-defeat and resignation. In its most prolonged state, as one hard-bitten regular said, being on tilt can be "a way of life."

Risk, in itself, does not necessarily lead to failure and lack of self-discipline. It can work for or against each player's survival. One pro summarized this conflict succinctly: "The need to take chances, even reckless chances, is an inherent characteristic of every successful gambler I've known. The difference between these winners and the would-be stars who bash themselves and their bankrolls into oblivion is this: *Winners have stopped denying that these dangerous urges exist within them. They have come to terms with themselves.*"[23]

3. *Life-style and Occupational Glorification versus Cynicism.* Glorification of the life of gambling abounds in the many public statements made by successful gamblers. One obvious benefit of the successful gambling life is material comfort: "Some professional gamblers, contrary to public conceptions, keep a low profile. Not me. I like the trappings that go along with the gambling life-style. I like fancy cars, fine clothes, and expensive houses. It's part of the dream."[24]

Indeed, winning gamblers are prone to fantasies and glorification of their lives because of the enormous and immediate payoffs of large sums of cash. But there exist also as permanent influences in the life of the professional gambler obvious stumbling blocks to the realization of such dreams. The daily association with offensive and ethically dubious players, the exhausting physical and emotional requirements, the big losses, and the occasional feelings of uncontrollability and uselessness all may burst out as loud, cynical deprecations of gambling, poker, and the pros' own lives. In exasperation, one pro who was losing heavily in a game complained: "We're all crazy doing this. It's insane. No normal person would let himself in for all this abuse and bullshit. There's got to be an easier way to make a living."

The professional poker player grows cynical quickly in this career. Other forms of institutional and occupational cynicism are determined by age and experience, but these are not prerequisites for the pessimism found in poker players.[25] Nor does cynicism in poker players arise from the discrepancy between public attitudes and private ones. Cynicism in poker derives primarily from the lack of fit between a player's financial aspirations and his actual standing. Always teetering between poker glory and poker hell, the player frequently pronounces himself "sick," "hooked on gambling," "suicidal," or "should be committed." The routine is almost a comedic parody of criticism from outside the poker world.

Self-derision and sarcasm about poker-playing are common conversational table topics, but they are not the only ones that should be taken seriously. Players speak disparagingly of the "low life" characters of the cardroom—the crude, the unemployed, the wheeler-dealers, the vulgar, the uneducated players with no "class," the bums and poker bums. They also admire those whom they trust and look up to, those with wealth and style. On some days the cardroom can be a dark, stank pit, the "asshole of the world," as some players put

90

it. On other days it provides, rewards, and encourages genuine feelings of belonging.

Despite the possibility of making thousands of dollars in a short period of time, cynical attitudes among poker players persist because a career in poker-playing demands unusual patience and planning. Every day the professional faces the daily battle to remain at the highest level that he has attained. Anything less would be a financial and psychological decline. Except when the pro is winning, he has little security and comfort. Cynicism, then, is a predictable response to work that is physically draining and that one day produces great rewards only to be lost the next. While cynicism is a recurrent outlook, it is usually not permanent; in the mind of the holder it takes its turns with career idealism.[26]

The professional poker player wavers between the polar ends of each of these sets of career tensions, depending on how he perceives his success or failure at the moment. When satisfied he leans toward group supportiveness, strong self-control, and the verbal and financial celebration of gambling glory. When losing he shifts without a moment's notice to the darker side: he places his own survival and bankroll above everything else, becomes prone to self-pity and self-destructive play, and voices loud pessimistic, sarcastic, and cynical judgments about his life, especially the harsh rut of poker-playing.

For the full-time career professional these tensions are persistent occupational hazards that are never resolved. As he oscillates between outdrawing others and being outdrawn, winning pots and losing pots, and standing in good shape and nearly busted, so he fluctuates in his moods, choice and depth of interpersonal relationships, and attitudes toward himself and his work.

5
Losers Walk

When you love the greenback dollar,
Sorrow's always bound to follow.
Reno dreams fade into neon amber.
And Lady Luck she'll lead you on,
She'll stay a while, and then she's gone.
You'd better go on home Kentucky gambler. *

Winning at poker creates a visible smugness and confidence in the fortunate player. And success, whether for one game or a streak lasting a month, lifts financial and psychological burdens at the same time. Even though winning players may savor their pleasurable state, they do not seem to dwell on *why* they have won. Winning requires no explanation or analysis; it is materially evident, and to seek deeper reasons would be anticlimactic. Losing, on the contrary, just once or many times, causes the unfortunate player to worry endlessly about strategy and to ask what went wrong. Possessing a large bankroll and better than average game skills and controlling luck and action do not ensure permanent cardroom survival. To keep in action a player must be able to raise money when he runs bad and he must use various rationalizations and supportive beliefs to reduce tension and console himself in losing streaks.

HOW MANY LOSE?

Known for many years as the "King of Gamblers," the legendary Nick the Greek Dandolas won and lost hundreds of millions of dollars playing poker, rolling dice, and betting on horses. In the 1920s and 1930s he challenged and gambled with some of the wealthiest businessmen and professional gamblers of his day. Nick loved action. His most quoted saying was "The next best thing to gambling and winning is gambling and losing." He is believed to have lost the largest stud poker pot ever—over $600,000—to Arnold Rothstein, a racketeer in New York City who was murdered in 1929 for not paying off his gambling debts. In his later years Nick the Greek was roundly beaten in many gambling games and ended up playing $5-10 draw poker in the cardrooms of Gardena. When asked by a fellow player if that was a comedown from his wealthy pinnacle, Nick replied, "It's action, isn't it?" He died broke on Christmas Day in 1966.[1]

Most occasionals, regulars, and social gamblers realize that losing is inevitable. In casino games of pure chance, where the house establishes a set edge or percentage over the player, it is unlikely that a gambler will win consistently. When the factor of player skill enters into consideration the chances for winning improve statistically but increased competition lowers the odds somewhat. Even professionals and winning regulars who do survive are subject to frequent, unavoidable downswings in daily fortunes. Indeed, within every poker club and cardroom, the majority of players will be losers *in the long run*. Providing exact figures for gambling losers and winners is difficult because it is not always possible to determine for individual players how long the "long run" may be and whether the player—for one reason or another—has misrepresented himself. Other factors add to the confusion: a player's changing frequency and level of play, unaccounted daily expenditures on collection fees, food, and drinks, lavish purchases when winning, and gains and losses in gambling other than poker.

I would estimate unhesitatingly that 95 to 99 percent of all cardroom poker players eventually lose more than they win.[2] And, of course, even professional poker players are not immune to devastating losses. In fact, they place themselves in a far more precarious position than the average social gambler by playing for enormous stakes nearly every day.

Losing at poker affects the occasional, regular, and professional differently. Most recreational occasionals (not the fallen regulars) do not risk more than they can afford to lose, and they come and go from the cardroom as they please. They can tolerate losing. Regulars adapt to losing quite differently

93

because they have made heavier social and affective investments in the cardroom. Many play until they lose heavily, then quit for a while or become occasionals, and return only when they have raised a new stake from working or from loans. The money-raising strategies for regulars usually are directed toward returning to cardroom play. When a professional loses, the consequences are more serious and greater adjustments must be made. Losing not only destroys the pro's playing stake but it also tarnishes his personal reputation and may reduce his capacity to borrow money from cardroom friends and other professionals. Furthermore, to himself, losses may completely erode his self-confidence and ability to operate as a "smart" money manager and winning player. To prevent this fate, every gambler must be aware of and contend with the devious, persistent dangers to his bankroll.

DANGERS TO THE BANKROLL

The foul taste of losing hits a player first in his pocket—in his bankroll, that wad of hard cash he must possess in order to stay in action. A gambler's bankroll can be exhausted with amazing rapidity because of three dangers to which professionals are most vulnerable.

Danger One: Setting No Limits on Time and Money. Full-time career gamblers with few interests or social obligations outside of the cardroom are in a particularly dangerous position with respect to their methods of money management and frequency of play. Many of them set no specific loss limits on any particular playing day, and disregarding warnings from other professionals and numerous advice-to-gamblers books, they sometimes play with most or all of their bankroll. Some do so out of sheer confidence in themselves, as one admitted:

> I am willing to take the maximum risks at all times. I'm willing to put
> my whole bankroll on the table at any given time. I think the top
> professional gamblers are not using an optimal approach if they protect
> their bankroll completely. It seems to me that this is not a very good
> strategy. Because in life itself there's more than a 1 percent chance that
> within the next year or two you'll come down with a serious illness, or
> something will annihilate your bankroll, or other life traumas will occur.
> If you risk only 1 percent you're not getting the most out of the ability to
> protect your life at any time. I think that those players are unduly
> conservative. I guess security is a big thing for them. It's not to me.
> Security doesn't mean anything to me. If anything, security means a lack
> of adventure. Something that's taken away from you.

Worse yet, some players may risk money that is not even their own, betting solely on their borrowing power and presumed credit with others. Unable to survive normal fluctuations of a stake and the run of cards, they fall victim to this insidious trap.[3]

Time, too, can be managed poorly. When professionals are stuck in a game, many of them play and play until they get even, or slightly ahead, or are too tired to continue. Some players sit continuously for days and nights at the table in a completely exhausted state, falling asleep between hands and rarely rising except to satisfy bodily needs. While losing their chips, they also lose their concentration and self-control, assets they normally rely on to win. Being stuck in a game forces most gamblers to stay and persist, but ironically so does winning quickly. Many poker players make a decent score within an hour or less of sitting down but do not quit and cash in. The feeling is that there is always the possibility of winning even more — making a gigantic hit — and that playing only an hour is not long enough. Accustomed to ten- to fifteen-hour all-night sessions, an hour's play is too short. A professional does not want to be accused of hitting and running since his friends and playing peers will be critical of this behavior.

Gamblers would like to believe that once they win a specific amount of money, one that "sounds right" to them, they will be comfortable and secure. That sum, however, never seems to be reached. Either the gambler increases the figure as he actually approaches it, or he modifies the goal in some other way, such as seeking to win an amount in round numbers. Casino stories are filled with incidents of gamblers who have tried to win a mere $2 to tip a doorman or waitress, only to lose thousands chasing it. Nor can gamblers stop at winning $99 or $19,000. The last push to reach a round sum, and then the plateau after that, has taken away hard-earned profits from many players.

For the full-time professional the social life in the cardroom is sometimes a more important reason to stay than the amount of money won or lost. At some point, however, every player must define his personal time limit and quit as close to a winner as possible. This limit, for most, is between three and twelve hours. While many players agree that decisions to quit should be made entirely on the basis of money won or lost rather than the length of playing time, they do not always follow their own advice. Many cardroom regulars complain that "There's nowhere to go" or "It's too early to sleep" (no matter what time it is). Time, like money, is a commodity to the full-time gambler that can be controlled wisely or spent foolishly.

Danger Two: The Escalation of Stakes. Gambling settings seem to encourage the escalation of stakes and the reliance on get-even strategies. When losing, many professional gamblers complain about the game by looking disgustedly at their lack of chips and asking, "How long are we going to play *this?*" Framed as a complaint, this question is heard at least once a night in high-stakes games where the winners have left and the losers remain to play among themselves. Escalating the stakes, of course, does not always save players from loss, nor does it guarantee that they will "bail out." More often than not, doubling-up results in more severe consequences. Some players lose months of hard-earned profit by moving up and losing at escalated stakes. And when a losing player is "out of his league" in a bigger game with the professionals at that level, he will generally not be given the same action.

The ability to build a working bankroll from small beginnings, in spite of loss, accounts for the continuing optimism among gamblers and adds to the folklore of the casinos and cardrooms. Take the case of Jack Straus, a professional gambler from Houston:

> Back in 1970, Jack was down to $40 after a run of bad luck in Vegas, and then he started playing 21. He quit after running it up to $500, took that and stretched it to $4,000 playing poker, then returned to 21 and hiked it up to $10,000. He bet that on the Kansas City Chiefs in the Super Bowl — and collected $20,000.[4]

Even though stories such as this one may lift the gambler's spirit and renew his confidence, successfully parlaying a small stake like this is quite difficult, for at each level the player must risk everything he has previously won. Gamblers feel, though, that until they cash out the chips, the profit they have made is temporary and not actually theirs. As long as chips remain on the table, they "play" and are subject to loss or gain.[5]

Danger Three: The Lure of Other Gambles. Few professional poker players do not at least occasionally gamble on sporting events, the horses, casino games, golf or pool shooting, or other on-the-spot propositions. Some, however, studiously avoid any of this "real" gambling if they do not have an edge. Other gamblers are knowledgeable and competent in many games and will gamble on almost anything. Compared to faster casino games where every throw or roll can be bet on, poker action is slow and drawn out. After losing at poker for hours and hours, many normally controlled players turn about-face completely and take extraordinary risks when they bet on other gambling games in order to get even. Commenting on one tight-playing regular, a pro said:

> I don't understand Joey S. In the club he just sits there playing the absolute nuts, but when I see him at the racetrack he's always trying to get even from the night before, and he's betting daily doubles and exactas like they were going out of style. And I mean making big bets. He never gambles when he's playing poker, but he sure goes crazy at the track. How can he gamble there and be so tight here?

Indeed, enormous losses on golf and sports betting almost destroyed or at least held back the careers of several publicly recognized professional poker players.[6] Some gamblers must virtually support their extra gambling habits by playing and winning at poker! Thus, it is easy, too easy, for gamblers to turn to other games that require less concentration and physical exertion. Each type of action, though, has its own merits and can be a handy alternative to losses elsewhere.

These three dangers to the gambler's bankroll tend to operate conjointly. Once in action after playing too long and raising money he does not have (Danger One), a gambler will often play beyond his means (Danger Two) and take too many chances in riskier games (Danger Three). More often than not, when these dangers deplete a player's stake, the professional as well as the regular and loser must search for practical alternatives in order to stay in action. And so the downward spiral of playing, losing, and raising a stake takes hold.

RAISING A STAKE

Considerable research has focused on the stresses and strains of life's untoward circumstances, but few studies include the sudden or even gradual loss of large sums of money.[7] Poker players, like others dealing with personal stresses, try to adapt to adverse situations and assuage immediate disturbances through a variety of plans to survive physically and emotionally. Psychiatrists have referred to these plans as coping strategies:

> Coping strategies are developed in many ways and from many sources: directly and indirectly, overtly and covertly, in fantasy and in action. Strategies for obtaining and utilizing information are formed at all levels of awareness and may be employed over long periods of time. Strategies that are established in a person's psychological repertoire, and that have served similar functions in earlier stressful experiences, are likely to be employed first.[8]

Losing players, if they are working regulars or full-time professionals, ordinarily would like to get back into action as soon as possible. Raising money is their first coping strategy: it is direct, overt, and practical. Among desperate gamblers, raising money is a fine strategic art and involves all the creativity and social diplomacy they can muster. If they have exhausted their own resources, they tend to rely first on established methods, namely, borrowing from friends and fellow gamblers within the cardroom. This can be done with little publicity, no credit checks, no papers to sign, and no involvement with outsiders or relatives.

To borrow money a losing player may directly ask another player over the table for a small loan just before or at the moment he taps out during a game. Or he may take a short walk around the cardroom on a "treasure hunt" to search out familiar players he can "hit up." Tapped-out players who do not want to give up sometimes become "railbirds," perched on the rail waiting for friends to arrive or for winners to leave the cashier's window. Short-term loans among friends and acquaintances in the cardroom are conducted quickly, quietly, and completely on the basis of personal trust. Gamblers share a general, unstated rule for lending money: a player can ask or expect to borrow money from a person from whom he has lent money in the past. If no such reciprocal history exists, a player's cardroom character, most notably his ability to win, and his assumed wealth are the major determinants of whether loans will be made. Wealthy regulars and pros with good reputations have the best chances of borrowing from others in the same category.

When a player loses increasingly more money and needs excuses for not paying off his loans at the agreed-on time, he may try to borrow money from other people, perhaps hiding his earlier debts. Some of the money can be used to pay off older debts or debts to close friends, while most, if not all, of it will probably be kept for a playing stake. At this point, as the financial seams of the losing gambler rupture, he must juggle five or more loans, including those outside of the cardroom, and sustain the tenuous trust of cardroom relationships.

Borrowing money in the cardroom is not an option open to everyone. Many players do not cultivate trustworthy reputations or playing friendships, so when such a player goes broke he can borrow or raise money only if he offers adequate security. Rings, watches, or other jewelry, for example, may be held as collateral for a short-term loan. Other times, the player can raise money by offering to write a personal check to an acquaintance. In contrast to short-term cash loans between friends, a loan certified by a check may carry interest. A losing player who believes he can get even by buying more chips may propose or be proposed "6 for 5" (a $600 check for $500 in cash). Accepting a check is risky, and rather than "eating" a bad check from an uncertain cardroom player, a regular would rather make, and be the recipients of, an interest-free cash loan based on personal trust and reputation.

Lacking jewelry, other merchandise, friends, or credit, the losing gambler can still cope with his losses by raising money in other ways. Within each cardroom the loan shark, also called a "Shylock" or "juiceman," who may or may not be a regular player, sits inconspicuously on the rail, in the coffee shop, or in a game. For his own protection the loan shark must be able to separate good customers from bad; he does not lend money indiscriminately. Most loan sharks set limits on the amount they lend, depending on the customer, who usually must be known or referred by another debtor as a kind of social security against default. Rates, from 5 to 20 percent of the borrowed amount per week or month, are much higher than rates for most other sources of money. To take one example: if a gambler borrows $1,000 on a 5 percent weekly loan, he must pay, in addition to the principal, $50 per week in "juice" (interest). If he is late on his payment he must sometimes pay additional interest not only on his loan but also on the juice. If debts are paid off promptly, a trusting relationship develops between the loan shark and his borrowers. Unlike banks, pawn shops, and curious relatives, the loan shark is always open for business, at all hours of the day and night. Most gamblers, however, avoid raising money in this manner because of the high interest rates and the fear of repercussions for late payments or default. The loan shark is a last resort for most players, sought only after all other sources of funds have been tapped.[9]

Another strategy for some cardroom regulars to raise a playing stake, though not on a one-night or emergency basis, is by occasional or full-time bookmaking. Often a player develops into a bookie by first accepting "friendly" bets from cardroom acquaintances, saving them time to drive to the race track or make a telephone call. Over the cardroom table, where sporting events are debated, this player might volunteer to "get down" (book) another player's pick if he thinks it might be a loser. For the few players who do choose this option, booking is only a temporary sideline activity until their poker-playing or other gambles generate more of a profit. These individuals are "opportunistic" bookies who take bets on the side when convenient.[10] Most cardroom bookies are of this type; they seldom resemble the professional, career bookie with an office and runners and connections with larger criminal syndicates.

When loans from many sources pile up, the indebted gambler must decide whether to cut back on all gambling or play for larger and larger stakes in a bid to erase all debts. At this point, many embark on a "chase." Henry Lesieur defines this situation as one in which "a gambler bets either to pay everyday bills that are due or to 'get even' from a fall."[11] A chase may be either short term or long term, the latter applying mainly to the permanently indebted gambler who has fallen deeper and deeper into debt in order to gamble more and pay off earlier debts.

The most obvious coping strategy for the losing regular or professional gambler is to raise money one way or another just to stay in action. An alternative to borrowing, if the player has a job, is to quit until he saves up enough money to begin playing again. A professional who does not work outside the cardroom may be forced to find a job or at least think about one. But for the career gambler, finding satisfying outside work may be a more difficult problem than raising a stake.

The ultimate coping strategy for some players is to quit gambling altogether and seek outside help. When this point is reached, decisions to play or not to play, to borrow or not to borrow, may not be made entirely by the gambler himself. Sooner or later, spouses, relatives, friends, and outside creditors will question the gambler's motivations and interests. In desperation, if he believes or has been told that he has a "problem," he may be encouraged to find help in the local chapter of Gamblers Anonymous[12] on the insistence of others who, by this time, have noticed erratic and inconsistent behavior in his life outside of the cardroom. This solution may not always be helpful. One man in his early fifties who used to be a regular, then quit, then became a regular again related his experience with Gamblers Anonymous:

> The meeting I went to was a joke. About half the people there were from Gardena, and I had played poker with a lot of them. Most of them were pretty depressed, and they asked me a lot of questions about some of their friends who were still playing. I only went one time because I couldn't stand seeing those same people. But now I see most of them here in the club. Maybe they think going there is just a joke. It's for their wives and relatives anyway. You know, gamblers fool themselves a lot. Once a poker player, always a poker player.

To sever further involvement a player or his close relatives may ask the manager of the cardroom to bar him from playing. The player might hope that he will be barred someday for getting drunk or fighting. One wealthy loser who lacked self-control admitted, "Getting barred is the best thing that could happen to me!" For regulars and pros who do extricate themselves from the cardroom, there is always the problem of recidivism and the hope that the cards will change after a short period of abstinence.

The losing regular or professional poker player who considers gambling a major part of his life must also face problems of self-identity and diminishing self-confidence when he goes busted and falls into debt. Some are able to talk themselves out of playing and quit for months, years, or forever. For those who are completely busted there is no choice. When debts have reached their limit and numerous promises have been broken, they cannot raise any more money. They cannot play without a bankroll. A few losing players have deliberately moved out of the Gardena area, and in several unfortunate cases some have even attempted suicide. The folklore of gambling highlights these mad moments of self-destruction that many losing gamblers openly talk about, even joke about, and secretly contemplate. But many losing gamblers cannot even take their own lives without failure. One such case concerns Hughie Rowan, a high-rolling, eccentric Australian who wagered millions of dollars per year at the racetrack:

> In 1947, when he was eighty years old and a feeble and penniless failure, he reached the end of his tether. From a West End hotel he sent a letter to a friend saying that he was going to commit suicide. When his hotel bedroom door was forced open Rowan was found dead—but the cause

was heart failure. In the bedroom was a hanging rope, but some minutes before he attempted to commit suicide, fate had stepped in and had cheated him of his last gamble. [13]

And a Gardena poker loser offers a standard cardroom joke: "After last night's loss I went to my car looking for a rope or a gun but I couldn't find them. When I did find the rope I tied it to a post and stuck my head in it. But the rope broke. So here I am."

Most cardroom losers are players for whom social, psychological, and monetary investments in gambling are not so large and intense that they risk more than they can afford to lose. Minor losses would not make them turn to illegal recourses or thoughts of self-destruction. Losing, however, is much more difficult for regulars and pros who have made the cardroom a daily part of their lives and a place where almost all social relationships and significant interests lie. A few realize that they will lose over time, based on their own history, but they continue to play because they enjoy it. They set daily loss quotas and give themselves a time schedule for playing so that they will not lose too soon and be left with nothing to do. Some can even laugh about their status as losers. One lowball loser remarked self-effacingly: "If I ever left Gardena fifteen people would have to quit playing poker and find jobs. I've supported a lot of these guys for years. You know that new car Gary bought? I paid for half of it. If it gets any worse I'll be able to deduct them off my income tax as dependents."

When losing regulars and professionals attend the cardroom less often than they used to, players who are still in action often gossip and joke about their absences:

Yeah, Joe's not here right now. He's in the repair shop getting his cards fixed.

Terry B.'s stuck on the freeway and trying to find his way back to Gardena, but he keeps missing the offramp.

A regular's personal adaptation to loss is touchy and sensitive, for he must cope with managing money, time, and outside social relationships. To many this means lying about paychecks, working overtime, and faking business conferences out of town. The gambler becomes secretive about portions of his life. Greg D., a stockbroker in his forties and an afternoon regular, said:

My wife doesn't know I come here every day. If she did she'd probably send me to a psychiatrist. She thinks that anyone who gambles is sick. I never keep a lot of money on me because she might go through my pants

101

and find it and ask me questions. I even have some extra clothes in the
car and change before I go home so she won't smell the stale smoke
on my shirt.

Even for pros—who do not have to explain their absences at home—the
irregular hours, heavy losses, and the obvious emotional changes that accompany losing affect the color of many social relationships, especially with
spouses and female friends. As one pro candidly saw the problem:

> Very few women would feel comfortable married to a professional
> gambler. It takes a special kind of lady. She has to live with chance. The
> capital her gambler accumulates through the years is volatile, subject to
> be risked at any time for the sake of great gain. She waits for him to
> come home. Games go on all night. Games go on for days, weeks. He
> travels. She waits. [14]

Hiding the actual severity of loss and the loser's identity is relatively easy in
the cardroom. Many players come and go with few gestures toward sociabil-
ity; they may be known only by their first names, initials, or faces. Running
between the poker cardroom, racetrack, casino, and bookies a player can lose
thousands of dollars without anyone's knowing the true state of his finances.
Moreover, most fellow gamblers are not likely to care or get involved, knowing that poker is a cutthroat game and that other players must lose in order
for them to win. Bearing sustained, heavy monetary losses cannot be accomplished without some degree of despair and much self-examination. Crazy
Mike explains:

> I cope with losing very badly. I think I have a feeling of persecution.
> That the unknown is persecuting me. I tend to think about mistakes a lot
> less when I've had a big loss. In fact I think I try to justify big losses by
> not wanting to think I've made any mistakes. It's already too painful to
> think about without the addition of mistakes.

Severe losses, more for the professional than any other poker player, mark a
significant turning point in his perception of self, others, and the game itself.
He must search long and hard for adequate explanation.

LOSS AND COMPULSION

Academic studies of gambling have almost universally assumed that losing at
gambling and compulsive gambling are one in the same problem and that the
latter could include many kinds of obsessive, neurotic, psychopathological,

and excessive behavior syndromes. Indeed, compulsion has become a familiar part of the public's image of the gambler. But the difficulty in assessing what exactly constitutes compulsive gambling is that scholars do not agree on its causes, manifestations, and definitions.[15] Generally the loose notion of compulsive gambling encompasses at least the following three familiar traits: living in a "dream world," a kind of addiction, and the subconscious love of losing.[16]

One sociologist contends that the United States is in the midst of a runaway gambling epidemic, and guesses that there are between four and ten million compulsive gamblers.[17] Jay Livingston believes that poker players, among gamblers as a group, are less likely to be compulsive gamblers because of peer-group monitoring and the value placed on smart and skillful play.[18] Livingston's sample of members of Gamblers Anonymous shows a high percentage of solitary gamblers, mainly racetrack bettors whose daily losses could not be calculated. An additional reason for the skewed distribution of so-called compulsiveness among different types of gamblers may be that games of pure chance could be more likely to produce repetitive losing behavior than games of mixed chance and skill or total skill. Games of chance offer little chance at all. As the story is told, several years ago the Sahara Hotel in Las Vegas received a bomb threat on an occasion when the casino was jammed with gamblers. Over the loudspeaker the manager advised everyone to leave the floor as soon as possible. What kind of gambler would be the most stubborn and stay? "The blackjack players were the first to go, then the crapshooters, then the baccarat players; finally the roulette players left. But the slot machines kept whirring and flashing, the players still throwing in their coins. Of the 1,000 players, only four would leave their machines."[19]

That monetary loss and compulsive gambling behavior are one and the same problem may not accurately represent the ethnographic facts. The accepted picture of the compulsive-loser gambler is drawn from many years of clinical study, but observations of bettors in their natural habitat provide examples of gamblers who are losers and not compulsive about their betting and, in contrast, of winning gamblers who bet far more recklessly. The former may lose for reasons other than compulsiveness, and the latter may win in spite of their "love of losing." In either case, when the label "compulsive gambler" is applied, we must carefully weigh the type and frequency of risk-taking and the sums at stake against what the player can afford to lose. Who is the compulsive gambler? Is it the once-a-year sure loser who buys an Irish Sweepstakes ticket, or is it the professional poker player who plays every day and earns his livelihood? Is it the player who loses one dollar when he cannot afford it, or the millionaire who drops ten thousand when he can? Is it the commodities speculator or the full-time twenty-one player? Gambling losers, like winners, show a wide range of observable differences and styles of play.

It may be even more accurate to speak of the professional poker player not as a compulsive gambler but as a "compulsory" gambler.

Losing may come at any time in a gambler's career, but it is much more likely that a winner will become a loser than the reverse transformation occur. Losers tend to have set gambling patterns and nonadaptive beliefs that are difficult to change and obviously not very successful. Given the varieties of gambling losers, the single causal factors normally advertised in the literature, such as a lonely childhood, the alleviation of guilt, the desire for self-punishment, escapism, or masturbatory substitutes, do not seem to provide sufficient explanation.[20] Moreover, losers and winners cannot even be separated easily into distinct groups. If we conceive of these states as a continuum rather than two tidy piles, the wide area of overlapping traits, strategies, and beliefs becomes obvious.

The moralistic or critical view of gambling, which links gambling with compulsion, also makes an explicit value distinction between acceptable (or "normal") and nonacceptable work, the former considered essentially more valuable than other kinds of livelihood in this society.[21] A further difficulty with treating gambling and losing from a judgmental and pathological perspective is that this point of view places primary emphasis on the amount of money a player loses, without seeing possible benefits. Writers as distant in time and as dissimilar in style as Dostoevski and Mario Puzo have confessed that gambling losses enabled them to be much more productive, because, being broke, they had to spend more time at their work in order to pay off debts.[22] Puzo, who made millions of dollars from his novels *The Godfather* and later *Fools Die*,[23] the latter his epic novel about gamblers, admitted candidly:

> Here is the terrible truth: I got more pure happiness winning 20 grand at the casino crap table than I did from a check many times that amount as the result of honest hard work on my book . . . I think that the magic power of gambling lies in its essential freedom from endeavor and its absence of guilt. No matter what our character, no matter what our behavior, no matter if we are ugly, unkind, murderers, saints, guilty sinners, foolish or wise, *we can get lucky.*[24]

Another voice, a university professor and recognized authority on several gambling games, has argued vociferously for the potentially beneficial aspects of occasional risk-taking and has praised gambling for saving him from a "misspent sabbatical."[25]

The behavior of poker players who lose regularly and heavily, and who are most likely to be labeled compulsive gamblers, does not invariably suggest an addiction, a love of losing, or a flight into fantasy. Contrary to popular and scholarly opinion, I maintain that the decision to gamble may be a *realistic* appraisal of the individual's situation and a reasonable way to dig himself out of debt. One losing pro, a man who has been playing poker for twenty-five years, said succinctly: "I can't afford to work. What would I do if I did? Make three bucks an hour? I'd have to work 200 years just to get even for the last month." Daily losses of thousands of dollars can sometimes be made up only by continued gambling, not by any other legitimate means. Many players in the highest-stakes games realize themselves that it is not possible to work at a conventional job, quit poker, and pay off debts of tens or hundreds of thousands of dollars. Gambling for such players is the cause of financial ruination, but it is the most likely road to salvation as well.[26]

Losing at gambling is an immensely complex and sensitive subject. The losing gambler's judgment of how to get out of debt may be *theoretically* realistic, but the *practical* strategies he uses may not be very successful. To be brief, he and everyone else knows how to get out of debt in an obvious sense — by gambling and winning — but for one reason or another, not necessarily compulsion, the loser cannot do this. The ultimate explanation for losing at gambling probably involves numerous interrelated social and psychological factors. I do not completely rule out gamblers' own admissions that they sometimes play recklessly to "punish themselves" (most gamblers are quite familiar with Bergler's thesis) or as a symbolic substitute for suicide. But these reasons may be only part of the symptoms.

Why Poker Players Lose

Recurring losses at poker can usually be attributed to at least one of the following three reasons. First, many losers are inexperienced, completely imperceptive, or simply bad players. They are unable to follow the game action and keep track of opponents' moves or they play too many "dog" (underdog) or "rag" hands that have little chance of winning. They play either too loose or too tight and do not adjust their style and game strategies to different situations and players.

Second, some players entertain patently erroneous ideas about the behavior of cards, dice, roulette balls, and horses and hold to common gambling fallacies, such as the belief in positive or negative recency, that is, that independent random events are somehow linked to each other and that they will continue as they have or change in the opposite direction. In roulette or dice, for example, the chance that certain numbers will appear in a series of long rolls can be predicted by the laws of distribution and probability. The greater the number of rolls, the more accurate the predictions. But no precise predictions can be made for the *next* number. After three reds turn up in a row on a roulette table, the probability of red turning up on the fourth roll is exactly the same as it was on the first, about 50 percent (on roulette tables "0" and "00" are "colorless"). Each roll or event is an independent trial. Gamblers, however, tend to perceive runs, patterns, and "hot" and "cold" streaks rather than random occurrence of events. An observer in the cardroom is apt to hear a complaint like "I've missed nine flushes in a row, but I know I've got to make one soon." This comment reflects the same confusion between a series of events and the occurrence of the next one to be bet on. Such cardroom players rely on two contradictory beliefs: (1) when things run bad, they've got to change, and (2) when things run bad, they stay that way. Either of these sayings may be called on to explain or prove a point. By holding either of these beliefs, all gamblers win, at least psychologically, by virtue of their incontestable dual system of logic. Whatever occurs, the gambler will be right.

The third cause for the downfall of many professional poker players is inept money management. Many excellent players lose over time simply because they risk too much of their entire bankroll in single playing sessions and do not give up gracefully when the chances of getting even are remote. Players who can avoid blowing back their winnings and getting stuck are praised as much as skillful game players. Money management itself must be considered a critical skill for the professional poker player. One regular commented: "Dory S. can't play worth a damn, but she's one of the best controllers of money in this town. She's not like you and me who sit here all night getting stuck and stucker and never get out. When she wins or gets near even she's out the door. We're stupid. She's smart."

My view of loss and compulsive gambling is simply that most poker players, amateur and professional, are unable to win consistently not because of an irrational dream state or a need for self-punishment but because of poor gambling skills, erroneous beliefs put into action, defective money management, or a deleterious combination of all three.[27] My position avoids the tautology that compulsion causes losing and losing causes compulsion because I have focused directly on various observable game, metagame, and coping strategies created not by the desire to lose but by the desire to stay in action.

STRATEGIES AS BELIEF SYSTEMS

The invention of strategies[28] to cope with problems reflects our need to confront the world and participate actively in controlling events around us. We may of course be deluding ourselves that control is possible. Whether our chosen strategies do or do not work, they at least temporarily alleviate the anxiety of not doing anything at all. Strategies, then, can be considered systems of belief because they act to comfort the user and give him the impression that the world is neither capricious nor random.

Both winning and losing gamblers rely on many different kinds of playing and survival strategies founded in personal beliefs or subculturally shared ritual. These strategies, as elaborated in earlier examples, range from changing decks to picking spots or borrowing money. Whether these recipes for success fleet by in a second or consume days of planning, they are held up on a sometimes shaky scaffolding of supportive beliefs. If a gambler carefully chooses a "good" game, he believes that he will have a better chance of winning than in a "bad" game; if he intimidates another player he thinks that this might loosen up that individual's play; if he borrows money, he hopes that he can win and recover his losses. Most practical strategies are directed toward social, psychological, or monetary gains. Whether they are rational or irrational, effective or not, is not entirely the point, for gamblers can always excuse themselves and their unsuccessful plays on extenuating circumstances or something faulty about the gaming setup. When the desired result is not forthcoming, the answer is that strategies yield probable rather than determinate causes and effects; players place hopes and beliefs above certainty. Strategies and beliefs are the gambler's adaptive mechanisms, but they are not perceived as fail-safe solutions. The gambling world is too chancy for ready formulas.

David Oldham refers to gamblers' strategies in play as "theories."[29] Although players may recognize that roulette, for example, consists simply of a rotating wheel and a small spinning ball whose behavior can be explained by the laws of mathematics and physics,[30] the theories players devise to win are completely negotiable and depend on the context of play, the player's role in the wider social structure, and the social organization of the gambling setting. Even though gambling games may limit strategic efficacy by their mathematical and physical features, players do not lack bold and inventive responses. Many kinds of strategies and systems for winning at poker have been published, but it is unlikely that an optimal strategy can be calculated accurately for each situation because of the astronomical number of card combinations coupled with the disordering factors of imperfect information, verbal and nonverbal lying, and deception.[31] These factors, and chance in particular, will always restrict the effective use of skills and strategies in poker. Nonetheless, poker players assert that strategies to change luck (or some similar notion like the "run of cards") do work, and gamblers can provide examples showing a direct relationship between an alteration in their behavior and a positive outcome. Experimental studies have shown that the more an individual prepares for an event, the more likely it is that he will believe that the anticipated event will actually occur.[32]

The phenomenon of the perceived contingencies of events and causality (or blame, as we shall examine) has been studied primarily by experimental psychologists. According to principles of behavioral psychology, successful strat-

107

egies and their rewarding payoffs can be described as a variable-ratio rein-forcement, which is characteristic of many gambling games.[33] In effect, strat-egies to change one's misfortunes are, by chance, reinforced at unpredictable intervals by periods of success. Although losing may continue in the long run, it still does not necessarily extinguish the belief that there is some causal con-nection between changing seats at a poker table, for example, and having better luck, or borrowing "fresh" money and beginning to win. B. F. Skinner refers to this as "superstitious behavior,"[34] the recognition of an accidental connection between a response and the appearance of a reinforcer. Other studies have shown that the degree of judged contingency between events is often a function of prediction, although the events in question may actually be independent of each other.[35] The "illusion of control"[36] is an apt descrip-tion for the beliefs many poker players hold. These illusory control beliefs are found in both games of pure chance and chance/skill and occur primarily whenever choice, familiarity, involvement, or competition are introduced into the play setting. These four conditions strongly typify professional poker-playing. Studies in the psychology of chance further suggest that individuals have a need to master their environment, to avoid the psychological unrest that may accompany the perception of having no control at all.[37]

Gamblers show remarkable persistence and originality under duress. To some, any strategy is better than none at all. Al C., a $10-20 draw player, offers an example: "When I'm running bad, I do anything to change my luck. It sounds silly but I start carrying around a turtle carved out of a rock that I bought in Mexico. Even if it doesn't work, there's no harm in trying." In fall-ing back on a variety of strategies to change his state, the gambler may inad-vertently begin to win. There are simple explanations: he may play better, compete against poorer competition, or receive more than a fair share of good hands in a short period of time. The favorable results perpetuate the belief that "something" can be done in unfortunate circumstances, at least some of the time.

As belief systems in action, strategies explain to the holder how and why players win and lose. The professional poker player is an active social agent who must continually revise his strategies for survival. Through a combina-tion of advantageous chance factors and acquired skills, he emerges repeat-edly to test his own "proven" principles of winning play and plausible beliefs over the poker table. To explain the gambler's behavior it is not sufficient to take a mere accounting of the rules of the game, its mathematical backbone, and the monetary stakes, for poker is a social, interactional game charged with sentiments and symbols. When poker players, like roulette players, en-gage in actual competition, they must battle difficult opponents, such as "bad luck"; they must deceive real-life tablemates; and, most of all, they must con-tend all of the time with their socially constructed theories of play.

108

Belief, Blame, and Justice

Gambling losers far outnumer winners. Strategies of all kinds apparently do not work all of the time, and beliefs are not always adaptive. Rather than search for the causes of these failures by outlining antecedent conditions and their effects, poker players more commonly phrase their experience and theories of play in blunter language. They often speak emotionally of poker "blame" and "justice."

When a loser returns home broke, he needs a reason, if not for himself, for friends from whom he has borrowed money and for relatives and spouses who cannot understand the long absences from home and unpredictable changes of mood. What the loser offers is a palpable verbal account[38] including both excuses for losing and justifications for continuing to gamble. Much of the gambler's vocabulary of losing is ritualized in blunt phrases: "It just wasn't my day," "Nothing went right," or "I couldn't hold any cards." Experimental research directed toward the individual's perception of events and their causes —in this context, where an individual lays the blame—is subsumed under the title attribution theory.[39] This theory analyzes how people attain cognitive mastery over their environment and develop causal schemas through their common-sense understanding of the world. As a first step, researchers classify reasons or attributes according to the locus of control: whether it is internal or external to the individual.[40] An internal locus of control refers to the belief that events are a direct consequence of personal involvement. A poker player, for example, might say, "I guess I was too tired and I played badly." External control means a belief that events are outside of or beyond the individual's manipulation. An example is the complaint "I couldn't help losing or do anything about it."

Fritz Heider,[41] an early contributor to these studies, further divided internal and external attributes into four subcategories: difficulty of the task, effort, ability, and luck (the acronym is DEAL). Ability and effort are considered features of an internal locus of control because the subject himself is responsible for what he knows and how hard he tries in a given situation. Task difficulty and luck are external to the individual and are characteristics of the situation rather than the subject. These concepts derived from attribution theory have not yet been applied extensively to natural settings, but they have far-reaching consequences for understanding gambling behavior because they attack the question every gambler would like answered: Who or what is responsible (can be blamed) for winning and losing? Is it mainly my knowledge and skill (ability), how hard I try (effort), the complex structure of the game (difficulty of the task), or the uncontrollable run of cards (luck): Is the reason inside myself or outside myself? In virtually every game I have played in, a player has commented on the relative merit of one or more of these attributes, naming one that is the real locus of control, the key to understanding poker.

Using the notion of locus of control and Heider's four attributes, I suggest that most consistent losing gamblers tend to be Externals who believe essentially that gambling, along with life's other problems, is ultimately beyond their control and that bad luck and bad games are the major causes of loss. Other studies confirm that a belief in the external locus of control is associated closely with broader fatalistic and pessimistic attitudes.[42] Losing players do not expect to win, and they can find a culpable external reason when they do not. Even when they do win, the reason is also likely to be external to themselves and traced to good luck or good timing.

Winners tend to be Internals who negate external causes who believe that winning is a result of their own effort, ability, and preparation for the game.[43] Even if an Internal admits to good luck, he will assert that he plays better when the "cards are coming" and plays badly when they are not. Often a winning player will say, "If I held half his cards I would have made twice as much money" or "If you had my hands, you would have lost much more." The implication in these statements is that skill or ability is the paramount factor in winning, even though such skill may work side by side with external factors.

Both winners and losers perceive patterns in the fall of cards and fit their beliefs to match their experiences. Winners emphasize their own ability and effort, and losers, because the idea of self-blame and incompetency is so damaging, find it easier to point to reasons outside themselves. Relegating reasons to events beyond the individual's control is understood by every losing gambler. As psychological states, winning and losing possess distinct sets of causes, beliefs, and folklore. Even from hand to hand, players alternate in their mode of explanation, first extolling their excellent play, then blaming "bad timing." Poker players risk more than money and character; they also deal in reasonable explanations.

Neither winning nor losing poker players believe that poker rewards and punishments are distributed randomly and fairly. But they both judge whether winning and losing is *just*. The idea of social justice, or a Just World, is a belief that "good things happen to good people and those who are suffering or deprived deserve their fate, are inferior in some important way."[44] Strong believers in a Just World tend to admire and support successful people and those in power while at the same time being unsympathetic toward victims of social injustice and suffering.[45] While the Just World concept may be relatively new to social science research, in poker it is as old as the game itself. Over the poker table players talk about the game as a fair meting out of poker justice, where the best players will (and should) win and the worst players deserve (and are expected) to lose. In succinct terms it has been written:

110

In poker, man is on his own. He must act as an individual. No one will help him. Success depends on the rational use of his mind. Success depends on exercising his positive qualities and overcoming his negative qualities. Success depends on him alone. In poker, man can function entirely for his own sake. The results are his own. The loser has made himself a loser. The winner has made himself a winner. Poker is sheer justice.[46]

Professional poker players feel upset or angry when they win less than they think they should or when the "wrong" players win, meaning players they do not like. It is, however, acceptable for an acknowledged loser to win in a game once in a while. Mert O. explains: "I'm really glad that Roger A. won that $2,000 yesterday. That'll make him come back and play and he'll probably end up blowing that and a lot more just trying to get even. I love it when I see him in a game with all the chips, 'cause I know that he'll eventually give it all back, and I want a shot at it." Attitudes like this show that players have a clear sense of distributive justice,[47] making moral judgments as to what is deserved and undeserved and who should be rewarded and not rewarded. Despite occasional outbursts to the contrary, such as crying "There's no justice!" when a bad player wins a hand or beats the game, poker winners and losers place their faith in a Just World — but for significantly different reasons. Winners believe that they deserve their payoffs because of their knowledge, competency, and effort; to them justice should or will prevail in the long run. But for longtime losers who believe that the world is controlled by the forces of fate or bad luck, the resultant negative outcome — losing — is also just. The justice of losing is completely congruent with the loser's belief that the downtrodden deserve what they get.

Losing gamblers continually express their belief in external blame and injustice and make negative predictions of doom and gloom in poker stories, excuses, jokes, and accounts of misfortune. Some losers even see their losses and the run of cards as a personal form of fate and retribution. In the heat and anger of losing, few believe that what they are going through has ever been experienced by others to the same degree. In desperation, one woman regular, unable to carry through a winning hand, looked up toward the ceiling and in anguish asked, "Why, poker god? Why me?" When losers console each other (if they even listen that closely), they perpetuate and mutually support their beliefs, and they are elated to find out that they have not been singled out for punishment by forces beyond their ken and control.

Why do players persist in gambling when they lose most of the time? One reason is that losers do win occasionally because of the chance run of cards, their improved play, or the ineptitude of other players. Winning at least some

111

of the time—it may be *this* time—creates hope; and the possibility of winning in the long run, however remote, appears to be strong enough motivation for continuing to gamble.[48] But all the reasons for returning to the poker card-room are no doubt more complex than weighing rewards (wins) and punishments (losses). It has been argued that gambling fulfills various monetary and nonmonetary needs, such as relief from daily boredom, the chance to extricate oneself from debt, the opportunity to make one's own decisions, the desire to be greedy, generous, or noble, and the quest for some form of organized social activity that is repetitive and ritualized and yet offers unpredictability and action.

Most players continue to play and lose not because of psychopathological masochism but because of "hopeless optimism"[49] that supports them after every win and even after every loss. Losers narrow their understanding of their circumstances and come to hold "overvalued" ideas. These are "beliefs of varying degrees of plausibility which are affectively loaded and tend to preoccupy the individual and dominate his personality. [Cognitively,] the person holding over-valued ideas over-schematizes his experience by elaborating only a few of the schemata available to him."[50]

Embracing a set of beliefs for each situation, losing gamblers are at the same time ultimate optimists and unsurprised pessimists.

6
Dealings Under the Table

You won't find a more honest group anywhere in the world.
They are tough, hard-bitten guys who have been around;
they know their way anywhere on this globe, and yet, in our
circle, we can lay down beside each other and sleep and leave
all our money in our pants pockets and not worry about it.
You can't do that with the square-johns.
—Amarillo Slim Preston*

A discussion of cheating[1] in a study of professional gamblers is likely to offend some players who proclaim and dutifully follow high ethical standards in their livelihood. But it would be naive to propose that cheating at cards rarely or never occurs in cardroom poker. It would be equally unfair to imply that cardrooms are sleazy dens of fleet-fingered dealers who are challenged by equally crooked patrons. The actual incidence of cheating, of course, lies somewhere between these two extremes, but its precise position is not easy to measure.

For the most part cardrooms are organized to protect the customer. Because cardrooms in Gardena earn their income from the collection fees paid

*Amarillo Slim Preston with Bill G. Cox, *Play Poker to Win* (New York: Grosset and Dunlap, 1973), p. 157.

by regular customers and do not employ house dealers, their relationship with players depends on an important combination of hospitality and security. At the request of a customer, the floorman, manager, or a club "spotter" will observe (through closed-circuit television cameras in the ceiling) a player who is suspected of cheating. If there is sufficient evidence against him, the suspect will promptly be barred from the cardroom.[2] Sometimes scrupulous regulars do report incidents of cheating, especially if they are involved in the losing end, but most of the time players merely attempt to avoid "bad" games and do not report suspected infractions to the management. This is tacit acknowledgment that "something funny" is going on but that they personally do not want to be part of it. Players accept the customary cardroom rule that they are "on their own" and must bear their own responsibility for policing others and protecting themselves.

It is possible to point to petty, habitual cardroom cheats and to highly ethical players who are extremely critical of any irregular behavior. Either type may be an occasional, regular, or full-time professional of any age or sex, but cardroom morality is a cloudy issue and goes beyond the easy separation of cheaters from noncheaters. For many players in the gray middle area, always looking for an advantage and never thinking of committing an illegal act, to cheat or not to cheat falls under the principle of distributive and situational morality.[3] This means first that moral guidelines are distributed differentially among cardroom players and groups, and second that the implementation of moral rules is dependent on the gravity of the situation at hand. Some players, including pros, view cheating as a completely unacceptable strategy among friends, but in other circumstances it is a routine tactic against specific players who are wealthy, loose, unobservant, offensive, disliked, or just "different" and fair game for exploitation. Cheaters can rationalize their actions and occasional financial devastation of other players by saying, "He can afford to lose," "He deserves to lose," or "He's eventually going to lose anyway so why shouldn't I get it?" This fluctuating morality, of course, favors longtime cardroom regulars and friends who have developed informal networks to protect one another's interest. Frank Wallace offers this explanation for cheating: "Many professional players who day after day lie and practice deceit in poker ironically do not grasp the *rightness* of their poker deception. To them, lying and deception in poker become little different from cheating in poker. Their ethics become hazy and ill-defined."[4]

Since the first die was tossed and the first wager offered, gambling and cheating have gone hand in hand. The tricks of the trade have passed down through the ages by word of mouth. Within the last hundred years the economy of print has made these techniques available to many, and dozens of books have been written that demonstrate how to spot cheaters. The detailed illustrations or photographs at the same time provide detailed instructions for cheating.[5] Historically, legitimate and illegitimate professional gamblers have needed to know how cheating occurs, at least in form, in order to protect themselves from amateur and professional cheats who might take advantage of them. These published manuals, as well as the widespread presence of security and surveillance equipment and cheaters' own testimonials, furnish incontestable evidence of the kinship between gambling and cheating. With this in mind, Las Vegas casinos have spent millions of dollars on surveillance devices to block the massive pilfering of chips both by customers and employees and to squelch the operation of practiced teams who have attempted to penetrate these barriers by every possible means from team-play to the use of electronically rigged roulette balls.[6] Casino owners can buy a "black book," compiled by a private detective agency, to keep track of actual and suspected cheaters. The book is filled with hundreds of photographs, physical descriptions, and methods of operation of cheaters. Several Las Vegas cardrooms have also had their operating licenses revoked because of illegal partnerships among shift bosses, dealers, and outside confederates.[7]

A number of factors can account for the methods and frequency of cheating in cardrooms and casinos: the social organization and physical layout of the gaming area, surveillance methods, individual tendencies, the likelihood of discovery, the player's degree of loss and desperation, feelings toward the intended victims, and the informal policy of the management.[8] Most cardroom cheating, I believe, is done primarily for financial gain and out of necessity rather than for any other purpose. Idealistic proclamations aside, the cardrooms are likely to harbor as wide a range of honest and dishonest people as elsewhere, and there is no reason to believe that regulars or professional poker players differ substantially from other types of poker players or the general population in terms of cheating, thievery, and profitable collusive entanglements.

WHO'S LIGHT?

Players generally must place their antes in or near marked circles designating seat number before the deal is begun. If players are inattentive about where they put their chips and lose track of the amount in a hefty pot, chips sometimes "move" or are misplaced. This is particularly noticeable when the winner of a large, scattered array of chips misses scooping in all of his profit, especially the chips on the fringe of the betting area lying next to the circles where players place their antes. Some of the winner's chips are simply left in place, becoming another player's next ante.

One of the commonest complaints at the poker table occurs when, accidentally or deliberately, a player is "light" or "short" in the pot, that is, he has not put in his ante or his betting chips. When raising or betting, some players

115

"forget" the number of raises, take the wrong change, or splash chips in the middle of the table on top of other chips where the correct sum cannot be counted without slowing down the game. To avoid shorting pots, sloppy bettors are warned to place their chips directly in front of them. These mistakes do not happen in Las Vegas cardrooms because the house dealer stacks and counts all bets before piling them together in the center of the table. Like "forgetting" to ante, shorting pots is a way for players to save money, albeit only a little at a time, by acts of omission in a kind of reverse thievery. Unsurprisingly, when a bettor puts too many chips in the pot, it is more likely to be overlooked by those in the hand, and regulars may joke about a "bonus" pot or a player "laying the odds."

Some chip thieves are more direct in their methods, stealing chips directly from another player's stack, collecting stray chips lying off to the side of the pot or in the discards, pretending to make change while distracted players are involved in a hand, or raking off chips in their palm while pushing the pot to the winner across the table. In 1975 an electrical failure blacked out the lights in a Gardena cardroom for several seconds. When the lights finally blinked on, most of the players were hunched protectively over their stacks. When the pot in progress was counted, two brown $20 chips were missing. A known chip thief was suspected, but with no evidence the pot was played "short." I once lost a $100 stack of chips, when I was absent from the table, to a player on my left who "accidentally" knocked over his stacks and one of mine. After fitting the fallen chips in a wooden chip rack he left the game and cashed out. The cardroom refunded my money when I complained.

Chip thieves who are caught in the act usually respond by denying the act or claiming that they committed an innocent mistake. They are less likely to make further "innocent" mistakes when observant and accusing players are at the table. Although some loner chip thieves steal from anybody, many of them, following the rule of distributive morality, steal only from the pots of those whom they consider undeserving winners or inattentive players. They will not steal from alert regulars or those whom they know well. Unless such thievery is caught in the act, little can be done to halt the practice. Most players in high-stakes games are more concerned with the money to be won and lost than with arguing endlessly about antes. While regulars consider chip thieves irritating, they are also thought to be pathetic, desperate losers. More dangerous to the survival of the regular and the legitimate professional poker player than the chip thief is the skillful card cheat.

THE SOLITARY CARD CHEAT

Some individuals cheat and make money by "playing" with the cards rather than stealing chips (although they may do a little of both). One of the oldest and most cumbersome methods of card-cheating involves the use of mechanical "holdout" equipment. The most complicated and effective mechanical holdout is a rig-and-pulley device attached around the arm and chest which allows a player to pull cards quickly up his sleeve and then reintroduce them into his palm at any time. Perhaps the most undetectable holdout device was perfected and used by P. J. Kepplinger, nicknamed "The Lucky Dutchman," around 1888. Playing with a group of observant, seasoned card professionals, his winning streak seemed remarkable:

> Holdouts in a game of that description would have been, one would
> think, useless encumbrances. The players were all too well acquainted
> with the signs and tokens of accompanying devices, and Kepplinger gave
> no sign of the employment of anything of the kind. He sat like a statue
> at the table, he kept his cards right away from him, he did not move a
> muscle as far as could be seen; his opponents could look up his sleeve
> almost to the elbow, and yet *he won*.[9]

Finally, after many losses, Kepplinger's fellow players decided to investigate. Grabbing his upper arm and chest, they discovered the equipment, but instead of harming him the three of them demanded that he make each of them an identical model. This ingenious contraption was not discovered until a gambling raid in Chicago where it was found under the shirt of one of the players. Various holdout devices, not all this complicated, are still in use today in public cardrooms and private home games, and they can be mail-ordered along with other cheating equipment, like marked cards, from supply houses around the country.[10]

Once or twice a year a player with a holdout device is found in Gardena cardrooms. But for card cheaters the heyday for the use of this equipment is over. Bold players sometimes holdout or palm cards without the use of any special equipment, just by sitting on cards or hiding them in their pockets or under their chips when other players are not looking. The more popular methods of card-cheating include a variety of card switching, manipulation, or marking techniques, many of which are over a century old. The experienced card manipulator, a *mechanic,* is able to shuffle, cut, and deal certain cards (usually "seconds" or "bottoms") to selected players, including himself. It is virtually impossible to detect the moves of an expert mechanic who, like a card magician, can skillfully stack a deck with false shuffles and cuts. Most cardroom players, however, are neither experienced card handlers nor mechanics and are likely to use less practiced methods of cheating. A player might, for example, "fish" for cards in the discards while pretending to throw away his own cards or tightly squeeze the deck when dealing and peek at the buckled top cards. Another cheat may slowly shuffle and observe the riffled cards; he may be a *locator,* a player with a good memory who can remember the approximate position and combination of certain cards and consequently adjust his draw of cards. These audacious methods, not nearly as smooth as those of the mechanic, do not require years of practice and can be performed any time other players are distracted.

In draw poker, discarding and then drawing different numbers of cards is also open to misconduct. A player may discard one card and ask the dealer for two, giving him six cards and a better chance of improving his hand. Technically, of course, he holds a dead hand and cannot win the pot, so he rids himself of the extra card by palming it and shoving it away from himself on top of the discards in a lightning-fast, natural hand motion. Like other forms of "playing" with the deck, the cheater leaves no hard evidence of impropriety, except in some instances when he successively displays "miracle" hands like two-card straights and flushes. Other cheating techniques deal with marking or creasing certain cards of high or low value. In the cardroom this is the most commonplace and least skillful kind of solitary card-cheating; it is also the most detectable. Creased or bent cards can be felt or seen from the back in different light angles. Almost every day I played in the cardroom, cards in the deck with a fingernail crease or other marking were discovered and commented on by other players. Since decks are changed at each table every half hour and are sometimes rotated from table to table, the card creaser may not necessarily be a player at the table of discovery. The offender could be almost any player in the club. More sophisticated methods of marking cards are also used, such as applying special paints and daubs that can only be seen with tinted glasses or contact lenses.

Every player handles the cards, making cheaters difficult to catch *flagrante delicto.* Direct, personal accusations of cheating are rare. If accused, a cheater can simply defend himself by denying the fact or claiming that a misunderstanding has taken place. It is difficult for accusers to offer tangible proof of misdoings. This is not to say that gossip and peer-group criticism are deterrents to individual cheaters. Established regulars and pros are likely to believe that their moral conduct is immune to reprobation and that the cardroom is unlikely to eject reliable customers. With this attitude, when they begin to lose they become more "dangerous" to other players. Their adept solo cheating is more of a defensive than an offensive tactic, that is, it is resorted to mainly to hold back heavy losses rather than to produce big wins. When winning, the cards "take care" of them, and these same players may be entirely scrupulous, in fact, zestful in their desire to play a "straight" game. Cheating, then, for even the most disreputable player is not usually practiced all of the time, in all games, against every player. In the same way that legitimate professionals pick their spots, cheaters select the place, the time, and the appropriate victim.

COLLUSION AND SCAMMING

Close friendships often develop between players who day after day spend long hours together in mutual enjoyment and suffering. These friendships, which may sometimes be solidified by reciprocal money-lending, borrowing, and personal obligations, directly affect at-the-table play. Collusive cheating, more so than any other method, is one of the most practiced and least detectable cardroom scams. There are two types: the first is an informal arrangement between friends who usually act appropriately and play independently but who at certain times develop a collusive "understanding";[11] the second type is a more formal collusion, built on a secretive, working partnership between players.

Informal collusions are not always "working" or "on" until one or both players is losing heavily. If collusive partners are seated adjacently, they carry great strategic advantage. Since poker action proceeds clockwise around the table, players must act in turn to call, raise, and fold. Adjacent partners can signal by leg, knee, or foot movements which one has the best hand and the greatest chance of winning without "burning up" his friend's money. One player called this the "underground telegraph system." To give each other an advantage on the draw, adjacent partners also may whisper their hands to each other, flash their discards or entire hand, or, if one is the dealer, peek at the cards on top of the deck. For collusive partners who are not seated next to each other (for game purposes, they say that this "looks better"), signals can be sent by the hands or face and helpful cards can be thrown in a partner's direction near the pile of discards. From these examples of informal collusion, we can separate *active* cheating methods, such as passing cards, from *passive* methods of cheating, like flashing part of a hand to a friend to help his decision on the draw.

Unlike informal collusive play, more formal collusions are always "on." These strategic setups, alternately termd a *scam, crew, combo,* or *setup,* are comprised of two to four players who function as a team to stage a single routine.[12] The routine, in this case, is winning money from "live" players by secret teamwork. The most prevalent method of cheating practiced by collusive pairs, whether they are seated adjacently or not, is the age-old method of "trapping" another player between raises. J. N. Maskelyne cites from a book written in 1894:

> The most common method of cheating at poker in clubs and private
> houses alike, but particularly in good society, is one which is
> accomplished by means of collusion, and in connection with that process
> of the game known as "raising out" . . . Two men, then, in secret
> partnership, upon sitting down to play, will contrive to get the man with

the most money, or the best player (their greatest antagonist) between them. Therefore, if these two men systematically raise their bets, whether they have good hands or not, they must eventually reach the point at which the other player will "go out."[13]

This tactic, called *middling,* means that collusive partners in a game will keep raising until a third or fourth unsuspecting player is "all-in" (has no more chips left) or has been forced to call numerous raises in order to stay in the pot. Middling is almost undetectable in Gardena games because there is no limit to the number of raises a player may make.[14] Some partners practice middling quite efficiently by raising just once or twice more than their hands actually warrant. This is sufficient to make a profit but not enough action to draw suspicion on themselves.

A team of two or three works best if one player is a fairly loose, action player who bets aggressively and likes to raise. The other one or two team members can be tighter, conservative bettors. These do not have to be charades; the operation in fact is smoother when players engage in their normal style of play. With these two playing types, much of the raising action can appear coincidental. Faced with this "two on one" predicament, the unaware player is easily trapped. Typically, in formal teamwork, partners space themselves deliberately at two or three to a table and avoid other scams and knowledgeable regulars who might give them trouble. Whether winning or losing as individuals, their shared goal is to extract as much money as possible from the other players. Sometimes they work from a common bankroll and split up the profits after playing, but to avoid being linked to a team performance members do not leave the table at the same time. One cashes out, and then the other plays on his own for a half hour or so longer. Other teamworkers retain independent bankrolls and profits but do their best to help each other win.

Formal collusive teams establish themselves in specific cardrooms where they run games, usually in the medium- to high-stakes range, to their satisfaction. Their playing hours are almost as regular and predictable as those of the employees. Like legitimate players, they pick their spots and demonstrate territorial rights by waving away friends and regulars who may interfere with their action and by drawing in loose players with noisy promises of a good game. Any cardroom player who sits down in their game and "gets in the way" is likely to be treated as a sucker, for sitting down in a team-run game is an open acknowledgment that a player does not know or does not care about the quality of the game and what is actually going on. Only friendly regulars, who know what is going on but do not say anything, are immune, and they will be given the "right" action.

Collusions, both informal and formal, are difficult to discover or prove, especially for occasional players and newcomers. House rules (see rule 5, appendix B) even forbid sitting innocently at the same table with a relative or spouse. As a clue to collusion, most experienced players can judge by the quantity of betting and raising action and the show of final hands whether players are raising and reraising on legitimate hands. The more formal the collusive relationship is, the less it has to employ obvious methods of active cheating, such as passing cards. If the method of middling is strong enough, it will break down the bankrolls of most players. Irate regulars have brought "heat" and complaints to the management about being cheated by collusive partnerships, and as a result several types of games at high stakes have been terminated. Speaking of one game, a floorman remarked:

> It really got bad because of all the scamming. I'm not talking only about two people. I mean they were three or four deep, involved in signaling and trapping other players in the pot. It got to the point where they practically had to issue knee pads there was so much knocking under the table. (Laughing) I bet you at least three of them players had to go in for knee surgery after those games.

Not all at-the-table cardroom friendships are expressed as deliberate collusive play and cheating. Other dealings under the table are grounded completely in legitimate or quasi-legitimate but accepted behaviors.

A LITTLE HELP FROM ONE'S FRIENDS

Almost every regular and pro in the cardroom has at one time or another depended strategically or financially on another player. Many of these relationships develop from participation in various types of noncheating collusive help or "protection." Regulars who are disliked, occasionals, and cardroom loners usually are not aware of supportive dealings under the table and are not considered trustworthy enough to be included. Female players, also, do not tend to establish long-lasting financial or strategic coalitions with other women or men in the cardroom, probably because they are outnumbered by men and are not as highly regarded as consistent or aggressive money-making players.

Social Relationships and Table Organization

Professional poker players and regulars would like to construct games to their liking. In friendly collusion with the floorman and other players, they steer familiar loose players and consistent losers to their table by advertising a "wide open" game with plenty of action. This may look like hustling, but it is not the same as the character deception practiced among pool sharks.[15] With eight players in a poker game, the accident of chance sometimes results in the live one "racking up" the game. Another difference between poker pros and pool hustlers is their style of self-presentation on first encounters. Ned Polsky[16] observes that pool hustlers lie low, not showing their "true speed" until the right moment, when the stakes are high. In pool-shooting, a game of complete skill, an able player may appear to be only a fair player by missing pockets by a fraction of an inch. Near misses of this kind are neither feasible nor particularly advantageous in poker, unless a person wants to set up another player by first losing to him and then raising the stakes. Most of the time, expert poker players would rather present a formidable front to their opponents, instilling fear in them and causing them to play defensively. Ron T., a Las Vegas pro, boasted: "When I sit down at the table I want people to think I'm the best. That way I can control the game and the other players and have them do what I want them to do. They'll all be looking at me. I want to be on the offense while they're there playing defense."

With these histrionic manipulations the professional poker player controls his own image and his relationships with other players. These relationships, of dislike and mistrust as well as of admiration and respect, develop to further affect the organization and conduct of table play. Hostile relationships, simply, are likely to cause complete avoidance or hostile poker play, the latter the preferred state, because as poker players usually say, "A little hostility is good for the game." But friendlier relationships create more delicate situations. To offer one example, new games are not likely to be called down from the board when the floorman sees that all of the players are on close, friendly terms and do not want to play hard against each other. Players will generally wait until at least one live one appears for a game to begin, and the game will only continue if he remains. Should he collect a noticeable stack of chips, this will be sure to attract other regulars and pros who see the "soft spot" and they will then be able to step in. Known losers and loose, action players who are independent of obligatory cardroom ties can attract other players no matter when or where they sit down. Games are built around them and will continue short-handed; they are even preferred short-handed. But if a short game is reduced to three or four hands, mutual friends will usually quit if both are winning. If one or both of them is stuck, however, they will keep the game intact so that they will have an extended chance to regain their chips. In addition, a regular will not sit down in a short game when he sees that a friend is severely beating one or more other players, or when the friend is losing terribly. In both cases the presence of an additional player could change the action in the game, perhaps for the worse. Such niceties of game construction are not accorded cardroom strangers or undesirables.

Friendships not only affect the composition of the table, they also constrain at-the-table play. Pros and regulars tend to be protective of one another. If one player should mention that he is "hurting" (for money) and does not want to be "messed with" in the game, this means that he wants to be given "normal" action, not too much or too little, and he will not be taken advantage of. If he wants less than normal action, friends will *softplay* one another, by not raising with the best hand, never bluffing, and generally not playing so rough. Softplaying is commonplace in poker-playing circles. As a matter of course, friendship ties, money-lending, and softplaying tend to fall together. If a player lends several hundred or thousand dollars to a friendly tablemate who is losing, the lender will be less likely to try to bluff and destroy him. Softplaying, then, creates obvious lines of favoritism among players, reduces action and robs others of potential winnings, and holds down losses among friends. For these reasons, many players consider softplaying the same as cheating and "bad for the game," but like so many other under-the-table cardroom dealings, softplaying lies in the shadowy area of propriety and morality.[17]

Ordinary, Acceptable Table Collusion

Other advertised forms of collusion contribute to the solidification of friendships and encourage mutual participation. Announcing themselves "on" for the collection fee, players agree that the first person to win a pot at the collection light pays both fees; or they *push antes,* meaning that each time a player wins a pot he antes up the other. In high-stakes games the sums of money involved in paying double collection fees and exchanging antes over a long period of time are substantial. Although these activities can be characterized as "supportive interchanges" based on the "ritualization of identificatory sympathy,"[18] they are open to advantageous abuse. Some tight players deliberately offer the loosest players the opportunity to be "on" for collection and to push antes knowing that a tight player will not have to contribute as much as a loose player. A newcomer who is aware of these practices can quickly spot the working friendships in a game and possible lines of nonbluffing and softplaying by observing the flow of antes and the payment of collection fees. One player joked about his experience: "I sat down in a game the other night and every time someone won a pot all of the antes stayed in place. Except mine. I was the only one putting up. I wondered what the hell was going on. Then I figured it out, and I got up from their game 'cause I didn't want to be their pigeon." More insidious collusive pairs and close friends do not advertise their ties in this manner or at all.

Backlining—sharing a percentage of winning pots, usually between two players—is another type of open financial collusion. Although technically not allowed it takes place when other players at the table do not raise objections. The loudest complaints against backlining are voiced when it is not conducted discreetly and when it slows down the game. Other objections to backlining are that players may play semicollusively and "kill" the action in the game because there is no great advantage to bluffing a partner or "getting out of line" with a bad hand. Backlining takes place mainly in high-stakes games among male regulars and pros. Each time a backline partner wins a pot he places 20 percent of it in a separate stack in back of his own chips. When one of the partners goes "short" during the game or decides to quit or declares himself "off," he and his partner split the entire backline in half. Backlining controls both the management of money and the quality of play for partners. Here again, as in pushing antes, it is advantageous for a tight player who plays few hands to backline with a loose player who plays many hands. It is also to the benefit of a bad player to seek out a solid, strong player for a partner. Backlining, while ideally a supportive interchange with no particular advantage to any player, is not an entirely altruistic proposition. Because one player usually contributes more than the other, this money-sharing strategy does not often break even, and at some point one partner will declare that he is "off" when he thinks that he has put in too many chips or when he is winning or losing too much in the game itself. In this temporary arrangement, conflicts between backlining partners often arise and sarcastic remarks are exchanged when one partner's perceived effort does not match the eventual parity of distribution.[19]

Another strategy of collusive cooperation permits players to raise cash immediately in order to get back into a game. Such players cruise by high-stakes tables and offer to sell gold jewelry, watches, rings, coins, television sets, and almost every other kind of merchandise. As gold necklaces and coins circulate around the table for inspection, three or more players will agree on the asking price, or offer one themselves, and will *pot out* for the goods. Once the participants state that they are "in," they set aside a predetermined amount or percentage (usually 20 percent) from each pot won by one of them until the selling figure has been reached. When the exact amount of money has been collected, it is paid to the seller. On the next deal the player dealt the lowest spade card wins the goods. With three or four players potting out, a player may contribute only $40-50 for $300 worth of merchandise. One night a player won the wares—a $300 microwave oven—but lost $2,700 in the game. Thinking about that night, he said, "Every time I see that damn thing in the kitchen I think about paying $2,700 for it, because that's all I got out of the game. It makes me sick to even think about it. But it's happened before. Let me tell you about the time I paid $1,500 for a hamburger dinner, or $1,000 just for coffee . . ."

Potting out also takes place when several players agree to bet collectively on a horse or sports event. When they raise the agreed-on sum, one player takes the money to the racetrack or places the bet with a bookie. Winnings are divided equally. Many players prefer to pot out with other players for outside gambling bets rather than pay outright the full amount themselves, for by doing so they can protect their losses and always hope to win big for a relatively small investment.

All of these forms of ordinary, acceptable table collusion are disallowed by house rules but are taken for granted by cardroom regulars who would like to cement friendships or gain a profitable edge. They are most important as a kind of symbolic side play where almost any player can feel that he is a part of the cardroom and a competent teamworker.

Loaners and Donors

The most frequent and important kind of social support among professionals and regulars is mutual lending and borrowing of money. Many of the methods these players use to raise a stake are the same general ones used by inveterate losers. Specific social circumstances surround short-term, daily loans and loans offered to the best players by donors.

Some regulars and pros maintain relationships of mutual trust or quasi partnerships with club chipgirls who lend them money to play. If a player goes broke during a game, he asks the chipgirl to supply him with more chips on the promise that the money to pay for the chips will be paid back sometime by the end of her shift. For a limited time a busted regular can *play out of the apron,* a practice not condoned by the cardroom, until he either wins enough money to pay off the apron or survives in the game and is able to borrow money when friends arrive. Cardroom friends, especially pros, who play every day lend one another money free of "juice" (interest), quite often without even knowing the borrower's last name or address: "Among professional poker players, you frequently extend credit, but you never accept a percentage. Juice isn't expected or paid. That's just the way it is in the world of poker professionals. You ask favors selectively, you do favors selectively."[20] Most pros have no difficulty acquiring a group of close friends on whom they can rely for social, financial, and moral support. As normally consistent winners, they are also lenders themselves. These ties of friendship and trust, expressed through reciprocal borrowing and lending, are essential to the survival of the professional, for without a stake to stay in action he has no way to earn a living and pay off other debts.

Gambling money in the cardroom is "easy." Hundred dollar bills come and go so fast in high-stakes games that they bear little relationship to the bill so coveted outside the cardroom. Cash loans of hundreds of dollars or more are made right over the table while a game is in progress. Daily gamblers are accustomed to lending one another money for playing rather than for paying off bills or buying material necessities. Most loans are made on the promise that the borrower will pay back the money the next day in person or will leave it in the cashier's cage.

Personal cardroom reputations are built on integrity in matters of borrowing and lending. An individual with a reputation for not paying back debts will find it difficult to reinstate old ties or form new ones unless he changes clubs and social networks altogether. For word of bad debts travels fast among regulars. When a player pays off his debts promptly, he establishes a credible personal reputation at the same time. If all he has to offer are excuses and stalling tactics, the gossip among the regulars will begin to corrode his reputation and capacity for borrowing. Some debtors, then, are forced to move to other cardrooms or play less regularly. As players go broke, incur bad debts, and cut previous trusted relationships, the social networks in the cardroom contract to exclude the insolvent or unreliable and expand to include a new batch of trustworthy regulars.

The frequency and scope of money-lending is greater for male pros and regulars than it is for women players and occasionals. These under-the-table mutual support systems, practically the lifeblood of the cardroom, operate totally under the condition of unwritten trust; they are extremely fragile. Lending money to one player also opens the channel for borrowing from that same person in the future. But as much as every pro has borrowed money at one time or another, every one of them also claims to have made loans that have not been or never will be paid off:

> Every time someone hits me up for a loan I should know better. But I know what it's like to be broke and wantin' to play so sometimes I give in anyway. I've sure learned a lot about human nature and who you can or can't trust, and sometimes even the most reliable people'll fool you. I mean you see 'em every day for a year and then they disappear.

"Getting burned" by bad debts discredits the idea of genuine trust and friendship in the cardroom, and some regulars choose to be loners, avoiding relationships that have no future or meaning beyond the walls of the cardroom. The loner avoids the sensitive issue of lending money to regulars, and he can always say that he has a strict policy against it. One loner justified his aloofness and summarized his fellow players thus: "You can't ever trust a gambler. They'll tell you one thing and then do another. As well as being sick in the head, most of them are compulsive liars. I wouldn't give anyone around here a dime for the time of day." This point is encapsulated in the cardroom wisdom "Money talks; bullshit walks." As much as loners protect themselves and their bankrolls from outside ruin, they also cannot exploit the full range of money-raising options available to only the most reputable and regular players. More than one destitute gambler has described the cardroom as a "cruel world" and a place where no one really cares about a loser, a place where social survival is predicated on beating another player before he beats you. One railbird summed it up: "This place can be mighty lonely if you're standing on the rail winking at guys you knew a couple of years ago, so that they'll lend you a few bucks. Nobody's going to give a loser nothing."

But winners or top players—the two do not necessarily go together—may get more offers than they need. In Las Vegas cardrooms, where some games reach high limits, many reputable skillful players who are busted or who lack an adequate personal bankroll are sought out by backers or the players themselves seek out backers. The object is fairly permanent play at high-stakes or play in specific games when sure losers and wealthy tourists are at the table. Player-backer relationships may be short term or long term and generally include a verbal agreement to share wins and losses equitably. News travels quickly by telephone and by word of mouth when wealthy losers have arrived in town, and games can be started very easily around one or two tourists and a handful of local pros hoping to cash in on the action. When games are extremely "juicy," some partner-players sit alternately as a "tag team," each member playing for eight to ten hours while the other rests. Players themselves, lacking donors, may pool their money and act as partners for one or more games; or a good player may simply offer a "piece of the action" to a friend or backer. These supportive arrangements in the cardroom involve more than trust and the exchange of money. They are an open acknowledgment of a player's poker capabilities and his ability to win and turn a profit. These arrangements are the cardroom's most telling display of interpersonal support.

In summary, I offer the opinion that most commercial cardroom poker games are completely straightforward, although from time to time various collusions and silent agreements are likely to be "on." These arrangements may be entirely secretive and unethical or public and legitimate. For some high-stakes games, which draw together a familiar lineup of daily regulars and pros, it would be unusual *not* to find some amount of softplaying, money-lending, past bonds of indebtedness, and milder forms of collusion. At the same time it would also be likely to find some extra-heated rivalries, when one player plays overaggressively against another, picking him out and giving him more action than anyone else.

The social organization of cardroom poker cannot avoid producing cooperative ties as well as divisive ones. The final effects of these various collusive linkages are unpredictable. They probably save as many cardroom lives as they destroy.

Conclusion:
"And the Days Are
Just So Many Decks"

Well, life is a gamble, and the days are just so many decks.
The hours are cards, they deal and you play what you get.
You think of the time you knew you could call so you raised.
You think of the time that you got out when you should have
  stayed . . .
Ah, the good thing about life is they shuffle and deal life
  again. *

Having looked at the work and career of the professional poker player, I
have one important, broad issue to examine: the meaning of professional
poker-playing. We can approach this topic from two perspectives. First, we
can judge professional poker-playing against a set of conventional sociological
criteria to determine what other work it is comparable to and how it measures
up as an actual profession. Second, we can probe further into the lives of the
participants themselves, into their experiences of playing poker as daily work
and as a lens for a larger view of the world. From the most mundane interactional movements of table play to the deepest confrontations with self, we
have come nearly full circle. It is time to turn up the final hand, to draw some

*Deal, words and music by Tom T. Hall. © Copyright 1975, Hallnote Music. All rights re-
served. Used with permission.

conclusions about the image of the professional card player and his reflection in society.

IS POKER-PLAYING A PROFESSION?

Throughout this study I have assumed quite uncritically that a full-time winning poker player could justifiably be called a *professional* poker player. He stands above other players in skill, knowledge, and profit. But when we isolate work activities and their characteristics from individual successful practitioners, a troublesome question of definition arises. Can the activity of poker-playing be considered a *profession?*

In the dozen or so textbooks in the sociology of work and occupations that I have consulted, none lists as an occupation (or profession) "poker player" or "gambler." The gambler's penchant for play and risk is more likely to be considered a suitable topic for students of deviance and psychopathology than for comparison with less controversial professions. The tack I take here is to see how profitable it is to judge poker-playing against some specific sociological criteria for professions. The notion of profession is more like a continuum than a self-contained state, and traits that apply to specialized professions show varying degrees of relevance to actual work.[1] In a survey and summary of professions discussed in other studies, George Ritzer[2] found six characteristics most frequently mentioned: (1) general, systematic knowledge, (2) authority over clients, (3) community rather than self-interest, (4) self-control rather than outside control, (5) recognition by the community and in law that the occupation is a profession, and (6) a distinctive culture.

Only the last characteristic — bearing a distinctive culture — applies fully to poker-playing. In preceding chapters we have seen how the beliefs, argot, strategies, and symbols of poker form a unique constellation of traits. These are its most noticeable features, although unlike other professions they are not encapsulated in detailed histories, code books, symbolic insignia, or dress. Indeed, the assumption of subcultural distinctiveness germinated much of this study.

Ritzer's third characteristic of professions — community rather than self-interest — does not apply at all to poker-playing, which has no pretensions to service ideals or those that may benefit others. Self-survival and self-interest rather than the fulfillment of social and symbolic needs of the wider society are in fact its raison d'être.

The remaining four criteria of professionalism apply only loosely, and I shall discuss them in turn. In poker-playing general but not systematic knowledge of poker is fairly well established and widespread. While the "scientific" aspect of gambling, its probability foundations, is not disputed, the other aspect of gambling knowledge, manifest in assorted beliefs, strategies, and

129

idiosyncrasies, is the topic of endless debate. Full-time poker players rather than amateurs are more likely to have mastered knowledge of the first type, but even among them its distribution is highly variable. Poker knowledge is specialized, but at the same time it is broad and freely accessible to any player who reads poker books and listens to table talk. Neither type of knowledge, of course, is acquired from a specialized training school or totally authoritative source. No full-time researcher or theoretician of poker labors in an office devising fundamentally new propositions or hypotheses to test; no distinction has arisen between player (worker) and researcher/scientist. Despite the regular appearance of "how to play poker" books, which, save for a few, tend to be repetitious rewritings of old knowledge, the limits of general and systematic poker knowledge seem to be severely constrained in comparison to other professions where the accepted knowledge changes constantly. "Good advice" is an equally apt term for most poker knowledge, for playing is an eminently practical kind of work.

In most professions a professional/client relationship emerges in which the former assumes the upper hand in knowledge and authority. The full-time poker player, however, has no actual client or customer whom he serves or who seeks him out. But the poker player must parry with other "social objects"[3] — amateur players — who support his existence. The relationship between full-time poker players and their "social objects" is not typically characterized by authority or exclusive jurisdiction.[4] Pros cannot claim an exclusive monopoly on skills, strategies, or winning. They cannot keep others from encroaching on their territory, nor can they make a protective claim on knowledge or upward mobility. Amateurs, losers, and novices quite regularly beat full-time poker players at their own game. As one notable example, the winner of the 1979 World Series of Poker was an amateur, and it was the first time this had happened. Many pros agreed that it was one of the best possible outcomes, because the success of an amateur would be sure to attract more amateurs and up-and-coming players to the tournament. One pro said bluntly, "That's going to prove to people that anyone can come in here and win a half a million dollars. It's not all Texas anymore."[5]

Over the poker table the players themselves are primarily responsible for social control in accordance with their own standards of table conduct. Enforcement of these standards is not supervised by specialized, outside personnel, except in blatant occurrences of cheating or fighting. Although public gaming institutions provide the paraphernalia and the setting for play, they do not completely control the incidences of rule-breaking and other petty troubles. Morality and social rules, as discussed in previous chapters, are open to different interpretations. Written rules may dictate the general structure of play, but situational decisions in the hands of the players do more to govern how and to whom rules should be applied. Professional poker players exercise their rules and ethics on their own in whatever way they deem appropriate, expedient, or profitable.

The history of professional poker-playing has shown an evolution from a profession composed largely of self-admitted cheaters to one in which public, elite professionals negotiate for respectability and public acceptance. Even though the law and community may recognize playing poker as a livelihood for some individuals, it is another matter to say whether society approves of it. If public opinion, though changing, and sociology textbooks are a measure, poker-playing is not yet considered a proper profession by most of society; it simply is not compatible with traditional ideas of work and it has not completely escaped the stigma of low-life.

By current sociological standards full-time poker-playing more resembles an occupation than a profession, and one that is deviant, free deviant (legal), quasi-deviant,[6] marginal, or incomplete. Full-time poker-playing is not only marginal by the criteria by which other true professions are judged but it also stands in physical and social isolation from the more accessible institutions of society. Other marginal occupations may cater to individuals in all segments of society, but this is not the case with the professional poker player. The non-gambler is not likely to seek out the services of the professional poker player or be a victim of his expertise by accident. My contention is that we can speak correctly of working professional poker players, that is, competent inside members, but by Ritzer's characteristics we have no authentic *profession* of poker-playing.[7]

The Individual Player as a Professional

This book was written under the assumption that the professional poker player does exist in flesh and blood, not just by definition or as a typology. But when we come to point out the poker player as an individual, the difficulty arises. Here we cannot apply sociological characteristics alone. Poker-playing as a career demands no formal socialization practices, special training programs, recruitment policies, identification cards, diplomas, or licenses. The lack of such career markers and distinctive physical signs, such as a uniform, make it difficult to tell who is and who is not a member. On the surface, one player may look like a professional, winning $25,000 per year, but he may consider the game no more than a hobby. Another player may hold strong convictions that poker-playing is a lifelong career and hang on exiguously at $2,000 per year or with no winnings at all.

Clearly, if the term *professional* is to be applied at all to individual poker players, it should not be based entirely on outside sociological or financial criteria. For deviant or marginal activities we need greater latitude. We should consider how the individual defines himself. Claiming professional status, too, is open to denials, false proclamations, endless negotiation, and sheer

131

self-delusion. One full-time gambler, for example, defines his professional status by reference to hard work:

> The whole problem with most players is that they want success without work. Their mental picture of a successful gambler is like the Hollywood image — some guy betting big money and doing nothing but win. Well, gambling is a *profession* that takes hard work to learn and skill to stay on top. You can't buy an education and say, "Stick it in my head." You can't become an athlete [by] sitting in your easy chair and watching sports events on television. It isn't until you turn away from the dream world and get down to real work that you get on the right track.[8]

The problem of self-identification and self-labeling only underscores the precariousness of the poker player's situation, the ephemerality of success and the high rate of failure. As occupations come closer to being professions as defined by Ritzer's six criteria, the subjective measure of self-claims may be less open to dispute. Whatever doctors and lawyers say, we know what they do and how they achieved their status. But for marginal occupations of all kinds, we must admit that individuals often certify themselves as members in the absence of social acceptance or formal, institutional criteria.

Professional Status, Social Stratification, and Mobility

Relative standing in the social and financial hierarchy of poker also bears professional status. The skills characteristic of poker-playing are most fully demonstrated at the upper levels of the pyramid, where a relatively permanent elite have carved out their niche. At lower levels reputations are known, but claims and disclaimers to professional status may not be such a significant issue. After all, for a player who is struggling to win just enough for daily survival, the cardroom can be an inhospitable place, not one conducive to self-glorification. For full-time players in the smallest games and for those who lose much of the time, applying the label professional to their state would not be entirely accurate, although it could be a fitting gesture to some. So if we dismiss instances of obvious self-deluded identification, we can find professional poker players at all levels of the pyramid of stakes, but they are more likely to be concentrated in the middle and upper ranks.

The status model of professional poker players is pyramidal: thin at the top end, wider in the middle, and broad at the base. Among the pros at the base we also find, in varying guises, new hopefuls and beaten veterans. Crowding around the base of the pyramid are thousands of regulars and amateurs who would like to be professional poker players, several hundred others who are struggling in self-delusion, and even some who are making an adequate

132

income but refuse to believe that they are anything more than recreational players.

Temporal and spatial movement within the status pyramid also touch on a player's professional status. For males in our society most careers follow a series of steps: preparatory period, initial period, trial period, stable period, and finally retirement.[9] The professional poker player passes through the first three stages during his early, informal playing years. Some move through these periods in months, others take years. No time limit on career transitions can be set. Reaching the fourth stage — the stable period — is the most difficult jump for aspiring players. But the name of this stage is misleading, for it is unlikely that any such stability exists for a professional poker player. Retirement from poker-playing may be a personal decision or a matter of financial necessity; rarely does it have much to do with chronological age.

Internal mobility in poker-playing is regulated mainly by the player himself. He may, of course, be forced to make decisions to quit or play because of losses, but if he has a viable playing stake, it is his choice alone whether to move up to bigger stakes. Most pros have some aspirations of career mobility in moving up to higher-stakes games and, perhaps, a more expensive life-style. Usually they cannot move horizontally to another occupation because there is none that demands the same skills. The mathematical competence and the long hours of patience and concentration the pro has cultivated may not necessarily be dependable assets for other tasks. Poker skills are not even entirely applicable from one gambling game to the next.

After the pro has conquered the task of simply surviving, his most difficult career choice is whether to move up. If he does, sustaining that movement is his most challenging activity. For every player at the top, hundreds or thousands are struggling to survive or have dropped out or busted out somewhere along the way. In many ways professional poker-playing is a "dream factory"[10] that manufactures myths of mobility and wealth. A few players in the limelight have realized these dreams of success. But to the inestimable number of strugglers and casualties of round-the-clock play and broken-down bankrolls, the career is more a chimerical delusion, more like a nightmare factory. Downward and outward mobility to smaller stakes or out of the competitive pyramid entirely is more the rule than upward mobility to wealth and stability. No player has a predictable line to success and status mobility.

Conflict is inherent in all occupations, and the nature of the conflict appears different at each stratum of the occupational hierarchy.[11] Using the pyramidal model of players again, we cannot say categorically that professional poker-playing is either a low- or high-status occupation because of the obvious inequities of fame and fortune. At the top there are players who have access to a ready playing stake of a million dollars or more and others who

133

have a difficult time trying to raise the minimum buy-in to any game. At each level the conflicts vary. In the middle and lower levels a player's main concern is financial security and viability. Lacking this he is out of the system entirely. Next he faces such strong barriers to upward mobility as better or wealthier players and his own ability to control himself and his bankroll. If he moves up the ranks and acquires relatively more financial stability, problems of positive face-work, status respectability, legitimacy, and self-image become greater, especially if the player is drawn into the public eye. The professional poker player, at this level, because he has prospered and invested much time and money, stands to lose much more than money if he slides downward. All of the associated decorations of reputation begin to deteriorate along with the player's identity as a self-sustaining professional of skillful card play.

ON LIFE AS A GAMBLE AND GAMBLING AS LIFE

"Life is a gamble" is a convenient metaphor spoken by gamblers and non-gamblers alike to emphasize the elements of risk and uncertainty in all our actions. Accidents, misfortune, and back luck may occur at almost any time to disturb our perceptions of order and control. The shared belief in the risky aspects of both life and gambling is a key subcultural symbol among gamblers. This belief orders the gambler's conceptual experiences, provides an orientation about the world, and is a basis for strategy-making.[12] There is good reason to believe that equating life with gambling, at least among full-time professional gamblers, is more than just a catchy metaphor that rationalizes play. I intend here to discuss how much life and gambling overlap into an indistinguishable set of experiences and meanings.

Many scholars have written of games and play as escapes or slices out of "real life," the paramount reality.[13] Games carry the aura of make-believe in their separation from ordinary life. Casinos and cardrooms, of course, deliberately provide this social insulation. The timelessness, the unstrained mechanical behavior of the employees, and the comfortable ambience can easily lull the outside visitor into feeling that he has stepped into a world so unlike the ordinary world that he can even believe his escape has been complete. This separation of the ordinary from the play world — the latter is usually presumed to be less real — is discussed fully in the writings of two notable European authors, Johan Huizinga and Roger Callois.[14] A further elaboration of this distinction appears in the writings of Erving Goffman, who offers the idea of a partitioning bracket:

> Activity framed in a particular way — especially collectively organized
> social activity — is often marked off from the ongoing flow of
> surrounding events by a special set of boundary markers or brackets of a

conventionalized kind. These occur before and after the activity in time and may be circumscriptive in space; in brief, there are temporal and spatial brackets. These markers, like the wooden frame of a picture, are presumably neither part of the context of activity proper nor part of the world outside the activity but rather both inside and outside, a paradoxical condition already alluded to and not to be avoided just because it cannot easily be thought about clearly. One may speak, then, of opening and closing brackets and bounding spatial brackets. [15]

Recognizing these artificial, constructed boundaries of games, most people commute back and forth easily between games and nongames, and they can separate their experiences, language, and even emotions. But I propose here that the professional poker player, who travels between temporal and spatial game brackets every day, reaches a perceptual point where his distinction between games and nongames becomes blurred or even negligible. The metaphor has become a serious statement about life.

Whereas most games stipulate a preset starting and ending point, determined by time or the agreed-on criterion of winning, poker-playing in commercial cardrooms has no such feature. Each player chooses his own beginnings and endings, moving in and out of games according to a private calculation of gain and loss. No rules govern how long or how briefly he plays. I have seen players sit down for three minutes or for three continuous days and nights. Although poker is a face-to-face interactional game, it is obviously also a private game in which each player determines whether he is satisfied with the conditions and outcome of play. "Having enough" of a game may be measured by financial gain, the limits of physical endurance, boredom, or purely aesthetic and affective judgments of satisfying play. While individual players come and go, often without a spoken word, the game itself is endless; it has no rigid temporal brackets. The game is always there.

There is an additional matter of temporal transcendence. Poker-playing, unlike regimented office or factory work, is extremely time-consuming. Many players say that it is a "waiting game." Poker does not generate a bet or action on every hand. Normally, in a "ring" (full) game that is neither too loose nor too tight, the average player will play up to the first bet only about 20-30 percent of the hands dealt to him. This means that he sits, waits, and watches the game up to 80 percent of the time. To win takes long hours at the table and deep concentration. Pros play and replay specific hands, games, and strategies in their heads, both at and away from the table, and they spend much time thinking about elaborate plays to exploit the weaknesses of others. Despite the skill and intellect they bring to a game, they cannot control how much they will win or when they will win in one particular sitting. Winning may occur instantaneously or after ten hours of waiting. Every professional poker player has at one time or another played "too long," stayed in a game longer than he planned or wanted to when either winning or losing. With no temporal brackets, game and life overlap much of the time, and sometimes, for professionals, it is the nonplaying life that is the escape, the time-out from the reality of poker.[16]

Money, the real-world commodity of play, is neutralized in the cardroom through the use of plastic chips. Money assumes many faces:

> It can be no more substantial than a figure scribbled on a bookmaker's game sheet or a series of cabalistic sounds on a telephone wire; it can be a gawdy stack of pastel-colored chips — cash at a camp costume ball where its behavior will be frivolous and unpredictable; it can be as ragged and hopeless as a year-old marker patiently waiting in the fold of one's wallet and subsisting on dreams of redemption; it can have the genteel, indeterminable status of a delicately signed personal check, or, finally, it can be its essential self, slips of numbered paper bearing the heavy countenances of statesmen.[17]

Gamblers do not recommend that a player think of chips in terms of cash or material substitutes; chips are only ammunition for play, anything but their "essential self."

But in actual practice many professional poker players determine when to play and when to quit by cold, practical urgencies — such as bills or loans due — rather than symbolic victories. In this frame of mind, when the tokens of gaming are not adequately perceived as separating real-world money from play money, when the translation between seriousness and fun has not been accomplished, professional poker players are not transported into a frivolous game world. Real-world monetary concerns are always apparent: "If the players feel that the betting is high in relation to their means and resources, their interest may be strangled, a participant in play flooding out of the gaming encounter into an anxious private concern for his general economic welfare. A player in these circumstances is forced to take the game 'too seriously.'"[18] This is precisely the point. Professional poker players must take the game "too seriously" much of the time. While handling chips may seem to be light work, walking to the cashier's window is not. Outside economic considerations weigh heavily in game matters as these comments reflect:

> I tighten up when the rent is due. Don't ever trail me with that piece of cheese again or you'll go busted.

> You guys haven't seen a rock yet. I'm really going to nut up to pay for this new car from you turkeys.

Games are said to consist of rules of relevance, which apply to play, and rules of irrelevance, which are not supposed to apply.[19] But professional poker players do not make such fine distinctions, or they include as relevant what many other gamesmen might reject. Poker players draw attention to the quality and look of the equipment at hand (e.g., the "sticky" cards or the imbalanced chair) as much as to gossip about another player's financial condition. Almost everything that is brought together in the confrontation of play—the equipment, setting, and participants—is relevant to the conduct of the game.

My argument then is that professional poker players make no clear distinction between games and nongames. In contrast to leisurely amateurs, pros quite often transcend the normally perceived "game brackets."

A complete gambling life-style, one that makes no clear distinction between work and play, also generates a unique cognitive outlook. When personal experiences of importance are defined, described, and interpreted through myopic lenses which filter out all but a few special traits, it is unavoidable that unrelated experiences will be interpreted in the same way. Full-time gamblers often perceive life outside the casino and cardroom as ruled more by chance than it actually is. The spillover from this interpretation of the world has a tendency to engulf ordinary experiences and explain them by the same principles of chance and skill, fortune and misfortune. For the gambler, almost everything, from raindrops rolling down windowpanes to the outcome of political elections, can be talked about and quantified in terms of action and odds.

Full-time players see the cardroom as much more than a place where games are played, and the games are more than a way to make a living. The rigors, adventures, and insecurities of full-time poker-playing produce a tight yet indefinable feeling of identity among players who share the same experiences. Like members of a collaborative secret society, only insiders can understand and appreciate fully this topsy-turvy existence. The pros, regulars, and employees can be said to form a subcultural core. Within this core social relationships are marked not only by a shared sense of being but also by mundane celebrations of social rites of passage: birthdays, marriages, divorces, and funerals. For members of this solid core, friendships and daily experiences center around card-playing and other players. The cardroom also serves its purpose as a kind of marketplace, offering a range of goods and services to its subcultural regulars. A player can watch television, eat, make outside gambling bets, and find drinking buddies and sexual companions all within the "office," as some pros have dubbed it. The cardroom is simultaneously a place of work and leisure. For more specific needs, it is easy to meet a sympathetic, card-playing discount jeweler, plumber, automobile salesman, tax accountant, house painter, clothing salesman, television repairman, drug dealer, doctor, or lawyer. For pros and regulars the cardroom is a nearly complete, multifunctional setting.

Life, obviously, is not a gamble to everyone. But the professional poker player sustains this metaphor both in his general outlook on life and in his everyday activities.[20] Metaphors and cognitive overlays are not limited to human thought processes. In practice they derive much of the solid texture of reality from those who translate thought into action and games into necessity.

THE EXISTENTIAL GAME

The gambler is the quintessential decision-maker and strategist. He is guided ultimately by his "brute being" in the world, by the "core of feelings and perceptions" that we call "our innermost selves, our beings."[21] He adapts and survives, not merely by his rational judgments but also because of the existence of intermediary feelings and emotions about how he should and would like to be:

> The uniqueness of poker consists of its being a game of chance where the element of chance is itself subordinated to psychological factors and where it is not so much fate as human beings who decide. In this respect poker is the game closest to the Western conception of life, where life and thought are recognized as intimately combined, where free will prevails over philosophies of fate or of chance, where men are considered free moral agents, and where—at least in the short run—the important thing is not what happens but what people think happens.[22]

Because of the relentless instability and uncertainty of day-to-day gambling, players continually examine and reexamine their motives, feelings, and entire state of being. If the life of the professional poker player were comfortable and predictable, I do not think that such extensive and persistent self-reflection would be required. Living, playing, and surviving in the chancy world of the cardroom repeatedly assaults the sensibilities, and several pros have openly commented on the difficulties of "lasting" and explaining what "all this means." Crazy Mike Caro singled out two vexing issues: "The most difficult aspects of playing poker professionally are coping emotionally with the losses and coping with the recurring idea that you're not doing anything worthwhile."

These questions about the meaning of worthwhile tasks can be traced to wider cultural values regarding what is appropriate, gratifying, and a constructive way to spend time and energy. Many people, including poker players themselves, do not see card-playing as particularly productive. Johan Huizinga,[23] for example, refers caustically to the proficiency of expert card players as a "sterile excellence," thinking that their time could be more profitably taken with other interests. Another writer offers further reservations about the ultimate value of poker, no matter how much money can be made:

> [The good player] must strive to surround himself with losers . . . with people who are constantly defaulting on the use of their minds — the opposite kind of people whom the good player could respect and enjoy. This cannot be a very satisfying or rewarding way for him to consume large, irreplaceable portions of his life. Indeed the good player may be the biggest loser in the game. He may be sacrificing valuable segments of his life to the neurotic and self-destructive needs of chronic losers.[24]

I believe that the criticisms of gambling made by outside observers and gamblers themselves stem basically from the unstructured nature of the gambler's temporal existence. His feelings about the finitude of time and the utility (or nonutility) of his activities hit the very core of the existential meaning of life and being.[25] To the full-time gambler time is not structured by clock-hours and rigid routines but rather by the unpredictable flow and pattern in the fall of cards. Time is experienced as passing very quickly from game to game, with virtually no change in the physical surroundings. The same old faces always seem to be there across the table.

The only change is the nearly three million possible combinations of five cards to which the gambler responds. But each hand is a fleeting moment, experienced only once, and usually discarded with no time to savor its satisfaction or uniqueness. The dangers or rewards of the next hand, and the one after, create an uneasiness, whether the gambler is winning or losing, and a wishful anticipation in the future. There is no finality of gain and no peak experience, except perhaps winning a major tournament. Even then neither the money nor the glory lasts for long. Hal Fowler, for example, winner of over a quarter of a million dollars in the 1979 World Series of Poker, lost $100,000 of it in a heads-up challenge match with actor Gabe Kaplan, a poker aficionado, just three months later.[26] The dimension of temporality, experienced as an undue prominence in the future, in what the next hand or thousand hands is likely to bring, manifests itself in an existential, if not socio-psychological, kind of imbalance.[27] While the social organization of time in outside work seems to tie a person to the here-and-now, generating some feeling of well-being and work satisfaction,[28] irregular and erratic hours of activity scramble the gambler's senses.

At least small, pleasurable tactile and kinesthetic jobs are always there to keep the player in touch with the present. Individuals continually indulge in various forms of self-satisfying chip-play. Holding a dozen chips in his hands, a player will click them together, then separate and stack them, make feigned bets and raises, and interweave them with a practiced grace. The most impor-

139

tant mundane table work, of course, concerns receiving and shuffling cards and doing chip-work. Except for drunks, no cardroom player ever leaves his chips scattered in a confused mess. Culling the right amount for each bet requires quick action so as not to slow down the game. Chip-work demands that the player make change, stack and restack his chips, sort them out by denomination and color, and rearrange them in structures of various sizes and shapes. Some players build huge, imposing walls; others construct miniature pyramids. These forms of work fulfill both practical and aesthetic needs. "Eyeballing" his stacks, a player knows at a glance exactly "where he's at" within a few dollars and he can "count down" others. Huge mounds of chips, as extensions of the self, also symbolize winning and the fun of play. Winning players in their betting, talking, and chip-work reek of self-confidence and revel in these public bodily and symbolic aesthetics of dominance.[29]

Around the green-felt tables, the professional poker player works and lives in an abstruse, technical "small life-world."[30] The poker player and his captivating interest are easy targets for critics. But perhaps it is unfair to question the ultimate meaning of any individual's way of life. In this respect I am in agreement with Jerome Skolnick: "If gambling and hedonism, like formal religion, provide solace from the ultimate certainty of death, they are perhaps justifiably considered 'universal neuroses.' But perhaps, too, they should not be presumed 'pathological' unless we regard as sickness any departure from the highest aspirations of human conduct."[31] A novelist delivers a similar judgment: "Well, man does not live by bread alone. He also does not live by art alone. Man needs his foolish dreams perhaps more than he needs anything else. For two reasons. He must forget the hardships and pain of life. He must forget that he must die."[32]

It is in these small life-worlds, with all their arcane symbols and skills, that the professional poker player tests his inventive adaptiveness at every moment. This barely explored world is a fertile field for the ethnographer, who himself is put to the test; for in order to learn the rules of the game, he too must plan, play, dream, and take his chances.

ANOTHER DAY, ANOTHER DECK

It is 7:15 in the morning, a Monday morning, and the sun, bright and clear, is a stark visual contrast to the inside of the cardroom. After sixteen hours of solid poker-playing I have just stepped outside of the Rainbow Club. Bone-weary and depressed, I'd been trying to get even the whole night but never succeeded. I'm looking forward to a good ten hours' sleep.

Walking to the car a friend approaches and says, "Look. I've got an idea. We're both stuck. Let's have some breakfast and then start the game at nine. The day crew is easy. We'll both get even."

I think about his offer for a short second, but all I can see is bad hand after bad hand dancing before my eyes. Uncertain feelings about the gains and losses of poker, and over ten thousand hours of ethnography-cum-poker-playing (or is it the reverse?) merge into one confusing mess. I take a deep breath and find some comfort in the crisp air. I straighten my back.

"You're on . . . let's go!"

Appendix A:
A Description of
Fieldwork Methods

There is a growing body of information on the personal experience of research by fieldworkers in the social sciences. Still a noticeable gap exists between the researcher's stated empirical and theoretical interests and his finished monograph. This gap—the methods and experiences of data collection and interpretation—can be closed only if researchers are willing to undertake a closer examination of their motives, involvement, and analytical procedures. Concerning the conduct of fieldwork, I agree strongly with John Johnson who writes that descriptions of purpose, involvement, roles, feelings, and especially entree deserve closer scrutiny as objects of study in their own right:

> The conditions under which an initial entree is negotiated may have
> important consequences for how the research is defined by the members
> of the setting. These social definitions will have a bearing on the extent
> to which the members trust a social researcher, and the existence of
> relations of trust between an observer and the members of a setting is
> essential to the production of an objective report, one which retains the
> integrity of the actor's perspective and its social context. [1]

I hope that the following personal digression into the world of poker players will considerably clarify the extent and nature of my involvement with this study.

GETTING INVOLVED

Growing up in an ethnically diverse neighborhood in Chicago, I came into daily contact with a rich mixture of peoples and ethnic subcultures. This valuable exposure probably helped stimulate my early fascination with different people and subsequently my becoming a cultural anthropologist. Nothing in my home environment, however, suggested my later interest in poker-playing. My parents, both first-generation immigrants from Japan, neither smoked, drank, nor gambled. I wondered, even then, about my own risk-laden proclivities. As a child I can remember playing card games with my brothers and sisters. Alone, I played solitaire or games with dice and had an active interest in magic and card tricks.

As in many urban, cosmopolitan cities, gambling in one form or another, from parlay cards to poker, was a natural and acceptable part of the cultural environment. Many of my high school friends took a great interest in the outcome of football and baseball games and studiously analyzed everything about a team and its players. This commanding interest was not simply for the love of the sport. Their lunch money was riding on the outcome of these games.

Throughout high school I played poker, usually on the weekends, with classmates and friends and did well enough to consider myself a fairly competent, if unstudied, player. The television portrayal of *Maverick*, even for an urban high school student living a century later, provided a seductive role model for me. I can still remember its catchy theme song.

> *Who is the tall dark stranger there?*
> *Maverick is the name.*
> *Riding the trail to who know's where*
> *Luck is his companion,*
> *Gambling is his game.*
> *Smooth as the handle on a gun,*
> *Maverick is the name.*
> *Wild as the wind in Oregon*
> *Flowing up a canyon, easier to tame.*
> *Riverboat ring your bell,*
> *Fare thee well Annabelle,*
> *Luck is the lady that he loves the best.*
> *Natchez to New Orleans, livin' on Jacks and Queens,*
> *Maverick is a legend of the West!**

I often fancied myself roaming from town to town playing poker and winning hundreds of dollars. Inside my expensive silk shirt, like Maverick's, was pinned a thousand dollar bill for emergencies.

Several years later in college there was usually a daily poker game in the cafeteria.[2] Although it was not permissible to gamble openly with money, sev-

---

*© Copyright 1957 Warner Bros. Used with permission.

eral female friends of the players patiently kept scores of wins and losses on a ruled sheet of paper. Most members of that undergraduate poker group lost their weekly allowances during that period and either flunked out or dropped out of college. With good fortune I survived both college and poker.

After graduating and then completing my master's degree in anthropology at the University of Illinois in 1965, I transferred to the University of California, Los Angeles (UCLA), to continue my doctoral dissertation work in cultural anthropology. I wanted eventually to undertake fieldwork in Papua New Guinea among one of the isolated villages in the highlands. During my early graduate training, I really had not given any attention to poker, and I had not even thought of playing in Los Angeles. Within the first two weeks of arriving in Los Angeles, however, I was invited to a "friendly" home game[3] by some friends. The stakes were small, and the beer-and-potato chips atmosphere was relaxing and convivial. One of the players offhandedly mentioned that public poker cardrooms were legal and abundant in California and that the largest ones were located in the suburb of Gardena, fifteen miles south of downtown Los Angeles. That was only a half-hour drive from UCLA, where I lived.

Weeks later I decided to venture out to the Gardena poker cardrooms one evening with several friends in order to "check out the action." I would take them for a lot of money, I thought. Because players in commercial card clubs pay "time," or collection fees, every half hour, the games are played at a feverish pitch so that as many hands as possible can be dealt. The first cardroom I entered seemed huge, smoky, and completely intimidating. My first experience with this brand of poker was not good: the game was too fast and the players were cold and impersonal. Not fully aware of the rules or accustomed to the speedy play, I was yelled at for not cutting the deck after it was shuffled (a mandatory practice), and my friend was reprimanded for "squeezing" his cards (peeking at each one slowly) and delaying the game by several important seconds. I continued to be harangued: "You can't take your money off the table!" "You can't play with cash in front of you!" "You have to let the person to your right cut the cards!" Most of the players in that small $1-2 draw game were elderly, and some even seemed to be senile, but they were quick enough to take advantage of any newcomer in their uncontested domain. That first night in Gardena in 1965 I lost my entire stake of $15.

This initial bad impression convinced me that commercial cardroom poker was not for me and I stuck solely to the more slow-paced, enjoyable home games with friends. Between 1966 and 1972 the pressing importance of my academic studies took over. During those years I spent a year of predoctoral study in anthropology at the London School of Economics, got married, went back to UCLA for a year, spent almost two years conducting anthropological fieldwork in the Papua New Guinea highlands as I had planned, and returned to Los Angeles to complete my doctoral dissertation in 1972. In the later stages of writing my dissertation I had secured a teaching job at a nearby university. While I played poker occasionally in a home game, poker was far from my mind.

In the fall of 1973, with my courses organized and more spare time, I decided again to pay a visit to the cardrooms of Gardena. I had been working hard at writing papers on my research in Papua New Guinea and I felt that I needed some kind of diversion and relaxation. With a small stake of $30 I walked into the Rainbow Club and heard the hawking, baritone voice of the floorman: "Seat open. $1 and $2 draw. Quarter ante. Seat open." I waved my hand to claim the seat and sat down in this small-stakes game. I looked around me. Even after many years' absence I recognized several of the faces I had seen there before. Some of the players — an old man with a cane, a wrinkled lady with dark glasses — appeared not to have left the club since I last left.

With my small stake I played a tight, cautious game to adjust to their style of play. Although a pair of jacks were the minimum openers, they almost never won. Sitting to my left an elderly man counseled me to play only "Gardena jacks." "You know, a pair of aces or better," he said. Within a few hours I doubled my money and left. For several nights after that my winning streak continued. Slowly I built up my confidence and my bankroll and, as I did, I moved up to bigger games, the $2-4, $3-6, and then the $5-10. Each level of play had its own set of regulars. One day in November 1973 I was waiting for a seat in the $5-10 game at the Horseshoe Club, but there was only an opening in the next biggest game, the $10-20. I did not feel like standing around and although I did not carry much money with me I decided to take a chance and sat down. Within an hour I won $295. That was my biggest win to date. Then a thought occurred to me. I could easily enjoy wins of this size, but what about the losses? It would be quite easy to lose as much or more in a game of that size. At these stakes repeated losses could wipe out my entire bankroll and could not be made up with my salary. Nobody I knew earned more than $300 per day at a job. Yet there were dozens, even hundreds of players in these and bigger games. How did they do it? How could *I* do it?

BECOMING A REGULAR

As the summer of 1974 began I started spending more time playing poker in Gardena. By the end of the summer I was known as a regular, part of a predictable group of players who came to play almost every day. As much as any regular my presence in the cardroom was expected and absences of a day or more were questioned by other players and employees. Floormen recognized me, boardmen knew my initials, and I was on a first name basis with many of the cardroom employees. "Put D. H. on the board. Come on, Dave. I'll buy you a cup of coffee." The recognition was flattering. The players I knew well even gave me a nickname, "The Arm," for the aggressive way I threw chips in the pot. I had become, in R. L. Gold's typology,[4] a complete participant in this poker-playing subculture.

Before, when I played in the small games, I did not even have to concentrate too much on the game itself. It was a matter of being a passive player and waiting until good hands were dealt to you and then taking action. The bigger games were much different. The people were not as old, they dressed in more expensive clothes, and many flashed expensive rings and watches. They also were generally better players, and the games included a greater proportion of working professionals. In fact, in some games, all of the players except myself were or eventually became full-time poker players. Often there was so much maneuvering and joking going on in these games that poker at this level seemed to be more a contest of outdoing one another than playing cards. Some players raised and reraised each other without even looking at their cards, or they "stood pat" (did not draw) with absolutely nothing at all. Many pros jokingly threatened to bust and send compatriots back to the small games to relearn the basics. High-stakes poker-playing was far more active and aggressive than any small game I had played in. Players did not always wait for hands; they "manufactured" them. I was learning the complex survival strategies of many of the best players in the cardroom and was adapting them for my own use.

Being a regular also meant becoming competent in the special argot of gamblers, including the terms they devised for various types of players, hands, cards, and playing styles. (Some of these terms are defined in the glossary.) I also became keenly aware of micromovements of the hands, head, and body as indications of how a player acted under stress and when he was or was not bluffing. Each player seemed to have his own style of putting together a poker-playing performance. As a regular I was learning about the intricacies of this century-old "art of civilized bushwhacking," as the legendary gambler Nick the Greek called poker. This would all help me later in my observations as an ethnographer.

THE TRANSITION FROM PLAYER TO PLAYER-ETHNOGRAPHER

About a year after my conferred status as a regular I thought that it might be both interesting and feasible to undertake a systematic social study—an ethnography—of the cardroom and its players. By that time, in June 1975, I had played solidly for almost a year and a half on an average of four playing sessions per week. I played in every club, tried out every type of game, and began to play regularly in the highest-stakes games. As a professional anthropologist

I had been trained to observe and analyze the behavior of peoples in the cultural setting where they lived, worked, and played. Here, all the time, was an exotic subculture of its own that had never been studied in depth. To be sure this would be unorthodox research. There were no official gatekeepers to confer permission for entry, I would not suffer from culture shock, and the research would not be funded by a government agency or foundation. (More precisely, on some days "field expenses" were covered and on other days they were not.)

I was especially curious about the players I saw every day who seemed to win most of the time. How did they do it? I posed this question originally out of a pure practical interest in surviving in the cardroom. From there the development of my problem focus meshed with the concepts provided in studies of face-to-face interaction and microethnography. Finally, my focus grew to larger questions about how such demanding table work could be sustained over time in order to become a career or profession to some players. This entire study arose essentially from one expanding question that derived more from self-preservation than science.

The ethnographer who enters an alien culture with the intention of studying its people generally attempts to approach the goals of full participant observation. These goals are (1) sharing in the subjects' world, (2) direct participation in the subjects' world, and (3) taking a role in subjects' interactions.[5] Because of my past involvement I had already satisfied these aims and had acquired a valuable head start in gaining entree, learning the vernacular of gamblers, and developing trust and rapport with many individual players. When my study suddenly accelerated in 1975 only a few of the players, despite daily social interaction, knew of my occupation as an anthropologist, and fewer still of my incipient ethnography.[6] But, as I discovered later, my "outside" identity did not seem to make a difference to the study in one way or another.

My immersion in the subculture of gamblers increased during the summer months when I was not teaching. With friends, many of them full-time gamblers, I made numerous excursions to Las Vegas, racetracks, and other poker cardrooms in Southern California. We pooled our money to bet on "inside tips" at the racetrack or on a football team and shared the same excitement of winning. At no point was it possible for me to consider these gamblers informants in the traditional ethnographic sense, for they were first and foremost fellow players with whom and against whom I competed every day. By this time I felt more comfortable sitting at a poker table than I did at faculty meetings and in my classes. Most of my social life focused on poker-playing, and often, especially after a big win, I felt the desire to give up my job as a university professor in order to spend more time in the cardroom.

During 1975-1976 with increasing personal and psychological involvement in the cardroom, I began to interpret many events from the gambler's perspective. That my own perceptions of luck, numbers, misfortune, and causality were changing was brought home to me by an accidental jolt. One night while driving to Gardena I followed a car with "777" on its license plate. To most people these numbers would probably bear no special significance. Seeing them would be a discarded perception, an irrelevant observation. For the inveterate gambler, however, combinations of numbers on license plates, clocks, dollar bills, the car odometer, checks from restaurants, almost anything, can take on special significance, usually as a portent that these same numbers will appear often in the future.

Three sevens, I thought. I could clearly recall the times in the past week when I held three sevens, how many times I had won or lost, who else was in the pot, where I was sitting, and the exact sequence of betting. I also wondered if I would be dealt many sets of sevens that night. Like many gamblers I sometimes incorporated this system of omens and warnings into nongambling circumstances. When I accidentally cut my finger in the kitchen I wondered if it were because I had been losing all week at poker. Was this just another indication that my luck was running bad? Who or what could be responsible for these misfortunes?

To my knowledge, the degree of intensity and involvement, empathy, and actual participation I had attained had rarely been duplicated in most ethnographic and sociological studies of subcultures. All ethnographic fieldwork involves immersion in a specific social group to some degree, but within several years I had virtually become one of the people I wanted to study! This process of self-identity change in social science fieldwork is a procedure that is only beginning to be recommended as one that might produce useful and valid information about other peoples:

If the purpose of research is to know the reality work of a phenomenon, then the researcher must begin by first becoming the phenomenon. The researcher must become a full-time member of the reality to be studied . . . Membership cannot be simulated. The researcher must not hold back. The researcher who holds back in the name of objectivity never comes to respect that reality or be respected by its practitioners . . . Traditional field work techniques counsel researchers to withhold a part of themselves to remain "objective" . . . this assumes that researchers will not experience as their subjects experience. The practical circumstances of the reality they are studying will not be their circumstance. As a result, they will only be able to infer the meanings events have for bona fide members. While this methodological aloofness protects researchers from becoming "merely one of them," it also effectively prohibits knowing any of them.[7]

"Becoming the phenomenon," as the phrase goes, requires disengagement from family, jobs, and friends. Those words are easy to say now, but the repercussions of actually living them can be felt still. An important adaptation to full-time gambling and fieldwork among gamblers is the irregular working hours. Some pros play only during the day and return to their families in the evening, attempting some semblance of regularity. Others, who have no restraining families, spouses, and social responsibilities, play well into the night, often until sunrise the next day. To follow the careers of many types of players my own schedule had to be adjusted to their prolonged hours of play. Over four years I played poker at different times, in the morning, afternoon, evening, and throughout the night, many times at fifteen-to-twenty-hour stretches or more. Because of these prolonged and unusual hours, many players assumed that I did not work at an outside job and was a full-time player. To my students at the university I sometimes appeared to be "tired," as if I had been up all night.

Spending vacation time with gambling friends often meant sleeping for a few hours in the late morning, driving to the racetrack in the afternoon, and rushing back to the cardroom in the evening. Many full-time gamblers, I discovered, did little else besides sleep, eat, and check out the available action at the racetrack or poker club. By observing the changing cycle of players I acquired a fairly comprehensive picture of both the "day shift" and the "night crew." Fatigue, a product of the irregular waking and sleeping hours, was initially one of the most difficult problems of adjustment. My social life and relationships outside of the cardroom also suffered. I was usually too tired or too busy to attend many social functions to which I was invited, and I was afraid that I was considered either unfriendly or too preoccupied to care. But at the time I do not think that many people, including my students and colleagues, realized the extent of my outside involvement and research. Had they done so I am certain that I would have been absolved of at least part of my erratic behavior and distant stance.

As the cardroom grew to become my major social and emotional outlet, I used it and the game as the depository for all of my moods. I attempted to keep on friendly terms with most of the players, for in the back of my head was the anthropological ideal of not detaching or alienating others who were one's "hosts" and informants. This was not always possible. In fast, aggressive poker games where relationships can easily reach breaking points, the only choice I had was to be forceful and boisterous in my dealings with others. As a player-ethnographer there would have been no other way to last in the field.

Elsewhere I have defined the term auto-ethnography to refer to a cultural study that is conducted among one's "own people."[8] In this sense this research can be described as an exercise in auto-ethnography because it is completely interwoven with my personal involvement and analysis of events as an inside member. At this stage it is not possible to separate subjects' strategies and realities from my own because of the many points of contact and similarity. I felt many "times of profound self-doubt"[9] about fieldwork since I had spent so much time playing and absorbing information on an informal level rather than conducting conventional inquiries as a stranger and unenlightened outsider. I was not even sure that the terms *fieldwork* or *research* could properly convey what I was involved with. Most of the time I did not carry a notebook, I had no predetermined list of questions to ask, and no strict time schedule. When my plans to formalize and extend my observations began, questions about my personal involvement and motivation began to plague me. Could I, did I want to, detach myself from the cardrooms? Had I become a compulsive gambler? Was I merely rationalizing my poker-playing, as several people (even some players) suggested, by considering it to be a "study"?[10]

By 1977 I began to play a little less frequently, formulate my ideas on an ethnography more clearly, and I wrote several papers on the cardroom which were published in scholarly journals.[11] I also wrote several short articles on the activities and rules of the cardrooms for popular gambling magazines.[12] Yet I was reluctant to discuss my findings and research in public, particularly to the classes I taught on field methods and ethnography. I thought that in order to make the subject matter more comprehensible to my students, many of whom had no knowledge or interest at all in poker and gambling, I would either have to frame the subject in the detached jargon of social science or spend a lot of time telling anecdotes about the players. Neither approach was acceptable to me. Almost any tack I took could not adequately portray the powerful personal feelings of frustration and elation and the many moods between that I had experienced in the thousands of long, hard hours in the cardroom.

Rumors about my study and preoccupation outside of the university had begun to filter through to the students and my colleagues, and I was often asked to present my information in a department colloquium. I finally relented. In November 1978 I delivered a short lecture, followed by many questions, to a jam-packed audience of students and faculty members. It was hurriedly titled "Rambling and Gambling," and I spoke on the subject mainly from what I had internalized as an insider. The talk was a success, apparently, and was picked up by the daily student newspaper and the university news service,[13] which in turn aroused the interest of a reporter for the *Los Angeles Times,* who requested an interview. I was shy (and still am) about this publicity, but I consented to a telephone interview. Several weeks later I read a well-balanced, complimentary article in the newspaper about my ethnograpic fieldwork among poker players.[14] The newspaper article generated even wider public interest, and I was asked to give several radio interviews and appeared on a local television program that filmed the Gardena cardroom scene. (At my request I was filmed discreetly from behind my head.)

After the publicity I had received and my absence of several months from the cardrooms in early 1979, I was curious to know of the players' reactions. When I appeared in the club, my faith in the engrossment of gamblers at play was firmly upheld. A few asked perfunctorily if it was really me on the radio and television. Others neither cared nor asked any questions. Most of the players only wanted to know if I wanted to be dealt in. I did and I was.

At present I have detached myself slightly from the cardroom and the subculture of poker players. My recurrent fantasies of a full-time gambling life have subsided somewhat, although I will probably remain a serious part-time player. Now when I am playing I no longer impose the burden on myself of capturing ethnographic tidbits at the same time. It is, however, admittedly difficult to cease hearing and seeing "data" whenever something new arises, as it does almost every time I play. Away from the table my interest in gambling and poker as a valid scholarly subject has increased tremendously. I see gambling behavior as an extremely influential but sorely neglected scholarly concern. In psychology and economics it has direct relevance to studies of risk-taking, decision-making under uncertainty,[15] and theories of causality and control. Its deserved place in sociological and ethnographic studies of face-to-face interaction, communication, and subcultural work and life-styles has scarcely been touched. I hope that this book will begin to fill this void.

TECHNIQUES OF DATA COLLECTION AND ANALYSIS

The drive from my house to Gardena consumed between forty minues and an hour, depending on the traffic. Most of the time I avoided the rush hours and drove unimpeded on the freeways in the early afternoon or late at night and at other uncongested hours. During those long solitary periods I thought a lot about the various poker hands I had seen played, the colorful collection of characters, and how I could systematically record and analyze what I had experienced. In 1974 I began to write down occasional "fieldnotes." Whenever I heard an interesting story about a player or some other gossip, I tried to remember the facts of the incident and jotted them down when I returned home. I wasn't sure of the ultimate purpose of those notes; perhaps it was anthropological habit that made me write them down in the first place. These initial notes were written haphazardly and at irregular intervals.

By June 1975 the long drive seemed a waste of valuable time: I was spending too much time thinking about winning and getting myself geared up to play. I decided then to be more productive and organized about collecting information; during the same time I had thoughts of formulating a larger ethnography. I purchased a small portable tape recorder and while driving to and from Gardena I dictated my observations and recollections. Most of this information was derived from *public* comments and conversations over the poker table. I did not find it necessary to deceive, play roles, eavesdrop, lurk, or deal in secrets. As a player-ethnographer I absorbed this information while at the table and memorized as much as possible of what went on during the game. I had no key informants; in fact, almost everyone I played with became a potential source of information and every event came under my scrutiny. My observations fit well into "native" analytic categories, such as how players selected cardrooms and games, how they labeled other players and controlled the extent of their table action, and how they perceived luck and misfortune.

While recording these observations I also began to survey all of the written publications on gambling by social scientists. To my surprise only a few books and papers were based on participant observation. I could find almost no detailed and comprehensive information on the life and work of the professional gambler, and virtually nothing describing the professional poker player. David Maurer, the author of *Whiz Mob,* a study of professional pickpockets, pointedly questioned this lack of academic breadth:

> We have more data on the behavior patterns of almost every obscure tribe than we have on these problem areas in our own culture. Perhaps an examination of thse subcultures has been neglected because of the aura of secrecy which has traditionally surrounded them; perhaps the fact that underworld areas have not been traditionally considered "respectable" for academic research has discouraged some investigators . . . At any rate, we need more light thrown into these areas, not so much to reform society as to understand it.[16]

In the twenty-five years since Maurer wrote that passage, the academic fascination with so-called deviant and alternative subcultures and life-styles in American society has grown tremendously, with the exception of naturalistic studies of gambling and gamblers, which has been left behind, the slow starter at the gate. The most familiar writings on poker players and the organization of the game are not written by academicians but by writers and players. They include several dozen "how to win at poker" books and autobiographical, anecdotal, and historical accounts of the game and its famous players. These publications contain little of direct ethnographic applicability, but they do provide a raw baseline as unanalyzed personal documents.[17] The scholarly contribution I hoped to make was an extended participant observation study of the life and career of the professional poker player in his natural environment seen largely from his perspective. For comparison, the closest I could come to ethnographic models were "classic" studies such as *The Professional Thief, Whiz Mob, Outsiders,* and more recent works like *Hustlers, Beats, and Others, The Racing Game, The Professional Fence, and Road Hustler.*[18] As fascinating and lively as these studies were, most of them touched only tangentially on the world of the legitimate professional gambler, and in only three cases (the works of sociologists Howard Becker, Ned Polsky, and Marvin Scott) did the researcher himself "become the phenomenon."

Committed to immersing myself in any and all available documents related to the history and ethnography of gamblers, I pored over dozens of novels about cheating gamblers and stealing gamblers, listened to popular songs about ramblers and gamblers, and viewed almost every movie about gamblers shown in theaters and on television between 1974 and 1978. (I still watch old *Maverick* reruns on local late-night television.) Later, in 1977, to supplement this indirect research and the data collected by participant observation, I conducted several structured interviews away from the cardrooms with professional poker players whom I knew on the inside as opponents.

In sum: most of the information collected in this study was derived from public table conversations that occurred while I was in play. The majority took place in Gardena cardrooms; the remainder came from playing in other poker cardrooms in Southern California and in Las Vegas. The many terse verbatim quips, comments, jokes, and retorts I have included as fairly typical of the setting reflect both the abruptness of actual table talk and the reliance on direct observation as the primary research technique. Longer, descriptive interview material is scarcer. My hope is that this stylistic thrust adequately satisfies the aims of good, qualitative ethnographic reporting while at the same time gives the reader the feeling of being there.

METHODOLOGICAL AND ETHICAL PROBLEMS OF FIELDWORK

Full-time professional poker players' drawn-out days and nights seem an endless assembly line of cards shuffled, hands dealt, pots won and lost. This apparent sameness, however, is deceptive, and for the ethnographer it poses both special temporal and observational challenges. He must spend long hours trying to make sense and patterns out of what can best be called repetitious variability. Most of what constitutes poker table interaction and the great mass of social life are surface reflections; the real core of rules and symbols are invisible to the eye. What the ethnographer cannot observe directly are the players' concealed gambits, decisions, and strategies made before every session of play and at every turn of the card. To see behind words and deeds, false leads, and lies and to interpret cultural meanings are the deepest prizes of studying others.

To achieve qualitative depth and comprehend game activities in this particular setting, an ethnographer can do no better than to employ a judicious mix of both participation and observation. Basically, this technique means hanging around with your eyes and ears open, relying on a hodge-podge of tactics, intuition, luck and some crude tools to expose a few rough stones. Hanging around involves long periods of inactivity, repetition, boredom, frustration, and second thoughts. Through the haze, however, the ethnographer occasionally sees the glimmer of an object or bit of talk that one has never thought of before in the same way. I take it to be the primary task of the ethnographer to understand and reconstruct how individuals experience and define their social lives. One way this may be accomplished is through the analysis and understanding of cultural symbols. According to Clifford Geertz, to understand others' symbolic forms does not necessarily require extraordinary awareness or capabilities. Rather:

> It comes from the ability to construe their modes of expression, what I would call their symbolic systems that such an acceptance allows one to work toward developing. Understanding the form and pressure of, to use the dangerous word one more time, natives' inner lives is more like grasping a proverb, catching an illusion, seeing a joke — or, as I have suggested, reading a poem — than it is like achieving communion.[19]

Yet in order to understand other worlds and — to invoke that equally troublesome phrase — "natives" who are closer to home, Geertz stops short methodologically. Here I have asserted that understanding poker players could not have possibly taken place in any way other than full, complete, long-term submersion, even communion, on the part of the ethnographer. With no formal texts to read, no protracted rituals to witness, and no works of art to admire, there is no other way the multiple layers of facticity, deception, and meanings could properly be interpreted and reconstructed.

I am not, of course, unqualifiably campaigning for the solipsist argument that researchers of illness must themselves be ill in order to develop a meaningful understanding of the problem. But in this case, a knowledge of the poker-playing subculture implies at least being in a physical position to see and hear what is going on. Nineteenth-century anthropologists who wrote tome after tome on the customs and habits of people they had never seen were rightly criticized for being "armchair anthropologists." A "rail anthropologist" peering over the playing area would be just as ludicrous. I belabor this point of firsthand involvement because an anthropologist colleague of mine once seriously asked me if it were necessary for me to play poker in order to understand cardroom behavior. Stunned, I do not think that I provided an adequate answer at the time. I was no longer an outsider, nor could I even hypothetically think like one in order to make a comparison of inside versus outside data collection. My attempt to present an insider's view of the work of professional poker players could only be accomplished by prolonged immersion and, most important, *by being a player*. I contend that the traditional methods of ethnography and naturalistic sociology have given no more valuable advice than instructing the researcher to gain "intimate familiarity"[20] with his subjects' social world.

Field methods and the design of research must be suited to specific places and peoples. I dismissed several methods in this study of cardroom gamblers not out of a cavalier disrespect for certain techniques but because of their relative uselessness. Copious on-the-spot note-taking, questionnaires, formal verbal elicitation techniques, and persistent and naive questioning would not have been feasible, or appropriate, in the ongoing social life of the cardroom.[21] Standard sampling methods were also not employed. It was not possible to circumscribe the universe of "poker players," which more resembles a loose collection of objects than a measurable, definable social entity. For most players, passage through the cardroom is the enactment of an "ephemeral role."[22] Players win and lose, appear and disappear, with surprising speed. Many whom I knew and played with every day in 1974 had completely vanished by 1979. The drawback of not sampling, however, is partly mitigated by my participation in all six Gardena cardrooms at one time or another. After a year or so I was familiar with hundreds of regulars in the various cardrooms and could see repetitive patterns of social interaction. Furthermore, I am confident that if a researcher remained in one seat at a table in one cardroom for at least six months, he would be confronted with such a shifting array of players, incidents, and poker hands to make valid external generalizations about other cardrooms.[23]

Research reliability is another matter. Anthropologists have traditionally been lax and even mysterious about the formulas they use to collect data. For one researcher to replicate another's study and arrive at the same conclusions is to conquer the Herculean task of the social sciences. One reason for the low rate of reliability and for the apparent messiness of human social life may be the ethnographer's method of collecting information. According to Gerald Suttles, "If anything distinguishes the ethnographic method, it is probably its shameless eclecticism, a willingness to draw on so many sources of data that contradictions and inconsistencies in human conduct are difficult to avoid or deny."[24]

"Shameless eclecticism" also touches on the final methodological obstacle: quantification. Questioning one player or the next, the researcher notes that wins and losses are routinely exaggerated or reduced to nothing. Figures for the various types of professionals, income over a year, rates of winning and losing, and rates of attrition and stability may never be precisely ascertainable. Some queries strike too uncomfortably into players' personal lives and finances; moreover informants themselves may not know their own gambling biographies in detail. Nonetheless, where appropriate, I have presented my best educated estimates and have provided corroborative opinion from other sources when available.

Fieldwork Ethics

Cardroom research posed several ethical problems. These derived from the unique conditions of research in this study, including the difficulties of participant observation, the structure of the setting, and the ever-changing movements of the "objects" of study. As a result I could follow no precedents set by previous investigators handling comparable situations.

The cardroom is a public social domain that anyone can enter. Players arrive and depart at any time and rarely give indications of future attendance. Gaining informed consent for research, a matter of protocol in most ethnographic undertakings, from such a transient population and announcing my intentions to observe and listen to talk for purposes of "research" (whatever the subjects might conceive that to be) would have been futile as well as impractical. Hence, my observations were unannounced. This procedure is not unusual in the social sciences:

> Scientists may routinely make observations about people without
> informing them. No disguises are involved; it is just that social scientists
> constantly observe others' behavior. These everyday observations of our
> family, friends, and self frequently become parts of the theories or data
> of the researcher. Certainly the social scientist cannot wear a warning
> sign: "You may be the subject of scientific observation." We can see,
> therefore, that many of our observations are not "open" and known to
> those we are observing.[25]

Like a many-angled mirror, the cardroom encourages, even necessitates, observing others and oneself from different perspectives.[26] It is an inherent part of the game to be attentive, make judgments, analyze other players' behavior, and to react to feigned or veridical images. In fact, for some players I was as much the object of their attention as they were mine. One professional, who keeps detailed written notes on the mannerisms of his opponents, had set aside a page on me in his notebook months before I knew of his observations. His detailed notations of my idiosyncratic gestures and betting habits were more exhaustive than my own notes!

The mutual influence of the researcher and his subjects is firmly implanted in the ethics of participation and penetration. There is no doubt that over the poker table I influenced others and they in turn were affected by me. These face-to-face confrontations were a significant aspect of the game, but I do not think that these relationships, good or bad, had a serious effect in skewing the data I collected or in altering the course of individual poker-playing careers. Involvement at this level also raised role conflicts. Certainly I had developed and cultivated friendlier relationships with some players over others. These bonds were cemented by mutual money-lending and borrowing as well as daily social interaction and shared drinks and meals. As a result I did not want to report illegal or unethical acts I had witnessed or was drawn into, and in some game disputes I knowingly sided with friends. At such times my role as an ethnographic observer, even though secondary to my interests as a player, forced me to think seriously about personal impartiality, and I tried to avoid those situations where this principle would have to be compromised.

In most instances, when citing verbatim remarks, I have respected the privacy and anonymity of the speakers by omitting or changing initials and first names. Although these statements were aired publicly and directed to anyone who cared to listen, I have assumed that most players would prefer to remain detached from their occasional slanderous or ludicrous outbursts.

Nosy players in the cardroom are rebuked sharply with the question: "Whadda you want from me? You writin' a book or somethin'?" I hope the reason for my curiosity can finally be understood.

Appendix B:
General House Rules

1. All collections are made in advance.
2. Each player shall ante before receiving cards.
3. Players may not ante for other players.
4. Five cards constitutes a playing hand; more or less than five cards after the draw is a foul hand. Before the draw, a player having less than five cards in his hand may receive additional cards, providing the stub of the deck is correct, and no action has been taken by the first player to act. If the stub of the deck is incorrect, or action has been taken, the play may draw the number of cards necessary to complete a five-card hand after the draw.
5. Husband and wife and immediate relatives are not allowed to play at the same table.
6. Players must act on hands in turn. Acting on a hand out of turn is not binding. A knock in turn constitutes a pass. If the player neglects to act in turn and three or more players act behind him, or the deck becomes out of action, he forfeits his right of action. To eliminate forfeiting right of action, player must stop the action by calling "time."
7. Any player, including the dealer, may draw five cards. At the discretion of the floorman, where there has been bona fide action and a hand is fouled by another player, the player fouled may draw five cards or have the number of cards fouled replaced.
8. Players must protect their hands at all times.
9. No one is allowed to play over anyone else's checks.
10. A player dropping a card on the floor out of his hand must still play that card.
11. Cards exposed face up in the deck are dead cards; dealer shall place boxed cards in center of table and continue to deal. Five or more boxed cards in a row, all hands are dead, providing there is no action.

12. Exposed cards must be face up. Dealer takes all exposed cards, except boxed cards. If dealer has not discarded and exposes any of his cards on the draw, his hand is dead.

13. On the draw, when player's card is exposed face up by the dealer, he shall receive another card after the deal is completed.

14. Cards must be cut before the draw but cannot be cut after draw except on floorman's request. Cut is made with one hand, straight out. Eight or more cards constitutes a legitimate cut. Any player may request the cutter to riffle the deck once before cutting.

15. Top card must be burned. Dealer's hand is dead if he takes the burn card. If the dealer deals burn card to player who places it in his hand, the card plays.

16. Dealer must tell amount of cards drawn by players only while deck is in action (until draw is completed and first bet is made). Dealer must always tell the amount of cards he has drawn.

17. Any card dealt off the table is a dead card except the dealer's card.

18. If cards are dealt from discards, players must keep same if they put them in their hands.

19. No games with less than three hands allowed.

20. On the draw, players may change number of cards called for, providing no cards have been dealt off the deck, or if the next player has not acted.

21. The dealer must take the number of cards he has laid off the deck for himself without interruption.

22. If two or more cards of the same suit and value, or cards of different color, appear in the deck, the deck is fouled and all hands are dead, providing the pot is still in play.

23. When a player miscalls his hand, causing another player to abandon his hand, the pot is awarded to the remaining participants. If a bettor is called, the bettor must showdown his hand first. If the bettor fails to show his hand and knocks on the table or makes a verbal statement conceding the pot, causing the caller to discard and foul his hand, the bettor forfeits the pot.

24. If a call is made behind a raise, player may withdraw call if unaware raise has been made.

25. Money in the pot denotes a player's action. However, a player raising a pot should verbally declare the raise. If the raise is not declared, the raiser must inform active players of the raise before the draw or during the showdown. No active playing hand still intact shall be fouled if player was unaware of a raise.

26. A knock in turn constitutes a pass, but a knock on the table may also mean the declaration of a pat hand. A player indicating a pat hand, not knowing the pot has been raised, may still play his hand, providing no hand has been discarded.

27. A short bet or call must be completed or forfeited. If player acting in turn releases checks on table with forward motion of the hand, it constitutes a bet or call.

28. Before the draw, a short bet must first be completed; it can be raised a full bet if opened for a half bet or more. After the draw a short bet may be called, or called and raised a full bet. Half a bet or more constitutes a raise. No string bets. When a player is "all-in" he must declare himself "all-in" in turn, before and after the draw.

29. After the draw, if a bet is made and called, or check and check, all players have a right to see both hands if desired.

30. All chips must be kept on the table. When money is placed on the table, chips must be requested.

31. Only one short buy is permitted after each full buy-in. One buy for less than "buy-in" is a short buy.

32. No playing behind.

33. If it is determined that the deal is out of position and there has been no action (as much as an opening bet), all hands are dead and the deal is adjusted. If pot has been opened, the play continues and the deal rotates.

34. No going the overs permitted.

35. *No potting* — except for refreshments and cigarettes.

36. Napkins, towels, or check-racks not permitted on table.

37. Players must be seated in turn from the board. *Absolutely no exceptions.*

38. No change in seating after new player has been seated or has placed the "buy-in" on table, or has been directed to the seat by the floorman, *except* when there is a change *written* on the board that has escaped the floorman's notice.

39. Player must have a full buy when changing table, except when leaving a broken table. When table breaks, cards are cut for choice of table to game of same denomination. Player leaving table, thus breaking same, is not allowed to return and cut for seat; name is to be placed on board.

40. When player in short game requests seat in next lower limit game, floorman must ascertain if balance of players desire to cut cards in order to show *fairness* to all players — four or less considered short game.

41. Once pot is out of play, no decision can be rendered by floorman.

RULES FOR HIGH DRAW

1. Jacks or better required to open pot. If pot opened by mistake is discovered before the draw, opener's money remains in pot and his hand is dead. If another player can show openers and has not passed same, the pot is declared open.

2. If the pot is opened falsely or the openers discarded, the pot will play if the pot was raised before the draw or if cards were drawn before it was discovered.

3. The opener must show openers at all times in order to win pot.

4. When splitting openers, player must declare same and protect split card by turning it face up under chip. If player declares he is splitting openers and on the showdown proves he has split falsely, his hand, at the discretion of the floorman, may be declared dead.

5. Player may check and raise.

6. Openers must hold openers until *after* action is completed and show same.

7. Joker is used with aces, straights and flushes.

8. Before draw, players take all exposed cards; on the draw, an exposed card cannot be taken.

9. Opening bet made with foul hand may be withdrawn only before next player acts.

10. A player calling the opener with less than a pair of jacks and not affecting action behind shall be reimbursed for the amount of the call.

11. Best hands *in turn* — first, five aces; second, royal flush; third, straight flush; fourth, four of a kind; fifth, full house; sixth, flush; seventh, straight; eighth, three of a kind; ninth, two pair; tenth, one pair.

RULES FOR LOW DRAW

1. Passing before the draw, player passes out.

2. After draw, player cannot check and raise.

3. Before draw, exposed cards of seven and under must be taken. After the draw, exposed cards cannot be taken. Player must accept a substitute card for an exposed card in order to act in turn.

4. No splitting blinds.

5. If a seven or less has been checked, the player checking same cannot win an additional bet. If a seven is checked, provided it is the best seven, all other action is void.

6. Best hand — 1, 2, 3, 4, 5 — with joker wild.

Notes

INTRODUCTION: "I HATE IT. NO, I LOVE IT!"

1. Commission on the Review of the National Policy Toward Gambling, *Gambling in America: Appendix 2: Survey of American Gambling Attitudes and Behavior* (Washington, D.C.: Government Printing Office, 1976).

2. Commission on the Review of the National Policy Toward Gambling, *Gambling in America,* p. 1.

3. Jerry Hulse, "Atlantic City in the Chips as Gamblers Flock In," *Los Angeles Times,* 13 May 1979.

4. Beth Ann Krier, "Legalized Bingo: Winners and Losers," *Los Angeles Times,* 3 August 1978; and "Maine Infested by Small-coin Gambling," *Los Angeles Times,* 18 February 1979.

5. John Barbour, "Gambling Becomes Part of U.S. Way," *Los Angeles Times,* 21 November 1976.

6. Tomas Martinez, "Gambling, Goods, and Games," *Society* 14 (1977): 79-81.

7. Myram Borders, "Interest in Casino Gaming Spreading Rapidly across U.S.," *Los Angeles Times,* 6 November 1977.

8. "European Nations Find a Sure Bet," *Los Angeles Times,* 14 October 1979. More detailed studies of European gambling include D. M. Downes, B. P. Davies, M. E. David, and P. Stone, *Gambling, Work and Leisure: A Study across Three Areas* (London: Routledge and Kegan Paul, 1976); and Nechama Tec, *Gambling in Sweden* (Totowa, N.J.: The Bedminster Press, 1964).

9. Irving Crespi, "The Social Significance of Card Playing as a Leisure Time Activity," *American Sociological Review* 21 (1956): 717-721; and his "Card Playing as Mass Culture," in *Mass Culture,* ed. B. Rosenberg and D. White (New York: Free Press, 1957), pp. 418-422.

10. A. D. Livingston, "'Hold Me': A Wild New Poker Game and How to Tame It," *Life* 65 (1968): 38-39, 42.

11. F. N. David, *Games, Gods and Gambling* (London: Charles Griffin, 1962), p. 26. For additional information on these historical ideas see Oystein Ore, *Cardano: The Gambling Scholar* (Princeton, N.J.: Princeton University Press, 1953); and Warren Weaver, *Lady Luck: The Theory of Probability* (New York: Doubleday, 1963).

12. Jim Scott, "The Greatest Poker Player of Them All," *Gambling Quarterly* (Summer/Autumn 1976): 11-12, 54. Further personal background on Johnny Moss can be found in Ted Thackrey, "He's a Rambler, Gambler—But Not Far from Home," *Los Angeles Times,* 27 May 1974; Jon Bradshaw, *Fast Company* (New York: Harpers Magazine Press, 1975), pp. 145-196; John Hill, "Johnny Moss: The Grand Old Man of Poker," *Gambling Times* 2 (1978): 22-25, 82-84; and Don Jenkins, *Champion of Champions* (Odessa, Texas: J. M. Publications, 1981).

ONE: THE IMAGE AND THE REALITY

1. Catherine Perry Hargrave, *A History of Playing Cards and a Bibliography of Cards and Gaming* (New York: Dover, 1966).

2. John Scarne, *Scarne on Cards* (New York: Signet, 1965), pp. 226-227.

3. Frank Wallace, *Poker: A Guaranteed Income for Life by Using the Advanced Concepts of Poker* (New York: Warner Books, 1977), p. 293.

4. Herbert Asbury, *Sucker's Progress* (New York: Dodd and Mead, 1938), pp. 310-324.

5. Ibid., pp. 310-311.

6. George Devol, *Forty Years a Gambler on the Mississippi* (Austin, Tex.: Steck-Vaughan Co., 1967 [orig. 1887]).

7. Three-card monte is still played on the streets of many big cities. According to one source, millions of dollars per year are lost to organized teams composed of a dealer, shill, and lookout. See "N.Y. Gives Warning on '3-Card Monte,'" *Los Angeles Times,* 4 November 1979.

8. Time-Life Books, The Editors, *The Gamblers* (Alexandria, Va.: Time-Life Books, 1978), p. 61.

9. See especially the essays in Jon Halliday and Peter Fuller, eds., *The Psychology of Gambling* (New York: Harper, 1974).

10. William F. Whyte, *Street Corner Society* (Chicago: University of Chicago Press, 1943); I. Zola, "Observations on Gambling in a Lower-class Setting," in *The Other Side: Perspectives on Deviance,* ed. Howard Becker (New York: Free Press, 1964), pp. 247-260; Marshall Clinard and R. Quinney, *Criminal Behavior Systems: A Typology* (New York: Holt, Rinehart and Win-

ston, 1967); Don C. Gibbons, *Society, Crime, and Criminal Careers* (Englewood Cliffs, N.J.: Prentice-Hall, 1968); and the collection of readings in
Robert Herman, ed., *Gambling* (New York: Harper and Row, 1967). A criticism of some of these sociological views on gambling and deviance can be
found in Jerome H. Skolnick, *House of Cards* (Boston: Little, Brown, 1978),
pp. 14-23.

11. Erving Goffman, *Stigma* (Englewood Cliffs, N.J.: Prentice-Hall, 1963),
pp. 143-144.

12. Howard Becker, *Outsiders: Studies in the Sociology of Deviance* (New
York: Free Press, 1963).

13. Amarillo Slim Preston with Bill G. Cox, *Play Poker to Win* (New York:
Grosset and Dunlap, 1973), pp. 157-158.

14. Martha Wolfenstein, "Movie Analyses in the Study of Culture," in *The
Study of Culture at a Distance,* ed. Margaret Mead and Rhoda Metraux (Chicago: University of Chicago Press, 1953), pp. 267-280.

15. Michael L. Burton and A. Kimball Romney, "A Multidimensional
Representation of Role Terms," *American Ethnologist* 3 (1975): 397-407.

16. David P. Campbell, "Who Wants to Be a Professional Gambler?" in
Gambling and Society, ed. William R. Eadington (Springfield, Ill.: Charles
C. Thomas, 1976), pp. 265-275.

17. Will Wright, *Sixguns and Society: A Structural Study of the Western*
(Berkeley, Los Angeles, London: University of California Press, 1975), pp.
5-6.

18. Time-Life, *The Gamblers,* p. 7.

19. For example, see the Bible-thumping convert in *Hellfire* (1948) and
also *The Mississippi Gambler* (1953), *The Gambler Wore a Gun* (1961), and
Arizona Bushwhackers (1968). Comedic and romantic portraits of gamblers
can be seen in *Frontier Gambler* (1958), *A Big Hand for the Little Lady*
(1966), and *5 Card Stud* (1968).

20. These topics are treated in *Gambling* (1939), *Lucky Losers* (1950) with
the Bowery Boys, *Johnny O'Clock* (1947), *Gambling House* (1951), *Man with
the Golden Arm* (1955), and *King of the Roaring '20's* (1961).

21. Ned Polsky, *Hustlers, Beats and Others* (New York: Anchor, 1969), pp.
34, 40.

22. This film is based on the book by Richard Jessup, *The Cincinnati Kid*
(Boston: Little, Brown, 1963). Of the few movies about poker players, this
one has been the most successful and has created the greatest controversy.
Most writers have criticized the accuracy of the final betting scene and the
way each man played his hand. See Allen Dowling, *The Great American Pastime* (New York: Barnes, 1970), pp. 196-208; Peter Arnold, *The Encyclopedia of Gambling* (Secaucus, N.J.: Chartwell Books, 1977), p. 166; David

Spanier, *Total Poker* (New York: Simon and Schuster, 1977), pp. 157-160; and Michael J. Caro, *Bobby Baldwin's Winning Poker Secrets* (Las Vegas: B & G Publishing Co., 1979), p. 31.

23. Frank Brady, "Chess in the Cinema," *Chess Life and Review* 34 (1979): 188-193.

24. Fyodor Dostoevski, *The Gambler* (Harmondsworth: Penguin, 1966 [orig. 1866]). The film *The Great Sinner* (1949) was based on an adaptation of this book.

25. Edmund Bergler, "The Psychology of the Gambler," *Imago* 22 (1936): 409-441. This thesis was later expanded by Bergler and presented in his *The Psychology of Gambling* (London: Hanison, 1958). Also see the earlier study by Sigmund Freud, "Dostoevski and Parricide," in Halliday and Fuller, *Psychology of Gambling*, pp. 157-174.

26. Later adapted as a book by Lou Cameron, *California Split* (Greenwich, Conn.: Fawcett, 1974).

27. For example, the countess in *The Queen of Spades* (1948) sells her soul to the devil in order to learn the secrets of winning at faro. A compulsive lady roulette player is featured in *Bay of Angels* (1964), and in *Hazard* (1948) Paulette Goddard plays a woman gambler in love and in debt.

28. A recent television movie, *Winner Take All* (1974), showed the same downhill destiny of gambling, compulsion, and debt for a lady gambler (played by Shirley Jones) who cannot stop betting on the horses and poker.

29. Preston, *Play Poker to Win*. Further profiles are in Jon Bradshaw, *Fast Company* (New York: Harpers Magazine Press, 1975); and Jim Scott, "How the Best Players in the World Play Poker," *Gambling Quarterly* (Winter 1976): 26-31, 60.

30. Bradshaw, *Fast Company*, p. 153.

31. Preston, *Play Poker to Win;* and Doyle Brunson, *How I Made over $1,000,000 Playing Poker* (Las Vegas: B & G Publishing Co., 1978). Brunson claims that he lost at least this amount playing golf.

32. Many of these were rigged propositions, such as lead-weighting a peanut and then throwing it over a building. These anecdotes and many more can be read in Bradshaw, *Fast Company*.

33. One admission is that of Pennsylvania Eddie, "Confessions of a Professional Poker Player," *Gamblers World* 1 (1974): 33-35, 66-69; also see the remarks of Bobby Baldwin in Caro, *Winning Poker Secrets*.

34. See the excellent ethnography by Robert Prus and C. R. D. Sharper, *Road Hustler* (Lexington, Mass.: D. C. Heath, 1977).

35. Reuben Fine, *The Psychology of the Chess Player* (New York: Dover, 1967), p. 9.

36. James K. Skipper, Jr., and Charles H. McCaghy, "Stripteasers: The Anatomy and Career Contingencies of a Deviant Occupation," *Social Prob-*

lems 17 (1970): 391-405; and James Bryan, "Apprenticeships in Prostitution," *Social Problems* 12 (1965): 287-297.

37. Ronald M. Pavalko, *Sociology of Occupations and Professions* (Itasca, Ill.: F. E. Peacock, 1971), pp. 85-86.

38. The outline of this typology was first presented in David M. Hayano, "The Professional Poker Player: Career Identification and the Problem of Respectability," *Social Problems* 24 (1977): 556-564. It is reprinted with permission.

39. James Carper and Howard Becker, "Adjustments to Conflicting Expectations in the Development of Identification with an Occupation," *Social Forces* 36 (1957): 51-55; and Becker, *Outsiders*, pp. 101-119.

40. David Newman, *Esquire's Book of Gambling* (New York: Harper and Row, 1962), pp. 20-22.

41. H. H. Gerth and C. Wright Mills, *From Max Weber: Essays in Sociology* (Oxford: Oxford University Press, 1946), p. 59.

42. There is an additional factor relevant to professional types which cannot be considered here without explaining the details of poker rules and play: a professional may be distinguished by his game-playing style and total demeanor at and away from the table. This had led Wallace, a popular poker writer, to conceive several subtypes of career professionals, such as the traditional public professional, the "new breed" public professional, and the advanced concept private professional. These types are obviously Weberian ideal, if not mythic, categories that admittedly include exceptions. See Frank R. Wallace, *"How I Made over $1,000,000 Playing Poker": An Obituary for the Professional Poker Player* (Las Vegas: I and O Publishing Co., 1978), pp. 11-13.

43. Another source quotes a wide figure of 100-200. See Frank R. Wallace, *Poker: A Guaranteed Income for Life by Using the Advanced Concepts of Poker* (New York: Warner Books, 1977), p. 216.

44. Erving Goffman, *Interaction Ritual* (New York: Anchor, 1967), pp. 5, 12.

45. Gale Miller, *Odd Jobs: The World of Deviant Work* (Englewood Cliffs, N.J.: Prentice-Hall, 1978), pp. 239-240.

46. Ibid., pp. 233-234.

47. James Bryan, "Occupational Ideologies and Individual Attitudes of Call Girls," *Social Problems* 13 (1966): 441-450; and Lawrence K. Hong and Robert W. Duff, "Becoming a Taxi-dancer: The Significance of Neutralization in a Semi-deviant Occupation," *Sociology of Work and Occupations* 4 (1977): 327-342.

48. J. Holtz, "The 'Professional' Duplicate Bridge Player: Conflict Management in a Free, Legal, Quasi-deviant Occupation," *Urban Life* 4 (1975): 131-148.

49. Clement McQuaid, ed., *Gambler's Digest* (Northfield, Ill.: DBI Books, 1971), p. 20; and L. G. Holloway, *Full-time Gambler* (New York: Lyle Stuart, 1969), p. 152.

50. Bruce Jackson, "Deviance as Success: The Double Inversion of Stigmatized Roles," in *The Reversible World: Symbolic Inversion in Art and Society,* ed. Barbara A. Babcock (Ithaca, N.Y.: Cornell University Press, 1978), pp. 258-275.

51. Len Miller, "From the Editor's Desk," *Gambling Times* 3 (1979): 5.

TWO: SOCIAL ORGANIZATION OF THE CARDROOM

1. Gaming a Misdemeanor, section 330 of the California Penal Code, reads: "Every person who deals, plays, or carries on, opens or causes to be opened, or who conducts either as owner or employee, whether for hire or not, any game of faro, monte, roulette, lansquenet, rouge et noir, rondo, fan, fan-tan, stud-horse poker, seven-and-a-half, twenty-one, hokey-pokey, or any banking or percentage game played with cards, dice, or any device for money, checks, credit, or other representative of value, and every person who plays or bets at or against any of the said prohibited games, is guilty of a misdemeanor, and shall be punishable by a fine not less than one hundred dollars and not more than five hundred dollars, or by imprisonment in the county jail not exceeding six months, or by both such fine and imprisonment. 1891.

Section 337s. Poker Parlours. (Invalidated by negative vote of the electors.)"

2. Las Vegas and other Nevada cardrooms mainly feature the major varieties of stud poker and the popular Hold 'Em, imported from Texas. For a survey of Las Vegas poker cardrooms and players, see Ian Andersen, *Turning the Tables on Las Vegas* (New York: Vanguard Press, 1976), pp. 130-141; and Frank Wallace, *Poker: A Guaranteed Income for Life by Using the Advanced Concepts of Poker* (New York: Warner Books, 1977), pp. 267-274.

3. David Shaw, "Gardena: Poker Draws Young and Old to the Tables," *Los Angeles Times,* 28 March 1971.

4. Since the cardrooms' inception, voters have gone to the polls six times to defeat their operation but have never been successful. See Shaw, "Gardena: Poker Draws Young and Old."

5. Mary Ann Lee, "Gardena Council Questions Card Club Licensing," *Los Angeles Times,* 22 December 1974.

6. For a general description of the playing atmosphere, see David M. Hayano, "DEAL—In Gardena We Play on Time," *Gambling Times* 1 (1977): 74-77.

7. Rebecca Trounson, "Poker Parlor Battle Heats Up as Bell Club Chimes In," *Los Angeles Times,* 14 December 1980.

8. In 1974 Pan, a rummylike game, was also made legal. A few cardrooms, moreover, offer two other varieties of draw poker, namely, California draw blind (which is opened "blind" for high by the player to the left of the dealer) and high-low (if the pot is not opened for high with a pair of jacks or better, the player to the left of the dealer must open "blind" for low).

9. There are forty-one general rules for Gardena poker and eleven more that pertain to high draw and six to lowball. These rules are listed in appendix B.

10. If the house does not charge the players and keeps the game together, new customers may walk in at any time and join the game. It is to the cardroom's advantage to keep high-stakes games going and occasionally give the players a "free roll," although each cardroom's policy is different.

11. A brief profile of the daily life of a Gardena poker prop is described by L. B. Taylor, "A Poker Prop," *Cavalier* 26 (1976): 61-62, 78.

12. "Voters Turn Down Poker Proposal [in Inglewood]," *Los Angeles Times,* 15 March 1978. In August 1980, however, the largest single cardroom in the world, the seventy-table California Bell Club, opened in the community of Bell, fifteen miles from Gardena. See Trounson, "Poker Parlor Battle," for some of the most immediate competitive effects.

13. Rules 3, 9, 13, 14, 19, 27, 29, 30, 31, 32, 34, 35, 36, 37, and 38.

14. For example, in a quarter-ante $1-2 game, the ante is one-fortieth of a player's buy-in of $10, but in a $40-80 game the $2 ante represents only one two-hundredth of a $400 buy-in.

15. John Lukacs, "Poker and American Character," *Horizon* 5 (1963): 57.

16. Shaw, "Gardena Poker Draws Young and Old."

17. Lawrence Dietz, "Gardena, California—Poker for the Geriatrics Set," *Holiday* 45 (1969): 22-24.

18. Jack Richardson, "Coming Down in Gardena," *Playboy* 21 (1974): 114, 158, 186-200.

19. See Patricia McCormack, "Race Tracks, Bus Depots: Social Centers for the Elderly," *Los Angeles Times,* 15 August 1979; Ken Stone and Richard A. Kalish, "Of Poker, Roles, and Aging: Description, Discussion, and Data," *International Journal of Aging and Human Development* 4 (1973): 1-13; and Rex Jones, "Poker and the American Dream," in *The American Dimension: Cultural Myths and Social Realities,* ed. William Arens and Susan P. Montague (New York: Alfred, 1976), pp. 170-177.

20. Felicia Campbell, "Gambling: A Positive View," in *Gambling and Society,* ed. William R. Eadington (Springfield, Ill.: Charles Thomas, 1976), p. 227.

21. Jones, "Poker and the American Dream," p. 178; also Stone and Kalish, "Of Poker, Roles, and Aging," p. 7.

22. Walter Wagner, *To Gamble, or Not to Gamble* (New York: World, 1972), p. 52.

23. William Hoffman, *The Loser* (New York: Funk and Wagnalls, 1968), p. 107.

24. Marvin Scott, *The Racing Game* (Chicago: Aldine, 1968).

25. See also the remarks of Amarillo Slim Preston with Bill G. Cox, *Play Poker to Win* (New York: Grosset and Dunlap, 1973), p. 161.

26. Kay Deaux and T. Enswiller, "Explanations of Successful Performance on Sex-linked Tasks: What's Skill for the Male Is Luck for the Female," *Journal of Personality and Social Psychology* 29 (1973): 80-85.

27. Sherri Cavan, *Liquor License: An Ethnography of Bar Behavior* (Chicago: Aldine, 1966).

28. Fred Davis, "The Cabdriver and His Fare: Facets of a Fleeting Relationship," *American Journal of Sociology* 63 (1959): 158-165; Katherine Carlson, "Reciprocity in the Marketplace: Tipping in an Urban Nightclub," in *Conformity and Conflict,* 3d ed., ed. James Spradley and David McCurdy (Boston: Little, Brown, 1977), pp. 337-347; and Odis Bigus, "The Milkman and His Customer: A Cultivated Relationship," *Urban Life and Culture* 1 (1972): 131-165.

29. Susan Boyd, "Poker Playing as a Dramaturgical Event: Bull Power, the Meaning and the Commitment for Efficacious Gamesmanship," in *The Anthropological Study of Play: Problems and Prospects,* ed. D. F. Lancy and B. A. Tindall (Cornwall, N.J.: Leisure Press, 1976), pp. 123-130.

30. See Tomas Martinez and Robert LaFranchi, "Why People Play Poker," *Trans-action* 6 (1969): 30-35, 52.

THREE: CONTROLLING LUCK AND MANAGING ACTION

1. Portions of this chapter were first presented in shorter form in David M. Hayano, "Strategies for the Management of Luck and Action in an Urban Poker Parlor," *Urban Life* 6 (1978): 475-488, and are reprinted here with the permission of Sage Publications, Inc.

2. Stanford Lyman and Marvin Scott, *A Sociology of the Absurd* (Pacific Palisades, Calif.: Goodyear, 1970), pp. 65-66.

3. See Erving Goffman, *Interaction Ritual* (New York: Anchor, 1967); and his *Strategic Interaction* (Philadelphia, University of Pennsylvania Press), 1969.

4. For example, see Lyle Stuart, *Casino Gambling for the Winner* (New York: Ballantine Books, 1978), p. 186.

5. John Cohen and Mark Hansel, "Preferences for Different Combinations of Chance and Skill in Gambling," *Nature* 183 (1959): 841-842; and Kay Deaux, L. White, and E. Faris, "Skill versus Luck: Field and Laboratory Studies of Male and Female Preferences," *Journal of Personality and Social Psychology* 32 (1975): 629-636.

6. John Cohen and Mark Hansel, *Risk and Gambling: The Study of Subjective Probability* (New York: Philosophical Library, 1956); and John Cohen, *Chance, Skill, and Luck: The Psychology of Guessing and Gambling* (Baltimore: Penguin, 1960).

7. Cohen, *Chance, Skill, and Luck,* p. 114.

8. See Edmund Bergler, *The Psychology of Gambling* (London: Hanison, 1958); Tomas Martinez and Robert LaFranchi, "Why People Play Poker," *Trans-action* 6 (1969): 30-35; and Igor Kusyszyn, "The Gambling Addict versus the Gambling Professional: A Difference in Character?" in *Studies in the Psychology of Gambling,* ed. Igor Kusyszyn (New York: Simon and Schuster, 1972), pp. 165-172.

9. Goffman, *Strategic Interaction,* pp. 85-86.

10. This is a 95.6-1 shot.

11. Louis Koullapis escaped a capital verdict but received five years to life imprisonment on a charge of second-degree murder. Since this incident Gardena cardrooms have boarded up their windows. See Allen Dowling, *The Great American Pastime* (New York: Barnes, 1970), pp. 156-169.

12. See, for example, Susan H. Boyd, "Anal Linguists, Cry Your 'I's' Out: Constructing a Metaphor of Poker," in *Studies in the Anthropology of Play: Papers in Memory of B. Allan Tindall,* ed. Phillips Stevens (West Point, N.Y.: Leisure Press, 1977), pp. 28-34. Further studies in the analysis of nonverbal communication and deception can be found in David M. Hayano's "Poker Lies and Tells," *Human Behavior* 8 (1979): 18-22, and his "Communicative Competency among Poker Players," *Journal of Communication* 30 (1980): 113-120. For specific game-related ploys, see John Fox, *Play Poker, Quit Work and Sleep till Noon!* (Seal Beach, Calif.: Bacchus Press, 1977), pp. 263-306.

13. William Labov, "Rules for Ritual Insults," in *Studies in Social Interactions,* ed. David Sudnow (New York: Macmillan, 1972), pp. 120-169.

14. To take a contrasting case, in England there are specific rules against any talk that is not related to the game action. Excessive talking is considered a kind of cheating. See Amarillo Slim Preston and Bill G. Cox, *Play Poker to Win* (New York: Grosset and Dunlap, 1973), p. 135.

15. A player who undercalls the value of his hand may still win the pot, but a player who *overcalls* his hand, that is, states that he holds a better hand than he actually does, will lose the pot if his declaration forced his opponent to throw away his hand. If, for example, a player has three aces (the best hand in this case) he will win the pot if he calls "aces" or "two aces," but he cannot win if he declares that he has "four aces" or any better hand than three aces. Verbally declaring hands generally speeds up the game, but it is subject to abuse and mishearings.

16. For representative opinions see John McDonald, *Strategy in Poker, Business and War* (New York: Norton, 1950); Herbert O. Yardley, *The Edu-*

cation of a Poker Player (New York: Simon and Schuster, 1957); and H. Levinson, *Chance, Luck and Statistics* (New York: Dover, 1963). A general survey of explanations of luck can be found in Max Gunther, *The Luck Factor* (New York: Macmillan, 1977).

17. See Warren Weaver, *Lady Luck: The Theory of Probability* (New York: Anchor, 1963). A controversial issue that cannot be discussed thoroughly here is whether randomness can actually be achieved by human shuffling. Thorp maintains that human shuffling is "decidedly nonrandom" and that players in card games who are aware of this may have an advantage. I have no doubt that poker players have known this for a long time. See Edward O. Thorp, "Probabilities and Strategies for the Game of Faro," in *Gambling and Society,* ed. William R. Eadington (Springfield, Ill.: Charles Thomas, 1976), p. 459.

18. Martinez and LaFranchi, "Why People Play Poker."

19. William H. McGlothlin, "A Psychometric Study of Gambling," *Journal of Consulting Psychology* 18 (1954): 145-149.

20. Peter Adler and Patricia A. Adler, "The Role of Momentum in Sport," *Urban Life* 7 (1978): 171.

21. Bronislaw Malinowski, an anthropologist who conducted fieldwork in the Trobriand Islands in the southwest Pacific in the World War I era, found that the villagers relied on magic more when embarking on deep-sea fishing excursions that were dangerous and unpredictable than for lagoon fishing, which was relatively more placid and successful. See Bronislaw Malinowski, *Magic, Science and Religion* (New York: Anchor, 1948). Later Malinowskian-type analyses can be found in James Henslin, "Craps and Magic," *American Journal of Sociology* 73 (1967): 316-330; and George Gmelch, "Baseball Magic," in *Conformity and Conflict,* 3d ed., ed. James Spradley and David McCurdy (Boston: Little, Brown, 1974), pp. 346-352.

22. Richard B. Felson and George Gmelch, "Uncertainty and the Use of Magic," *Current Anthropology* 20 (1979): 587-589.

23. Ken Uston, *Two Books on Blackjack* (Wheaton, Md.: The Uston Institute of Blackjack, 1979), p. 42.

24. See Louis Zurcher, "The 'Friendly' Poker Game: A Study of an Ephemeral Role," *Social Forces* 49 (1970): 173-186.

25. Another reason for changing seats, unrelated to luck strategies, is for position vis-à-vis other players. For pros this means taking advantage of having certain types of players on the right, where they must act first, and other types on the left.

26. Goffman, *Interaction Ritual,* p. 186.

27. Brunson is quoted in Maurice Zolotow, "How to Hold All the Cards in a Friendly Poker Game," *Los Angeles* 23 (1978): 97.

28. See the further remarks of Doyle Brunson in Zolotow, "How to Hold All

the Cards," and those of Amarillo Slim Preston in Preston, *Play Poker to Win.*

29. Frank Wallace, *Poker: A Guaranteed Income for Life by Using the Advanced Concepts of Poker* (New York: Warner Books, 1977), p. 227.

FOUR: WINNERS TALK

1. See Igor Kusyszyn, "The Gambling Addict versus the Gambling Professional: A Difference in Character?" in *Studies in the Psychology of Gambling,* ed. Igor Kusyszyn (New York: Simon and Schuster, 1972), pp. 165-172; and Joseph N. Bell, "World Series Revelations: How to Win at Poker," *Coast* 17 (1976): 19-20.

2. Edwin Silberstang, "Ask Our Experts," *Gambling Times* 3 (1979): 8.

3. Wallace guesses the new average earning for professional poker players in Gardena to be closer to $10,000. See Frank Wallace, *Poker: A Guaranteed Income for Life by Using the Advanced Concepts of Poker* (New York: Warner Books, 1977), p. 211.

4. Ian Andersen, *Turning the Tables on Las Vegas* (New York: Vanguard Press, 1976), pp. 133-134.

5. Wallace, *Poker: A Guaranteed Income for Life,* p. 214.

6. Ibid., p. 213.

7. Julian Block, "Gambling and Taxes," *Gambling Times* 2 (1978): 31-33.

8. George Ritzer, *Man and His Work: Conflict and Change* (New York: Appleton-Century-Crofts, 1972).

9. Andersen, *Turning the Tables,* pp. 132-133.

10. For a written criticism of this type of rivalry see David Sklansky, *Sklansky on Poker Theory* (Las Vegas: Gambler's Book Club, 1978), p. 164.

11. Doyle Brunson, *How I Made over $1,000,000 Playing Poker* (Las Vegas: B & G Publishing Co., 1978), p. 419.

12. His biography can be found in Jimmy Snyder, *Jimmy the Greek* (Chicago, Ill.: Playboy Press, 1975).

13. Subsequent winners include: 1972, Amarillo Slim Preston; 1973, Puggy Pearson; 1974, Johnny Moss; 1975, Brian (Sailor) Roberts; 1976, Doyle (Texas Dolly) Brunson; 1977, Doyle (Texas Dolly) Brunson; 1978, Bobby Baldwin; 1979, Hal Fowler; 1980, Stu Ungar; 1981, Stu Ungar. A photographic study of some of these players in tournament action is in Ulvis Alberts, *Poker Face* (Hollywood, Calif.: Angel City Books, 1981).

14. In a recent year these games included: Ace-to-five Lowball Draw, High Draw, Seven-card Razz, Seven-card High-low Split, Seven-card High (preliminary), Seven-card High (world championship), Deuce-to-seven Lowball, Mixed Doubles Seven-card High, Women's Seven-card High, Non-profes-

sional Hold 'Em, and the Preliminary Hold 'Em. Gardena cardrooms began lowball tournaments in August 1979.

15. David M. Hayano, "The First Annual World Draw Poker Tournament," *Gambling Times* 2 (1978): 22-23, 93.

16. "Seven Named to Poker Hall of Fame," *Gambling Times* 3 (1979): 84. An eighth player, Tracie (Blondie) Forbes, has since been added.

17. For example see Leonard Wise, *The Big Biazarro* (Garden City, N.Y.: Doubleday, 1977); Christopher Keane, *The Crossing* (New York: Arbor House, 1978); and Ernest Tidyman, *Table Stakes* (Boston: Little, Brown, 1978).

18. Clifford Geertz, "Deep Play: Notes on the Balinese Cockfight," in *The Interpretation of Cultures,* ed. Clifford Geertz (New York: Basic Books, 1973), pp. 412-453.

19. Martin Bevans, "Playing Poker to Win," *Club* 4 (1978): 52-54, 66.

20. Erving Goffman, *Interaction Ritual* (New York: Anchor, 1967), pp. 239-258.

21. Peoples in many cultures and subcultures live under the same conditions of contradiction and strain. Also see the study by Barbara G. Myerhoff, "We Don't Wrap Herring in a Printed Page: Fusion, Fictions, and Continuity in Secular Ritual," in *Secular Ritual,* ed. Sally F. Moore and Barbara G. Myerhoff (The Netherlands: Van Gorcum, 1977), pp. 199-224.

22. For a good collection of articles on this topic and its relevance to social research, see Irwin Deutscher, ed., *What We Say/What We Do* (Glenview, Ill.: Scott, Foresman and Co., 1973).

23. Michael J. Caro, *Bobby Baldwin's Winning Poker Secrets* (Las Vegas: B & G Publishing Co., 1979), pp. 202-203.

24. Ibid., pp. 96-97.

25. For contrasts see Fred H. Goldner, R. Richard Ritti, and Thomas P. Ference, "The Production of Cynical Knowledge in Organizations," *American Sociological Review* 42 (1977): 539-551; and Robert M. Regoli, Eric D. Poole, and Jeffrey L. Shrink, "Occupational Socialization and Career Development: A Look at Cynicism among Correctional Institution Workers," *Human Organization* 38 (1979): 183-187.

26. Howard Becker and Blanche Geer, "The Fate of Idealism in Medical School," *American Sociological Review* 23 (1958): 50-56.

FIVE: LOSERS WALK

1. Cy Rice, *Nick the Greek* (New York: Funk and Wagnalls, 1969).

2. Rex Jones guesses that only 2 percent of the players in Gardena cardrooms emerge as winners. In another commercial cardroom in northern Cali-

fornia two observers calculated that a scant 10 out of 300 people were consistent winners over a four-year period. If other, more chancier gambling games are included, winning rates are adjudged even lower; as few as 1 in every 5,000 gamblers may end up with a profit. Rex Jones, "Poker and the American Dream," in *The American Dimension: Cultural Myths and Social Realities,* ed. William Arens and Susan P. Montague (New York: Alfred, 1976), pp. 170-180; Tomas Martinez and Robert LaFranchi, "Why People Play Poker," *Trans-action* 6 (1969): 30-35, 52; and Oswald Jacoby, *Oswald Jacoby on Gambling* (Garden City, N.Y.: Doubleday, 1963).

3. For a further explanation of this problem, see Allan N. Wilson, *The Casino Gambler's Guide* (New York: Harper and Row, 1970), pp. 259-260.

4. "Winners," *Winning* (January 1977): 51.

5. A joke among gamblers illustrates this attitude nicely. At the racetrack a player starting with a $2 bet in the first race was able to build up his bankroll to several thousand dollars by the eighth race. On the ninth and final race he placed the entire amount on his favorite horse to win. But it lost. When asked by a friend how he did at the race track, the gambler replied, "Not bad. I only lost $2."

6. See the admissions of Doyle Brunson, *How I Made over $1,000,000 Playing Poker* (Las Vegas: B & G Publishing Co., 1978), pp. 12-13; and Michael J. Caro, *Bobby Baldwin's Winning Poker Secrets* (Las Vegas: B & G Publishing Co., 1979), pp. 138-141.

7. Several recent books have discussed the equally distressing problem of people who have suddenly earned, inherited, or won hundreds of thousands of dollars. See Jerry and Rena LeBlanc, *Suddenly Rich* (Englewood Cliffs, N.J.: Prentice-Hall, 1978); and H. Roy Kaplan, *Lottery Winners* (New York: Harper and Row, 1978).

8. David A. Hamburg, John E. Adams, and H. Keith H. Brodie, "Coping Behavior in Stressful Circumstances: Some Implications for Social Psychiatry," in *Further Explorations in Social Psychiatry,* ed. Berton H. Kaplan, Robert N. Wilson, and Alexander H. Leighton (New York: Basic Books, 1976), p. 172.

9. Henry R. Lesieur, *The Chase: Career of the Compulsive Gambler* (Garden City, N.Y.: Anchor, 1977), pp. 155-157. A more specific account of the "connected" loan shark and the loan shark industry can be cound in John Seidl, *"Upon the Hip": A Study of the Criminal Loan-shark Industry* (Washington, D.C.: Law Enforcement Assistance Administration, U.S. Department of Justice, 1969).

10. Michael J. Hindelang, "Bookies and Bookmaking: A Descriptive Analysis," *Crime and Delinquency* 17 (1971): 245-255.

11. Lesieur, *The Chase,* p. 1.

12. Recent sociological studies of Gamblers Anonymous include Lesieur, *The Chase;* and Jay Livingston, *Compulsive Gamblers* (New York: Harper and Row, 1974).

13. J. Philip Jones, *Gambling Yesterday and Today* (Devon, England: David & Charles, 1973), pp. 170-171.

14. Caro, *Winning Poker Secrets,* p. 122.

15. Livingston, *Compulsive Gamblers,* p. 3; and Robert D. Herman, *Gamblers and Gambling* (Lexington, Mass.: D. C. Heath, 1976), p. 103.

16. David Oldham, "Compulsive Gamblers," *The Sociological Review* 26 (1978): 349-371.

17. The sociologist is Tomas Martinez of the University of Colorado. His view is reported in "Gambling in U. S. Judged Epidemic," *Los Angeles Times,* 6 February 1977.

18. Livingston, *Compulsive Gamblers,* p. 42.

19. Mario Puzo, "Standing Up for Las Vegas," *Playboy* 23 (1976): 224.

20. The criticism of single explanatory causal factors is discussed by Herman, *Gamblers and Gambling,* p. 103.

21. Oldham, "Compulsive Gamblers," p. 358.

22. Jerome H. Skolnick, *House of Cards* (Boston: Little, Brown, 1978), p. 18; and Mario Puzo, *Inside Las Vegas* (New York: Grosset and Dunlap, 1977), p. 16.

23. Mario Puzo, *Fools Die* (New York: G. P. Putnam's, 1978).

24. Puzo, "Standing Up for Las Vegas," p. 224B.

25. Igor Kusyszyn, "How Gambling Saved Me from a Misspent Sabbatical," in *Gambling and Society,* ed. William Eadington (Springfield, Ill.: Charles C. Thomas, 1976), pp. 255-264.

26. This is a sociological rather than a personal conclusion. Taking this line of argument, I am not, of course, condoning or encouraging gambling for anyone, whether he or she wins or loses. But I do believe that individuals must be free to make their own choices and proceed knowing all of the attendant risks.

27. Also see Oldham, "Compulsive Gamblers," pp. 369-370.

28. Part of this argument was first presented in David M. Hayano, "Strategies for the Management of Luck and Action in an Urban Poker Parlor," *Urban Life* 6 (1978): 475-488.

29. David Oldham, "Chance and Skill: A Study of Roulette," *Sociology* 8 (1974): 407-426.

30. There is a controversial dissenting view that states that roulette dealers may have individual "signature" patterns in spinning the ball which result in nonrandom runs. Unfortunately, there is little other research on the "human element" in casino games of chance. See Stephen Kimmel, "Roulette and Randomness," *Gambling Times* 3 (1979): 48, 94.

31. R. A. Epstein, *The Theory of Gambling and Statistical Logic* (New York: Academic Press, 1967).

32. R. Yaryan and Leon Festinger, "Preparatory Action and Belief in the Probable Occurrence of Future Events," *Journal of Abnormal and Social Psychology* 63 (1961): 603-607.

33. B. F. Skinner, *Science and Human Behavior* (New York: Free Press, 1953), p. 104; and James Henslin, "Craps and Magic," *American Journal of Sociology* 73 (1967): 316-330.

34. Skinner, *Science and Human Behavior,* pp. 84-87.

35. For example, H. A. Jenkins and W. C. Ward, "Judgment of Contingency between Responses and Outcomes," *Psychological Monographs* 79 (1965): 1-17.

36. Ellen Langer, "The Illusion of Control," *Journal of Personality and Social Psychology* 32 (1975): 311-328; and Ellen Langer and J. Roth, "Heads I Win, Tail's It's Chance: The Illusion of Control as a Function of the Sequence of Outcomes in a Purely Chance Task," *Journal of Personality and Social Psychology* 32 (1975): 951-955.

37. Ellen Langer, "The Psychology of Chance," *Journal for the Theory of Social Behaviour* 7 (1977): 185-207.

38. Marvin Scott and Stanford Lyman, "Accounts," *American Sociological Review* 33 (1968): 46-62.

39. There is a vast literature in this field. See, for example, Edward E. Jones et al., *Attribution: Perceiving the Causes of Behavior* (Morristown, N.J.: General Learning Press, 1972); and Kelly G. Shaver, *An Introduction to Attribution Processes* (Cambridge, Mass.: Winthrop, 1975).

40. Julian B. Rotter, "Generalized Expectancies for Internal versus External Control of Reinforcement," *Psychological Monographs,* vol. 80, no. 609, 1966; and Herbert M. Lefcourt, *Locus of Control: Current Trends in Theory and Research* (New York: Wiley, 1976).

41. Fritz Heider, *The Psychology of Interpersonal Relations* (New York: Wiley, 1958).

42. Lefcourt, *Locus of Control,* pp. 151-152.

43. For purposes of argument I have simplified the issue of locus of control. In the general population, as well as among gamblers, individuals tend to be neither exclusively Internals or Externals; see Lefcourt, *Locus of Control,* p. 153.

44. Melvin J. Lerner, "The Justice Motive in Social Behavior: Introduction," *Journal of Social Issues* 31 (1975): 1-19.

45. Zick Rubin and Letitia Anne Peplau, "Who Believes in a Just World?" *Journal of Social Issues* 31 (1975): 65-89.

46. Frank R. Wallace, *Poker: A Guaranteed Income for Life by Using the Advanced Concepts of Poker* (New York: Warner Books, 1977), p. 291.

47. This term is taken from George Homans, *Social Behavior: Its Elementary Forms* (London: Routledge and Kegan Paul, 1961), pp. 72-78.

48. Experiments in social learning theory have shown that behaviors are less likely to be extinguished when they are rewarded at rates of partial reinforcement, say, at 50 percent, than at 100 percent reinforcement. See W. H. James and Julian B. Rotter, "Partial and 100 Percent Reinforcement under Chance and Skill Conditions," *Journal of Experimental Psychology* 55 (1958): 397-403.

49. Oldham, "Compulsive Gamblers," p. 367.

50. Graham Reed, *The Psychology of Anomalous Experience* (Boston: Houghton Mifflin, 1974), pp. 136, 138.

SIX: DEALINGS UNDER THE TABLE

1. Rather than relying on innuendo and gossip, I include in this chapter mostly actual incidents of cheating and collusion that I myself observed in the course of fieldwork. My attention is on the general social organization of cheating, not the details of technique.

Cheating violates what Harold Garfinkel has called the "constitutive order of events" of games in an unacceptable, furtive manner. In poker, however, not only the rules are tampered with. The actual material of play as well as opponents' mental states may be manipulated. This opens the way for interesting questions of structure, such as how and why some games are easier to cheat at than others. A preliminary attempt to sort out the possibilities and consequences of rule-breaking can be found in Harold Garfinkel, "A Conception of, and Experiments with, 'Trust' as a Condition of Stable Concerted Actions," in *Motivation and Social Interaction,* ed. O. J. Harvey (New York: The Ronald Press, 1973), pp. 187-238.

2. Morehead estimates that about 100 cheaters are barred from Gardena cardrooms each year. I can neither verify nor deny this figure. See Albert Morehead, "The Professional Gambler," *Annals of the American Academy of Political and Social Science* 269 (1950): 90.

3. For a nonwestern example, see Kenneth Read, "Morality and the Concept of Person among the Gahuku-Gama," *Oceania* 25 (1955): 233-282.

4. Frank R. Wallace, *Poker: A Guaranteed Income for Life by Using the Advanced Concepts of Poker* (New York: Warner Books, 1977), p. 239.

5. Some of the best available books include John Nevil Maskelyne, *Sharps and Flats* (Las Vegas: Gambler's Book Club, 1971 [orig. 1894]); S. W. Erdnase [E. S. Andrews], *The Expert at the Card Table* (Las Vegas: Gambler's Book Club, n. d. [orig. 1902]); Michael MacDougall, *Gamblers Don't Gamble* (New York: Garden City, 1940); Frank Garcia, *Marked Cards and Loaded Dice* (New York: Bramhall House, 1962); John Scarne, *The Odds against Me:*

An Autobiography (New York: Simon and Schuster, 1966); and A. D. Livingston, Dealing with Cheats (New York: Lippincott, 1973).

6. Ken Uston with Roger Rappaport, The Big Player (New York: Holt, Rinehart, and Winston), 1977; Lawrence Linderman, "Cheating the House," Penthouse 8 (1977): 55-56, 78; and Bill Boyarsky, "Casinos Stalk the Big Game—Cheaters," Los Angeles Times, 25 April 1977.

7. Jerome H. Skolnick, House of Cards (Boston: Little, Brown, 1978), p. 248; and Wallace, Poker: A Guaranteed Income for Life, p. 237.

8. Frank Wallace also believes that there is more player cheating in higher-stakes games. He guesses that about 60 percent of Las Vegas pros and 40 percent of Gardena pros cheat at poker. The extent to which individual card-rooms know of this behavior or condone it is not ascertainable. See Wallace, Poker: A Guaranteed Income for Life, p. 240.

9. Maskelyne, Sharps and Flats, p. 99.

10. Garcia, Marked Cards, p. 31; and E. L. Mahigel and Gregory P. Stone, "How Card Hustlers Make the Game," Trans-action 8 (1971): 40-45.

11. A further discussion on this point is made by Erving Goffman, The Presentation of Self in Everyday Life (New York: Anchor, 1959), p. 80.

12. Goffman, Presentation of Self, p. 79.

13. Maskelyne, Sharps and Flats, pp. 170-171.

14. Middling is more likely to occur in lowball rather than in high-draw poker because of the structure of "blind" bets in the game. Las Vegas card-rooms deter middling to some extent by limiting the number of raises when three or more players are in the same pot.

15. Ned Polsky, Hustlers, Beats, and Others (New York: Anchor, 1969).

16. Ibid., pp. 42-44.

17. Also see G. Bobby Ilson, "The Soft Play Hustle," Gambling Times 3 (1979): 16-18.

18. Erving Goffman, Relations in Public (New York: Basic Books, 1971), p. 65.

19. For a game theory analysis of this principle, see Byron M. Roth, "Competing Norms of Distribution in Coalition Games," Journal of Conflict Resolution 23 (1979): 513-537.

20. Michael J. Caro, Bobby Baldwin's Winning Poker Secrets (Las Vegas: B & G Publishing Co., 1979), p. 49.

CONCLUSION

1. Ronald M. Pavalko, Sociology of Occupations and Professions (Itasca, Ill.: F. E. Peacock, 1971), pp. 17-27.

2. George Ritzer, Man and His Work: Conflict and Change (New York: Appleton-Century-Crofts, 1972), pp. 56-63.

3. Norman K. Denzin and Curtis J. Mettlin, "Incomplete Professionalization: The Case of Pharmacy," in *Sociological Perspectives on Occupations,* ed. Ronald M. Pavalko (Itasca, Ill.: F. E. Peacock, 1972), pp. 56-66.

4. Harold Wilensky, "The Professionalization of Everyone?" *American Journal of Sociology* 70 (1964): 137-158.

5. John Hill, "Highlights of the World Series of Poker," *Gambling Times* 3 (1979): 25.

6. See, for example, J. Holtz, "The 'Professional' Duplicate Bridge Player: Conflict Management in a Free, Legal, Quasi-deviant Occupation," *Urban Life* 4 (1975): 131-148.

7. Studies in the sociology of deviance have long considered insider specialists "professional" (e.g., the professional thief, fence, and hustler). I use this loose labeling here but advocate further study into how professionalization in deviant occupations is attained, using both external and internal traits.

8. L. G. Holloway, *Full-time Gambler* (New York: Lyle Stuart, 1969), pp. 88-89.

9. George Ritzer, *Man and His Work,* p. 42.

10. Powdermaker used this term to describe the Hollywood movie industry. See Hortense Powdermaker, *Hollywood, The Dream Factory* (Boston: Little, Brown, 1950).

11. Ritzer, *Man and His Work,* pp. 6-11.

12. Sherry Ortner, "On Key Symbols," *American Anthropologist* 75 (1973): 1338-1346.

13. Examples can be found in Stanley Cohen and Laurie Taylor, *Escape Attempts: The Theory and Practice of Resistance to Everyday Life* (Harmondsworth: Penguin, 1976).

14. Johan Huizinga, *Homo Ludens: A Study of the Play Element in Culture* (Boston: Beacon Press, 1950); Roger Callois, *Man, Play, and Games* (New York: Free Press, 1961).

15. Erving Goffman, *Frame Analysis* (New York: Harper and Row, 1974), pp. 251-252.

16. A parallel example is attributed to Karl Wallenda, the high-wire circus performer, who is reputed to have said: "To be on the wire is life: the rest is waiting." Quoted in Erving Goffman, *Interaction Ritual* (New York: Anchor, 1967), p. 149.

17. Jack Richardson, *Memoir of a Gambler* (New York: Simon and Schuster, 1979), p. 91.

18. Erving Goffman, *Encounters: Two Studies in the Sociology of Interaction* (Indianapolis: Bobbs Merrill, 1961), p. 69.

19. Ibid., pp. 19-26.

20. James W. Fernandez, "Persuasions and Performances: Of the Beast in

Every Body . . . and Metaphors in Everyman," in *Myth, Symbol, and Culture,* ed. Clifford Geertz (New York: Norton, 1971), pp. 39-60.

21. Jack Douglas, "Existential Sociology," in *Existential Sociology,* ed. Jack Douglas and John Johnson (New York: Cambridge University Press, 1977), p. 3.

22. John Lukacs, "Poker and American Character," *Horizon* 5 (1963): 56.

23. Huizinga, *Homo Ludens,* p. 199.

24. Frank R. Wallace, *Poker: A Guaranteed Income for Life by Using the Advanced Concepts of Poker* (New York: Warner Books, 1977), pp. 283-284.

25. See William Barrett, *What Is Existentialism?* (New York: Grove Press, 1964); and Gary Schwartz and Don Merten, "Participant Observation and the Discovery of Meaning," *Philosophy of Social Science* 1 (1971): 279-298.

26. Fowler's win is discussed in Scott Harris, "Does He Like His Work? You Bet!" *Los Angeles Times,* 9 July 1979; and Len Miller, "Filling the Straight," *Gambling Times* 3 (1979): 14-22; his loss is noted by Carol Crotta, "Welcome Back, Cardshark," *Los Angeles Herald Examiner,* 17 August 1979.

27. John Macquarrie, *Existentialism* (Harmondsworth: Penguin, 1973), p. 157.

28. Marie Jahoda, "The Psychological Meanings of Unemployment," *New Society* 49 (1979): 492-495.

29. This term is used in reference to ballet movements in G. B. Straus, "The Aesthetics of Dominance," *The Journal of Aesthetics and Art Criticism* 37 (1978): 75-79.

30. Benita Luckmann, "The Small Life-worlds of Modern Man," *Social Research* 37 (1970): 580-596.

31. Jerome H. Skolnick, *House of Cards* (Boston: Little, Brown, 1978), pp. 22-23.

32. Mario Puzo, "Standing Up for Las Vegas," *Playboy* 23 (1976): 224B.

APPENDIX A

1. John Johnson, *Doing Field Research* (New York: Free Press, 1975), pp. 50-51.

2. For a further discussion of college poker, see David McKenzie, "Poker and Pop: Collegiate Gambling Groups," in *The Participant Observor,* ed. Glenn Jacobs (New York: Braziller, 1970), pp. 161-178.

3. The organization of home games is described by Louis Zurcher, "The 'Friendly' Poker Game: A Study of an Ephemeral Role," *Social Forces* 49 (1970): 173-186.

4. R. L. Gold, "Roles in Sociological Field Observations," *Social Forces* 36 (1958): 217-223.

5. Norman K. Denzin, *The Research Act,* 2d ed. (New York: McGraw-Hill, 1978), pp. 184-186.

6. Many lay people erroneously believe that the cultural anthropologist studies only ancient or nonwestern cultures, digs in the ground, or observes primates. A passage from a book by card authority John Scarne stood out in my mind as a prime example: "The observation of crooked card players is my business, as the observation of nonhuman primates is the anthropologist's" (John Scarne, *Scarne on Cards* [New York: Signet, 1965], p. 4). Cultural anthropology is the study of extant human cultures and societies around the world. As a branch of cultural anthropology, ethnography is devoted to the scientific description of one particular culture or group of people. So although some players knew that I was some kind of an anthropologist, they could not quite tie it in with a study of themselves.

7. Hugh Mehan and Houston Wood, *The Reality of Ethnomethodology* (New York: Wiley, 1975), p. 227.

8. David M. Hayano, "Auto-ethnography: Paradigms, Problems, and Prospects," *Human Organization* 38 (1979): 99-104.

9. John Johnson, *Doing Field Research,* p. 1.

10. I was glad to discover that other researchers who have studied gamblers in their natural setting also found that their colleagues suspected their motivations. See Darrell W. Bolen, "Gambling: Historical Highlights and Trends and Their Implications for Contemporary Society," in *Gambling and Society,* ed. William R. Eadington (Springfield, Ill.: Charles Thomas, 1976), p. 14.

11. David M. Hayano, "The Professional Poker Player: Career Identification and the Problem of Respectability," *Social Problems* 24 (1977): 556-564; and David M. Hayano, "Strategies for the Management of Luck and Action in an Urban Poker Parlor," *Urban Life* 6 (1978): 475-488.

12. David M. Hayano, "A Complete Guide to Playing Poker in California," *Winning* (May 1977): 36-38, 56-57. This magazine is now defunct. And David M. Hayano, "DEAL—In Gardena We Play on Time," *Gambling Times* 1 (1977): 74-77.

13. Ross Shuben, "Gambling Prof Worries about Study Involvement," *The Daily Sundial,* 15 November 1978; and Treva Dean, "The Poker Misconception: Professor Studies Effects," *Insight* (November 1978): 6.

14. Ken Lubas, "Scientist and Poker," *Los Angeles Times,* 3 December 1978.

15. See, for example, Nicholas Findler, "Computer Poker," *Scientific American* 239 (1978): 144-151.

16. David Maurer, *Whiz Mob* (New Haven: College and University Press, 1955), p. 12.

17. I have relied heavily on books and popular articles primarily written about and by poker players and have cited them as the personal documents

through which poker pros portray their lives. For a description of the use of this method see Robert Bogdan and Stephen J. Taylor, *Introduction to Qualitative Research Methods* (New York: Wiley, 1975), pp. 95-124.

18. *The Professional Thief,* annot. and interp. Edwin H. Sutherland (Chicago: University of Chicago Press, 1937); Maurer, *Whiz Mob;* Howard Becker, *Outsiders: Studies in the Sociology of Deviance* (New York: Free Press, 1963); Ned Polsky, *Hustlers, Beats, and Others* (New York: Anchor, 1969); Marvin Scott, *The Racing Game* (Chicago: Aldine, 1968); Carl B. Klockars, *The Professional Fence* (New York: Free Press, 1974); and Robert Prus and C. R. D. Sharper, *Road Hustler* (Lexington, Mass.: D. C. Heath, 1977).

19. Clifford Geertz, "'From the Native's Point of View': On the Nature of Anthropological Understanding," in *Meaning in Anthropology,* ed. Keith Basso and Henry Selby (Albuquerque: University of New Mexico, 1976), pp. 236-237.

20. John Lofland, *Doing Social Life* (New York: Wiley, 1976), pp. 8-9.

21. For example, researchers in one group were "firmly rebuffed" when they attempted to hand out questionnaires inside of the clubs. Ken Stone and Richard Kalish, "Of Poker, Roles, and Aging: Description, Discussion, and Data," *International Journal of Aging and Human Development* 4 (1973): 1-13.

22. See Zurcher, "The 'Friendly' Poker Game."

23. As a matter of record, I spent about 70 percent of my time playing California draw blind, 15 percent in lowball, 10 percent in high draw, and 5 percent in high-low. While it is apparent that some elements of the folklore, strategies, and social organization of play vary with game stakes, location of the poker cardroom, and the variety of poker played, I believe that these differences lie at a specific level rather than at the general one I have attempted to discuss here.

24. Gerald D. Suttles, "Urban Ethnography: Situational and Normative Accounts," in *Annual Review of Sociology,* ed. Alex Inkeles (Palo Alto, Calif.: Annual Reviews, Inc., 1976), vol. 2, p. 3.

25. Edward Diener and Rick Crandall, *Ethics in Social and Behavioral Research* (Chicago: University of Chicago Press, 1978), pp. 118-119.

26. For this reason I do not think that this research could be considered "disguised" or "secret" in its controversial usage. See, for example, Kai T. Erikson, "A Comment on Disguised Observation in Sociology," *Social Problems* 14 (1967): 366-373; and Julius A. Roth, "Comments on 'Secret Observation,'" *Social Problems* 9 (1962): 283-284.

Glossary

Advertise. Deliberately showing a bluff or bad hand to give the impression of loose play.

All-in. Betting all of one's remaining chips.

Angle shooter. A player who takes advantage of others by bending the rules of the game.

Ante. The required fee a player places in front of him so that he may be dealt a hand.

Backline. 1. An agreement between two or more players to split a percentage of each other's pots. 2. A stack of chips placed behind a player's regular playing stack.

Bad beat. 1. Losing a pot with a good hand. 2. A big loss.

Bet on the finger. Making a verbal declaration of playing without having bought chips.

Bicycle (or *Wheel*). An A-2-3-4-5, the best possible hand in California lowball.

Blind. A mandatory bet, usually by a player or players to the dealer's left, in lowball and in some high games.

Blow back. Losing back most or all of one's profits.

Board. The large, visible blackboard in the cardroom where players' initials are recorded by the boardman.

Brain surgeon. Players who analyze every bet or play in detail.

Burn card. A card dealt off the top of the deck into the discards preceding the draw.

Bust. A worthless or incomplete hand.

Busted. Broke, tapped out.

Buy-in. The minimum amount of money required to sit down in a game. Sometimes called a change-in.

California draw blind.   A form of high poker where the player to the dealer's left must open the pot blind.

Calling station.   A player who calls many bets and is difficult to bluff.

Card rack.   A player who holds many good hands.

Case money.   A player's last money.

Checks.   Cardroom chips.

Cheese (a piece of).   A bad hand.

Cherry patch.   An easy table filled with live ones.

Crying call.   A hesitant or unsure call.

Dead hand.   By house rules an unplayable hand.

Down to the cloth.   A player who has only a few remaining chips in front of him.

Garbage.   1. A bad hand. 2. The discards.

Gardena miracle.   Making a good hand out of an improbable draw.

Go south.   To take chips off the table.

Heads-up.   A poker game of two players.

High-draw.   A form of poker in which the highest hand wins.

High-low.   A form of poker in Gardena cardrooms where if the pot is not opened for high with a pair of jacks or better, the player to the left of the dealer must open blind for low. This can also be played as *high-low declare* when the player to the dealer's left looks at his cards and then states whether the game is high or low. In either variation of Gardena high-low, there is no split pot.

Hit and run.   Winning and leaving the game quickly.

Hold-out.   Hiding cards out of the deck and using them at the right time.

Hot and stuck.   Losing badly in a game.

Juice.   1. Interest on a loan. 2. Influence with other people.

Juiceman.   A loanshark; a person who lends money and charges interest.

Juicy.   A term used to describe an easy player or game.

Live one.   A bad or loose losing player.

Loose.   An action-giving style of play.

Lowball.   A form of poker where the lowest hand wins.

Mechanic.   An experienced cheat who manipulates cards in the deck.

Middling.   Trapping a player between raises and re-raises.

Miscall a hand.   To verbally misstate the value of a hand.

Monster.   1. An extremely good hand. 2. A huge pot.

Needle.   Insults directed to another person and his play.

No brainer.   A good hand that requires no decision on how it should be played.

Nut up.   Tighten play; give less action.

Nuts.   Strong or good hands.

On tilt.   An unsteady financial and emotional state caused by losing.

Paint. Any "picture" card (jack, queen, or king).

Pat hand. A complete hand, such as a straight, flush, or full house, requiring no draw of cards.

Play behind. To play with money that has not been placed on the table.

Play out of the apron. To play on borrowed money from the chipgirl.

Pot out. Taking a percentage out of each pot to buy some merchandise or place a bet.

Professor. A smart player or one who thinks he knows it all. Often used pejoratively.

Prop. A house-employed shill.

Pumped up. In possession of a gambling stake after being broke.

Push antes. Exchanging antes after winning pots.

Rack up the game. Winning enough chips to have to carry them to the cash-out window in wooden racks.

Rail. The section of the cardroom where spectators watch the games.

Railbird. A (usually) broke player who stands on the rail.

Rake-off. A percentage of the pot that is taken by the dealer and goes to the house.

Ring game. A full game.

Rock. A tight, conservative player.

Running bad. On a losing streak.

Running good. On a winning streak.

Rush. A more-than-normal good run of cards.

Scam. An illegal, collusive partnership among players.

Scared money. The description for a player who plays cautiously and is afraid to lose money.

Shill. A house-employed player who fills in short games.

Short. Lacking one's usual bankroll.

Showdown. When all bets have been met and players lay down their hands.

Side bet (or *proposition*). Making bets on cards or hands not related to the game itself.

Slowroll. Showing down the best hand last, after other players have shown theirs.

Slowplay. Playing a strong hand with moderate strength to trap others in the pot.

Softplay. Playing easily against a friend.

Stand pat. To not draw cards.

Steam. To lose control and play wildly.

Stuck. Losing.

Tap city. Busted, broke.

Tell. A player's giveaway mannerism about his hand.

Throw a party. To lose heavily.

Ticket.   A card.

Tight.   A cautious and conservative style of play.

Time.   The house collection fee.

Timing.   Having the best hand when it really counts—in the biggest pots.

Treasure hunt.   Looking around the cardroom for a person who might lend money.

Wide open.   A player who has changed to a loose, wild style of play.

Bibliography

Adler, Peter, and Adler, Patricia A. "The Role of Momentum in Sport." *Urban Life* 7 (1978): 153-176.

Alberts, Ulvis. *Poker Face.* Hollywood, Calif.: Angel City Books, 1981.

Andersen, Ian. *Turning the Tables on Las Vegas.* New York: Vanguard Press, 1976.

Arnold, Peter. *The Encyclopedia of Gambling.* Secaucus, N.J.: Chartwell Books, 1977.

Asbury, Herbert. *Sucker's Progress.* New York: Dodd and Mead, 1938.

Barbour, John. "Gambling Becomes Part of U.S. Way." *Los Angeles Times,* 21 November 1976.

Barrett, William. *What Is Existentialism?* New York: Grove Press, 1964.

Becker, Howard. *Outsiders: Studies in the Sociology of Deviance.* New York: Free Press, 1963.

Becker, Howard, and Geer, Blanche. "The Fate of Idealism in Medical School." *American Sociological Review* 23 (1958): 50-56.

Bell, Joseph N. "World Series Revelations: How to Win at Poker." *Coast* 17 (1976): 19-20.

Bergler, Edmund. *The Psychology of Gambling.* London: Hanison, 1958.

———. "The Psychology of the Gambler." *Imago* 22 (1936): 409-441.

Bevans, Martin. "Playing Poker to Win." *Club* 4 (1978): 52-54, 66.

Bigus, Odis. "The Milkman and His Customer: A Cultivated Relationship." *Urban Life and Culture* 1 (1972): 131-165.

Block, Julian. "Gambling and Taxes." *Gambling Times* 2 (1978): 31-33.

Bogdan, Robert, and Taylor, Stephen J. *Introduction to Qualitative Research Methods.* New York: Wiley, 1975.

Bolen, Darrell W. "Gambling: Historical Highlights and Trends and Their

Implication for Contemporary Society." In *Gambling and Society,* edited by William R. Eadington, pp. 7-38. Springfield, Ill.: Charles Thomas, 1976.

Borders, Myram. "Interest in Casino Gaming Spreading Rapidly across U.S." *Los Angeles Times,* 6 November 1977.

Boyarsky, Bill. "Casinos Stalk the Big Game—Cheaters." *Los Angeles Times,* 25 April 1977.

Boyd, Susan. "Anal Linguists, Cry Your 'I's' Out: Constructing a Metaphor of Poker." In *Studies in the Anthropology of Play: Papers in Memory of B. Allan Tindall,* edited by Phillips Stevens, pp. 28-34. West Point, New York: Leisure Press, 1977.

———. "Poker Playing as a Dramaturgical Event: Bull Power, the Meaning and the Commitment for Efficacious Gamesmanship." In *The Anthropological Study of Play: Problems and Prospects,* edited by D. F. Lancy and B. A. Tindall, pp. 123-130. Cornwall, New Jersey: Leisure Press, 1976.

Bradshaw, Jon. *Fast Company.* New York: Harpers Magazine Press, 1975.

Brady, Frank. "Chess in the Cinema." *Chess Life and Review* 34 (1979): 188-193.

Brunson, Doyle. *How I Made over $1,000,000 Playing Poker.* Las Vegas: B & G Publishing Co., 1978.

Bryan, James. "Apprenticeships in Prostitution." *Social Problems* 12 (1965): 287-297.

———. "Occupational Ideologies and Individual Attitudes of Call Girls." *Social Problems* 13 (1966): 441-450.

Burton, Michael L., and Romney, A. Kimball. "A Multidimensional Representation of Role Terms." *American Ethnologist* 3 (1975): 397-407.

Callois, Roger. *Man, Play, and Games.* New York: Free Press, 1961.

Cameron, Lou. *California Split.* Greenwich, Conn.: Fawcett, 1974.

Campbell, David P. "Who Wants to Be a Professional Gambler?" In *Gambling and Society,* edited by William R. Eadington, pp. 265-275. Springfield, Ill.: Charles Thomas, 1976.

Campbell, Felicia. "Gambling: A Positive View." In *Gambling and Society,* edited by William R. Eadington, pp. 218-228. Springfield, Ill.: Charles Thomas, 1976.

Carlson, Katherine. "Reciprocity in the Marketplace: Tipping in an Urban Nightclub." In *Conformity and Conflict,* 3d ed., edited by James Spradley and David McCurdy, pp. 337-347. Boston: Little, Brown, 1977.

Caro, Michael J. *Bobby Baldwin's Winning Poker Secrets.* Las Vegas: B & G Publishing Co., 1979.

Carper, James, and Becker, Howard. "Adjustments to Conflicting Expectations in the Development of Identification with an Occupation." *Social Forces* 36 (1957): 51-55.

Cavan, Sherri. *Liquor License: An Ethnography of Bar Behavior.* Chicago: Aldine, 1966.

Clinard, Marshall, and Quinney, R. *Criminal Behavior Systems: A Typology.* New York: Holt, Rinehart and Winston, 1967.

Cohen, John. *Chance, Skill, and Luck: The Psychology of Guessing and Gambling.* Baltimore: Penguin, 1960.

———. *Psychological Probability.* London: Allen and Unwin, 1972.

Cohen, John, and Hansel, M. "Preferences for Different Combinations of Chance and Skill in Gambling." *Nature* 183 (1959): 841-842.

———. *Risk and Gambling: The Study of Subjective Probability.* New York: Philosophical Library, 1956.

Cohen, Stanley, and Taylor, Laurie. *Escape Attempts: The Theory and Practice of Resistance to Everyday Life.* Harmondsworth: Penguin, 1976.

Commission on the Review of the National Policy Toward Gambling. *Gambling in America.* Washington, D.C.: Government Printing Office, 1976.

———. *Gambling in America: Appendix 2: Survey of American Gambling Attitudes and Behavior.* Washington, D.C.: Government Printing Office, 1976.

Crespi, Irving. "Card Playing as Mass Culture." In *Mass Culture,* edited by B. Rosenberg and D. White, pp. 418-422. New York: Free Press, 1957.

———. "The Social Significance of Card Playing as a Leisure Time Activity." *American Sociological Review* 21 (1956): 717-721.

Crotta, Carol. "Welcome Back, Cardshark." *Los Angeles Herald Examiner,* 17 August 1979.

David, F. N. *Games, Gods, and Gambling.* London: Charles Griffin, 1962.

Davis, Fred. "The Cabdriver and His Fare: Facets of a Fleeting Relationship." *American Journal of Sociology* 63 (1959): 158-165.

Dean, Treva. "The Poker Misconception: Professor Studies Effects." *Insight* (California State University, Northridge) (November 1978): 6.

Deaux, Kay, and Enswiller, T. "Explanations of Successful Performance on Sex-linked Tasks: What's Skill for the Male Is Luck for the Female." *Journal of Personality and Social Psychology* 29 (1973): 80-85.

Deaux, Kay; White, L.; and Faris, E. "Skill versus Luck: Field and Laboratory Studies of Male and Female Preferences." *Journal of Personality and Social Psychology* 32 (1975): 629-636.

Denzin, Norman K. *The Research Act.* 2d ed. New York: McGraw-Hill, 1978.

Denzin, Norman K., and Mettlin, Curtis J. "Incomplete Professionalization: The Case of Pharmacy." In *Sociological Perspectives on Occupations,* edited by Ronald M. Pavalko, pp. 56-66. Itasca, Ill.: F. E. Peacock, 1972.

Deutscher, Irwin, ed. *What We Say/What We Do.* Glenview, Ill.: Scott, Foresman and Co., 1973.

Devol, George. *Forty Years a Gambler on the Mississippi.* Austin, Texas: Steck-Vaughan Co., 1967 (orig. 1887).

Diener, Edward, and Crandall, Rick. *Ethics in Social and Behavioral Research.* Chicago: University of Chicago Press, 1978.

Dietz, Lawrence. "Gardena, California — Poker for the Geriatrics Set." *Holiday* 45 (1969): 22-24.

Dostoevski, Fyodor. *The Gambler.* Harmondsworth: Penguin, 1966 (orig. 1866).

Douglas, Jack. "Existential Sociology." In *Existential Sociology,* edited by Jack Douglas and John Johnson, pp. 3-73. New York: Cambridge University Press, 1977.

Dowling, Allen. *The Great American Pastime.* New York: Barnes, 1970.

Downes, D. M.; Davies, B. P.; David, M. E.; and Stone, P. *Gambling, Work and Leisure: A Study across Three Areas.* London: Routledge and Kegan Paul, 1976.

Epstein, R. A. *The Theory of Gambling and Statistical Logic.* New York: Academic Press, 1967.

Erdnase, S. W. [E. S. Andrews]. *The Expert at the Card Table.* Las Vegas: Gambler's Book Club, n.d. (orig. 1902).

Erikson, Kai T. "A Comment on Disguised Observation in Sociology." *Social Problems* 14 (1967): 366-373.

"European Nations Find a Sure Bet." *Los Angeles Times,* 14 October 1979.

Felson, Richard B., and Gmelch, George. "Uncertainty and the Use of Magic." *Current Anthropology* 20 (1979): 587-589.

Fernandez, James. "Persuasions and Performances: Of the Beast in Every Body...and Metaphors in Everyman." In *Myth, Symbol, and Culture,* edited by Clifford Geertz, pp. 39-60. New York: Norton, 1971.

Findler, Nicholas V. "Computer Poker." *Scientific American* 239 (1978): 144-151.

Fine, Reuben. *The Psychology of the Chess Player.* New York: Dover, 1967.

Fox, John. *Play Poker, Quit Work and Sleep till Noon!* Seal Beach, Calif.: Bacchus Press, 1977.

Freud, Sigmund. "Dostoevski and Parricide." *The Psychology of Gambling,* edited by Jon Halliday and Peter Fuller, pp. 157-174. New York: Harper, 1974.

"Gambling in U. S. Judged Epidemic." *Los Angeles Times,* 6 February 1977.

Garcia, Frank. *Marked Cards and Loaded Dice.* New York: Bramhall House, 1962.

Garfinkel, Harold. "A Conception of, and Experiments with, 'Trust' as a Condition of Stable Concerted Actions." In *Motivation and Social Interaction,* edited by O. J. Harvey, pp. 187-238. New York: The Ronald Press, 1963.

Geertz, Clifford. "Deep Play: Notes on the Balinese Cockfight." In *The Interpretation of Cultures,* edited by Clifford Geertz, pp. 412-453. New York: Basic Books, 1973.

——. " 'From the Native's Point of View': On the Nature of Anthropological Understanding." In *Meaning in Anthropology,* edited by Keith Basso and Henry Selby, pp. 221-237. Albuquerque: University of New Mexico Press, 1976.

Gerth, H. H., and Mills, C. Wright. *From Max Weber: Essays in Sociology.* Oxford: Oxford University Press, 1946.

Gibbons, Don C. *Society, Crime, and Criminal Careers.* Englewood Cliffs, N.J.: Prentice-Hall, 1968.

Gmelch, George. "Baseball Magic." In *Conformity and Conflict,* 3d ed., edited by James Spradley and David McCurdy, pp. 346-352. Boston: Little, Brown, 1974.

Goffman, Erving. *Encounters: Two Studies in the Sociology of Interaction.* Indianapolis: Bobbs Merrill, 1961.

——. *Frame Analysis.* New York: Harper and Row, 1974.

——. *Interaction Ritual.* New York: Anchor, 1967.

——. *The Presentation of Self in Everyday Life.* Garden City, N.Y.: Anchor, 1959.

——. *Relations in Public.* New York: Basic Books, 1971.

——. *Stigma.* Englewood Cliffs, N.J.: Prentice-Hall, 1963.

——. *Strategic Interaction.* Philidalphia: University of Pennsylvania Press, 1969.

Gold, R. L. "Roles in Sociological Field Observations." *Social Forces* 36 (1958): 217-223.

Goldner, Fred H.; Ritti, R. Richard; and Ference, Thomas P. "The Production of Cynical Knowledge in Organizations." *American Sociological Review* 42 (1977): 539-551.

Gunther, Max. *The Luck Factor.* New York: Macmillan, 1977.

Halliday, Jon, and Fuller, Peter, eds. *The Psychology of Gambling.* New York: Harper, 1974.

Hamburg, David A.; Adams, John E.; and Brodie, H. Keith H. "Coping Behavior in Stressful Circumstances: Some Implications for Social Psychiatry." In *Further Explorations in Social Psychiatry,* edited by Berton H. Kaplan, Robert N. Wilson, and Alexander H. Leighton, pp. 158-175. New York: Basic Books, 1976.

Hargrave, Catherine Perry. *A History of Playing Cards and A Bibliography of Cards and Gaming.* New York: Dover, 1966.

Harris, Scott. "Does He Like His Work? You Bet!" *Los Angeles Times,* 9 July 1979.

Hayano, David M. "A Complete Guide to Playing Poker in California." *Winning* (May 1977): 36-38, 56-57.

———. "Auto-ethnography: Paradigms, Problems, and Prospects." *Human Organization* 38 (1979): 99-104.

———. "Communicative Competency among Poker Players." *Journal of Communication* 30 (1980): 113-120.

———. "DEAL—In Gardena We Play on Time." *Gambling Times* 1 (1977): 74-77.

———. "The First Annual World Draw Poker Tournament." *Gambling Times* 2 (1978): 22-23, 93.

———. "The Professional Poker Player: Career Identification and the Problem of Respectability." *Social Problems* 24 (1977): 556-564.

———. "Poker Lies and Tells." *Human Behavior* 8 (1979): 18-22.

———. "Strategies for the Management of Luck and Action in an Urban Poker Parlor." *Urban Life* 6 (1978): 475-488.

Heider, Fritz. *The Psychology of Interpersonal Relations.* New York: Wiley, 1958.

Henslin, James. "Craps and Magic." *American Journal of Sociology* 73 (1967): 316-330.

Herman, Robert, ed. *Gambling.* New York: Harper and Row, 1967.

Herman, Robert. *Gamblers and Gambling.* Lexington, Mass.: D. C. Heath, 1976.

Hill, John. "Highlights of the World Series of Poker." *Gambling Times* 3 (1979): 24-29.

———. "Johnny Moss: The Grand Old Man of Poker." *Gambling Times* 2 (1978): 22-25, 82-84.

Hindelang, Michael J. "Bookies and Bookmaking: A Descriptive Analysis." *Crime and Delinquency* 17 (1971): 245-255.

Hoffman, William. *The Loser.* New York: Funk and Wagnalls, 1968.

Holloway, L. G. *Full-time Gambler.* New York: Lyle Stuart. 1969.

Holtz, J. "The 'Professional' Duplicate Bridge Player: Conflict Management in a Free, Legal, Quasi-deviant Occupation." *Urban Life* 4 (1975): 131-148.

Homans, George. *Social Behavior: Its Elementary Forms.* London: Routledge and Kegan Paul, 1961.

Hong, Lawrence K., and Duff, Robert W. "Becoming a Taxi-dancer: The Significance of Neutralization in a Semi-deviant Occupation." *Sociology of Work and Occupations* 4 (1977): 327-342.

Huizinga, Johan. *Homo Ludens: A Study of the Play Element in Culture.* Boston: Beacon Press, 1950.

Hulse, Jerry. "Atlantic City in the Chips as Gamblers Flock In." *Los Angeles Times,* 13 May 1979.

Ilson, G. Bobby. "The Soft Play Hustle." *Gambling Times* 3 (1979): 16-18.

Jackson, Bruce. "Deviance as Success: The Double Inversion of Stigmatized Roles." In *The Reversible World: Symbolic Inversion in Art and Society,* edited by Barbara A. Babcock, pp. 258-275. Ithaca, N.Y.: Cornell University Press, 1978.

Jacoby, Oswald. *Oswald Jacoby on Gambling.* Garden City, N.Y.: Doubleday, 1963.

Jahoda, Marie. "The Psychological Meanings of Unemployment." *New Society* 49 (1979): 492-495.

James, W. H. and Rotter, Julian B. "Partial and 100 Percent Reinforcement under Chance and Skill Conditions." *Journal of Experimental Psychology* 55 (1958): 397-403.

Jenkins, Don. *Champion of Champions.* Odessa, Texas: J. M. Publications, 1981.

Jenkins, H. A., and Ward, W. C. "Judgment of Contingency Between Responses and Outcomes." *Psychological Monographs* 79 (1965): 1-17.

Jessup, Richard. *The Cincinnati Kid.* Boston: Little, Brown, 1963.

Johnson, John. *Doing Field Research.* New York: Free Press, 1975.

Jones, Edward E., et al. *Attribution: Perceiving the Causes of Behavior.* Morristown, N.J.: General Learning Press, 1972.

Jones, J. Philip. *Gambling Yesterday and Today.* Devon, England: David & Charles, 1973.

Jones, Rex. "Poker and the American Dream." In *The American Dimension: Cultural Myths and Social Realities,* edited by William Arens and Susan Montague, pp. 170-180. New York: Alfred, 1976.

Kaplan, H. Roy. *Lottery Winners.* New York: Harper and Row, 1978.

Keane, Christopher. *The Crossing.* New York: Arbor House, 1978.

Kimmel, Stephen. "Roulette and Randomness." *Gambling Times* 3 (1979): 48, 94.

Klockars, Carl B. *The Professional Fence.* New York: Free Press, 1974.

Krier, Beth Ann. "Legalized Bingo: Winners and Losers." *Los Angeles Times,* 3 August 1978.

Kusyszyn, Igor. "The Gambling Addict versus the Gambling Professional: A Difference in Character?" in *Studies in the Psychology of Gambling,* edited by Igor Kusyszyn, pp. 165-172. New York: Simon and Schuster, 1972.

———. "How Gambling Saved Me from a Misspent Sabbatical." In *Gambling and Society,* edited by William R. Eadington, pp. 255-264. Springfield, Ill.: Charles Thomas, 1976.

Labov, William. "Rules for Ritual Insults." In *Studies in Social Interaction,* edited by David Sudnow, pp. 120-169. New York: Macmillan, 1972.

Langer, Ellen. "The Illusion of Control." *Journal of Personality and Social Psychology* 32 (1975): 311-328.

———. "The Psychology of Chance." *Journal for the Theory of Social Behavior* 7 (1977): 185-207.

Langer, Ellen, and Roth, J. "Heads I Win, Tails It's Chance: The Illusion of Control as a Function of the Sequence of Outcomes in a Purely Chance Task." *Journal of Personality and Social Psychology* 32 (1975): 951-955.

LeBlanc, Jerry, and LeBlanc, Rena. *Suddenly Rich.* Englewood Cliffs, N.J.: Prentice-Hall, 1978.

Lee, Mary Ann. "Gardena Council Questions Card Club Licensing." *Los Angeles Times,* 22 December 1974.

Lefcourt, Herbert M. *Locus of Control: Current Trends in History and Research.* New York: Wiley, 1976.

Lerner, Melvin J. "The Justice Motive in Social Behavior." *Journal of Social Issues* 31 (1975): 1-19.

Lesieur, Henry R. *The Chase: Career of the Compulsive Gambler.* Garden City, N.Y.: Anchor, 1977.

Levinson, H. *Chance, Luck and Statistics.* New York: Dover, 1963.

Linderman, L. "Cheating the House." *Penthouse* 8 (1977): 55-56, 78.

Livingston, A. D. *Dealing with Cheats.* New York: Lippincott, 1973.

———. "'Hold Me': A Wild New Poker Game and How to Tame It." *Life* 65 (1968): 38-39, 42.

Lofland, John. *Doing Social Life.* New York: Wiley, 1976.

Lubas, Ken. "Scientist and Poker." *Los Angeles Times,* 3 December 1979.

Luckmann, Benita. "The Small Life-worlds of Modern Man." *Social Research* 37 (1970): 580-596.

Lukacs, John. "Poker and American Character." *Horizon* 5 (1963): 56-62.

Lyman, Stanford, and Scott, Marvin. *A Sociology of the Absurd.* Pacific Palisades, Calif.: Goodyear, 1970.

MacDougall, Michael. *Gamblers Don't Gamble.* New York: Garden City, 1940.

Macquarrie, John. *Existentialism.* Harmondsworth: Penguin, 1973.

Mahigel, E. L., and Stone, Gregory P. "How Card Hustlers Make the Game." *Trans-action* 8 (1971): 40-45.

"Maine Infested by Small-coin Gambling." *Los Angeles Times,* 18 February 1979.

Malinowski, Bronislaw. *Magic, Science and Religion.* New York: Anchor, 1948.

Martinez, Tomas. "Gambling, Goods, and Games." *Society* 14 (1977): 79-81.

Martinez, Tomas, and LaFranchi, Robert. "Why People Play Poker." *Trans-action* 6 (1969): 30-35, 52.

Maskelyne, John Nevil. *Sharps and Flats.* Las Vegas: Gambler's Book Club, 1971 (orig. 1894).

Maurer, David. *Whiz Mob.* New Haven: College and University Press, 1955.

McCormack, Patricia. "Race Tracks, Bus Depots: Social Centers for Elderly." *Los Angeles Times,* 15 August 1979.

McDonald, John. *Strategy in Poker, Business and War.* New York: Norton, 1950.

McGlothlin, W. H. "A Psychometric Study of Gambling." *Journal of Consulting Psychology* 18 (1954): 145-149.

McKenzie, David. "Poker and Pop: Collegiate Gambling Groups." In *The Participant Observor,* edited by Glenn Jacobs, pp. 161-178. New York: Braziller, 1970.

McQuaid, Clement, ed. *Gambler's Digest.* Northfield, Ill.: DBI Books, 1971.

Mehan, Hugh, and Wood, Houston. *The Reality of Ethnomethodology.* New York: Wiley, 1975.

Miller, Gale. *Odd Jobs: The World of Deviant Work.* Englewood Cliffs, N.J.: Prentice-Hall, 1978.

Miller, Len. "Filling the Straight." *Gambling Times* 3 (1979): 14-22.

———. "From the Editor's Desk." *Gambling Times* 3 (1979): 5.

Morehead, Albert. "The Professional Gambler." *Annals of the American Academy of Political and Social Science* 269 (1950): 81-92.

Myerhoff, Barbara G. "We Don't Wrap Herring in a Printed Page: Fusion, Fictions, and Continuity in Secular Ritual." In *Secular Ritual,* edited by Sally F. Moore and Barbara G. Myerhoff, pp. 199-224. The Netherlands: Van Gorcum, 1977.

Newman, David. *Esquire's Book of Gambling.* New York: Harper and Row, 1962.

"N.Y. Gives Warning on '3-card Monte.'" *Los Angeles Times,* 4 November 1979.

Oldham, David. "Chance and Skill: A Study of Roulette." *Sociology* 8 (1974): 407-426.

———. "Compulsive Gamblers." *The Sociological Review* 26 (1978): 349-371.

Ore, Oystein. *Cardano: The Gambling Scholar.* Princeton: Princeton University Press, 1953.

Ortner, Sherry. "On Key Symbols." *American Anthropologist* 75 (1973): 1338-1346.

Pavalko, Ronald M. *Sociology of Occupations and Professions.* Itasca, Ill.: F. E. Peacock, 1971.

Pennsylvania Eddie. "Confessions of a Professional Poker Player." *Gamblers World* 1 (1974): 33-35, 66-69.

Polsky, Ned. *Hustlers, Beats and Others.* New York: Anchor, 1969.

Powdermaker, Hortense. *Hollywood: The Dream Factory.* Boston: Little, Brown, 1950.

Preston, Amarillo Slim, with Bill G. Cox. *Play Poker to Win.* New York: Grosset and Dunlap, 1973.

The Professional Thief. Annotated and interpreted by Edwin H. Sutherland. Chicago: University of Chicago Press, 1937.

Prus, Robert, and Sharper, C. R. D. *Road Hustler.* Lexington, Mass.: D. C. Heath, 1977.

Puzo, Mario. *Fools Die.* New York: G. P. Putnam's, 1978.

———. *Inside Las Vegas.* New York: Grosset and Dunlap, 1977.

———. "Standing Up for Las Vegas." *Playboy* 23 (1976): 178, 200, 224-224B.

Read, Kenneth. "Morality and the Concept of the Person among the Gahuku-Gama." *Oceania* 25 (1955): 233-282.

Reed, Graham. *The Psychology of Anomalous Experience.* Boston: Houghton Mifflin, 1974.

Regoli, Robert M.; Poole, Eric D.; and Shrink, Jeffrey L. "Occupational Socialization and Career Development: A Look at Cynicism among Correctional Institution Workers." *Human Organization* 38 (1979): 183-187.

Rice, Cy. *Nick the Greek.* New York: Funk and Wagnalls, 1969.

Richardson, Jack. "Coming Down in Gardena." *Playboy* 21 (1974): 114, 158, 186-200.

———. *Memoir of a Gambler.* New York: Simon and Schuster, 1979.

Ritzer, George. *Man and His Work: Conflict and Change.* New York: Appleton-Century-Crofts, 1972.

Roth, Byron M. "Competing Norms of Distribution in Coalition Games." *Journal of Conflict Resolution* 23 (1979): 513-537.

Roth, Julius A. "Comments on 'Secret Observation.'" *Social Problems* 9 (1962): 283-284.

Rotter, Julian B. "Generalized Expectancies for Internal versus External Control of Reinforcement." *Psychological Monographs,* vol. 80, no. 609, 1966.

Rotter, Julian B.; Liverant S.; and Crowne, D. P. "The Growth and Extinction of Expectancies in Chance Controlled and Skilled Tests." *Journal of Psychology* 52 (1962): 161-177.

Rubin, Zick, and Peplau, Letitia Anne. "Who Believes in a Just World?" *Journal of Social Issues* 31 (1975): 65-89.

Scarne, John. *Scarne on Cards.* New York: Signet, 1965.

———. *The Odds against Me: An Autobiography.* New York: Simon and Schuster, 1966.

Schwartz, Gary, and Merten, Don. "Participant Observation and the Discovery of Meaning." *Philosophy of Social Science* 1 (1971): 279-298.

Scott, Jim. "The Greatest Poker Player of Them All." *Gambling Quarterly* (Summer/Autumn 1976): 11-12, 54.

———. "How the Best Players in the World Play Poker." *Gambling Quarterly* (Winter 1976): 26-31, 60.

Scott, Marvin. *The Racing Game.* Chicago: Aldine, 1968.

Scott, Marvin, and Lyman, Stanford. "Accounts." *American Sociological Review* 33 (1968): 46-62.

Seidl, John. *"Upon the Hip": A Study of the Criminal Loan-shark Industry.* Washington, D.C.: Law Enforcement Assistance Administration, U.S. Department of Justice, 1969.

"Seven Named to Poker Hall of Fame." *Gambling Times* 3 (1979): 84.

Shaver, Kelly G. *An Introduction to Attribution Processes.* Cambridge, Mass.: Winthrop, 1975.

Shaw, David. "Gardena: Poker Draws Young and Old to the Tables." *Los Angeles Times,* 28 March 1971.

Shuben, Ross. "Gambling Prof Worries about Study Involvement." *The Daily Sundial* (California State University, Northridge), 15 November 1978.

Silberstang, Edwin. "Ask Our Experts." *Gambling Times* 3 (1979): 8.

Skinner, B. F. *Science and Human Behavior.* New York: Free Press, 1953.

Skipper, James K., Jr., and McCaghy, Charles H. "Stripteasers: The Anatomy and Career Contingencies of a Deviant Occupation." *Social Problems* 17 (1970): 391-405.

Sklansky, David. *Sklansky on Poker Theory.* Las Vegas: Gambler's Book Club, 1978.

Skolnick, Jerome H. *House of Cards.* Boston: Little, Brown, 1978.

Snyder, Jimmy. *Jimmy the Greek.* Chicago, Ill.: Playboy Press, 1975.

Spanier, David. *Total Poker.* New York: Simon and Schuster, 1977.

Stone, Ken, and Kalish, Richard. "Of Poker, Roles, and Aging: Description, Discussion, and Data." *International Journal of Aging and Human Development* 4 (1973): 1-13.

Straus, G. B. "The Aesthetics of Dominance." *The Journal of Aesthetics and Art Criticism* 37 (1978): 75-79.

Stuart, Lyle. *Casino Gambling for the Winner.* New York: Ballantine Books, 1978.

Suttle, Gerald D. "Urban Ethnography: Situational and Normative Accounts." In *Annual Review of Sociology,* edited by Alex Inkeles, vol. 2, pp. 1-18. Palo Alto, Calif.: Annual Reviews, Inc., 1976.

Taylor, L. B. "A Poker Prop." *Cavalier* 26 (1976): 61-62, 78.

Tec, Nechama. *Gambling in Sweden.* Totowa, N.J.: The Bedminster Press, 1964.

Thackrey, Ted. "He's a Rambler, Gambler—But Not Far from Home." *Los Angeles Times,* 24 May 1974.

Thorp, Edward O. "Probabilities and Strategies for the Game of Faro." In *Gambling and Society,* edited by William R. Eadington, pp. 443-463. Springfield, Ill.: Charles Thomas, 1976.

Tidyman, Ernest. *Table Stakes.* Boston: Little, Brown, 1978.

Time-Life Books, The Editors. *The Gamblers.* Alexandria, Virginia: Time-Life Books, 1978.

Trounson, Rebecca. "Poker Parlor Battle Heats Up as Bell Club Chimes In." *Los Angeles Times,* 14 December 1980.

Tversky, Amos, and Kahneman, Daniel. "Belief in the Law of Small Numbers." *Psychological Bulletin* 76 (1971): 105-110.

Uston, Ken. *Two Books on Blackjack.* Wheaton, Md.: The Uston Institute of Blackjack, 1979.

Uston, Ken, with Roger Rappaport. *The Big Player.* New York: Holt, Rinehart and Winston, 1977.

"Voters Turn Down Poker Proposal" [in Inglewood]. *Los Angeles Times,* 15 March 1978.

Wagner, Walter. *To Gamble, or Not to Gamble.* New York: World, 1972.

Wallace, Frank R. *"How I Made over $1,000,000 Playing Poker": An Obituary for the Professional Poker Player.* Las Vegas: I and O Publishing Co., 1978.

———. *Poker: A Guaranteed Income for Life by Using the Advanced Concepts of Poker.* New York: Warner Books, 1977.

Weaver, Warren. *Lady Luck: The Theory of Probability.* New York: Anchor, 1963.

Whyte, William F. *Street Corner Society.* Chicago: University of Chicago Press, 1943.

Wilensky, Harold. "The Professionalization of Everyone?" *American Journal of Sociology* 70 (1964): 137-158.

Wilson, Allan N. *The Casino Gambler's Guide.* New York: Harper and Row, 1970.

"Winners." *Winning* (January 1977): 51.

Wise, Leonard. *The Big Biazarro.* Garden City, N.Y.: Doubleday, 1977.

Wolfenstein, Martha. "Movie Analyses in the Study of Culture." In *The Study of Culture at a Distance,* edited by Margaret Mead and Rhoda Metraux, pp. 267-280. Chicago: University of Chicago Press, 1953.

Wright, Will. *Sixguns and Society: A Structural Study of the Western.* Berkeley, Los Angeles, London: University of California Press, 1975.

Wykes, Alan. *The Complete Illustrated Guide to Gambling.* New York: Doubleday, 1964.

Yardley, Herbert O. *The Education of a Poker Player.* New York: Simon and Schuster, 1957.

Yaryan, R., and Festinger, Leon. "Preparatory Action and Belief in the Probable Occurrence of Future Events." *Journal of Abnormal and Social Psychology* 63 (1961): 603-607.

Zola, I. "Observations on Gambling in a Lower-class Setting." In *The Other Side: Perspectives on Deviance,* edited by Howard Becker, pp. 247-260. New York: Free Press, 1964.

Zolotow, Maurice. "How to Hold All the Cards in a Friendly Poker Game." *Los Angeles* 23 (1978): 90-104.

Zurcher, Louis. "The 'Friendly' Poker Game: A Study of an Ephemeral Role." *Social Forces* 49 (1970): 173-186.

Index

Designer: Gayle Birrell and Michael Sheridan
Compositor: Janet Brown
Printer: Edwards Brothers
Binder: Edwards Brothers
Text: 10/12 Baskerville, Compuwriter II
Display: Kabel Bold